Praise for *Home on the Road*

"It's tempting to think Catherine Watson has seen it all. She has established herself over the past thirty years or so as one of the truly gifted travel writers in American journalism. Yet in this dazzling collection of travel pieces there isn't a taint of been-there/done-that. The eye is keen and kind, the writing by turns sharp and lyrical, the destinations ever a surprise. Whether she's mushing with sled dogs in Alaska, mourning loss in Tibet or visiting old Fort Snelling at home in Minnesota, this is a writer of grace and curiosity. And rare passion. What's best—you can trust her to be the traveler you wish you could be. She has the uncanny grace of one truly at home in the world. A magic carpet collection by one of our best."

Patricia Hampl, author,
A Romantic Education, Virgin Time, Blue Arabesque

"In *Home on the Road*, Catherine Watson explores the world with a refreshing warmth and compassion, revealing as much about people as she does about place. She is a poetic storyteller, a wise observer, an intimate companion—the best guide anyone could want."

Larry Habegger, executive editor, *Travelers' Tales Books*

"All travel writers should have Catherine Watson's curiosity. She travels far and wide, and often into people's homes and lives. Her stories get beneath the surface, grab hold of you and linger."

Michael Yessis, co-founder,
the on-line travel magazine, *World Hum*

"*Home on the Road* indeed! What obscure corner of the planet has Catherine Watson not investigated with her eyes open, her notebook ready and her wits alive and thrumming? Mongolia, Tibet, the Falklands, the Canadian Arctic, the Jordan desert following Lawrence of Arabia. Do you wonder what the human mind does with a scorpion sting in Costa Rica? Even the ancestral cabin in Minnesota becomes a place rich, strange and productive of wisdom. Though journalism gave birth to these essays, they are, in fact, literature, little windows into the mystery of how human beings live on this planet, and what insight we can harvest from traveling among them."

Bill Holm, author, *The Heart Can Be Filled Anywhere on Earth,*
Coming Home Crazy, Windows of Brimnes

"Other writers may evoke the sights and sounds of a place, but Catherine Watson captures the soul."

John Flinn, executive travel editor, *San Francisco Chronicle*

"I think I'd go all over the world with Catherine Watson—and through her honest, perceptive and inviting essays, I probably have. This collection shines with the enthusiasm of a traveler who looks for the best, not the worst, wherever she goes. Her curiosity, humor, warmth and openness to new experience enliven every account of her travels to places as diverse as Tibet, Alaska, Bimini and Death Valley. *Home on the Road* also displays a polished writer's grace and finesse. A beginning writer could find an education simply by studying each carefully crafted opening sentence—and then, reading on, learn about shape, tone and style. In writing as well as traveling, Catherine Watson clearly knows how to get where she wants to go."

Susan Allen Toth, author, *Blooming, My Love Affair with England*

"This is a must-read book for all of you who need to stop dreaming about travel and just go do it! It encourages you to eliminate the word 'later' from your vocabulary and see the world. So burn those travel brochures and read Watson's adventures—stories that take you beyond the well-known icons to the real experiences that make travel so wonderfully addictive."

Peter Greenberg, travel editor, NBC Today Show

"As she did in *Roads Less Traveled*, Catherine Watson touches on details that illuminate an over-all sense of the culture of her subject. If you savor armchair traveling or appreciate good writing, don't miss this book."

Joan Drury, founder, Norcroft Writing Retreat for Women; author, *Those Jordan Girls*

"I left each essay imbued with a sense of having been there with her, of experiencing the peoples, traditions, history and culture of the places she writes about, and I could not help but respond with similar joy."

Beryl Singleton Bissell, author, *The Scent of God*

"Catherine Watson has a unique talent for writing about her experiences in a way that appeals to both those who travel and those who just dream of travel. A rare combination of insight and heart."

Gerry Spiess, sailor and author, *Alone Against the Atlantic*

Home on the Road

Further Dispatches from the Ends of the Earth

Catherine Watson

To Mary — Iff — may all your travels bring you joy — Catherine Watson

SYREN BOOK COMPANY

Minneapolis

Most Syren Books are available at special quantity discounts for bulk purchases for sales promotions, premiums, fund-raising, and educational needs. For details, write:

Syren Book Company
Special Sales Department
5120 Cedar Lake Road
Minneapolis, Minnesota 55416

Published by
Syren Book Company
5120 Cedar Lake Road
Minneapolis, Minnesota 55416

Printed in the United States of America on acid-free paper

ISBN 978-0-929636-76-4

LCCN 2007929630

Cover photo: *Sunset, the Galapagos,* by Catherine Watson
© *Star Tribune.* Used by permission.
Cover design by Kyle G. Hunter
Book design by Wendy Holdman

To order additional copies of this book, please go to www.itascabooks.com

For the young ones—deep breath now—
Jonathan, Rebecca, Emily, Elizabeth, James, Charlie,
John, Helen, Will, Andrew, Matthew, David and Joe.

Contents

Author's Note

I WAS FIVE when I took my first long trip, going on the train with my mother, from Minneapolis to Grand Forks, to see my uncle and aunt and cousin Mark. What I remember best is that my mother sewed me a pretty blue suit for the journey, and I got to wear snow-white gloves.

When I took my next long trip—and my first alone—I was sixteen, an exchange student bound for Germany, and white gloves weren't on my packing list. By then I knew that travel was more than a matter of new clothes, but I hadn't yet learned that it was also more than landscape and architecture. The essence of travel turned out to be people, and the more I let the world's people into my life, the happier I became, until I truly felt more at home on the road than anywhere else.

I got homesick on that first overseas trip—still do, every time I'm out of the country, until I get over my jet lag and get into the experience. But even while I *missed* home, I don't think I really wanted to *go* home. And once home again, I didn't want to stay.

I used to believe that this push-pull tension would burn itself out, and I would be one-hundred-percent happy in just one place. But that hasn't happened. There are still too many places to go, too many people to meet, too many good stories to hear, and they all tug at my imagination—and my heart. Home and away, I see now, are the yin and yang of travel. Both are part of the same journey.

Many people are responsible for my permanently impermanent state of being. Some of them I thanked in my earlier collection, *Roads Less Traveled,* but there are many more to whom I owe debts I can never repay:

First, for sheer inspiration, my peripatetic uncle, Louis Geiger, who was one of the best travelers I have ever known.

For patience (and help hefting luggage and holding spare lenses), my indefatigable fellow travelers Mary Ann Ringwelski, Jim Bjorkman and Jonathan Rist and, from time to time, each of my brothers and sisters.

Supportive friends, advisers and editors Al Sicherman, Trudi Hahn Pickett, Jane O'Reilly, Deb and Phil Ford, Jarrett Smith, Mike Zika, Deb and Ken Moss, Linda Myers, Kathy Coskran, Judy Krauss, Jenni Pinkley and Lynn Brun, all here at home. And Brian Mitchell, John and Margaret Rodgers and Penny Inglish de Abreu in London.

Also my collective cheerleaders from the Split Rock Arts Program and The Loft Literary Center, my colleagues in the Society of American Travel Writers and—among many mentors at the *Minneapolis Tribune*—Stu Baird, Larry Batson, Dick Cunningham, Frank Premack and Beverly Kees, great journalists all.

Finally, heartfelt thanks to the people to whom I've been talking in print for the better part—the *best* part—of thirty years. We haven't met face to face, but even so, we know each other. Keep traveling, friends. Be curious. Be open. Be peacemakers. And always ask for a window seat.

Catherine Watson
May 2007

Home on the Road

Further Dispatches from the Ends of the Earth

Healing in the Himalayas

1987

MY MOTHER HAD DIED, and in the emptiness that followed, all I wanted was to be far from home. Travel has
curative powers for me, and I turned to it now as if to a healing
drug. I craved a place so distant and so difficult that it would
take full concentration to survive the present moment, with
nothing left for the future or the past. I chose Tibet.

My friend Jim and I left Kathmandu, Nepal, by bus, just
after dawn on the morning of the Lord Buddha's 2,531st birthday. It seemed auspicious. All sorrow comes from craving, the
Buddha taught: Extinguish craving, and you extinguish sorrow. That is a good banner to travel under; travelers who expect nothing are never disappointed.

Our budget tour followed valleys at first, heading east, then
north, into the foothills of the Himalayas and along the Sun
Kosi River—part of Nepal's border with Tibet—and finally
across it, via the Chinese-built Friendship Bridge. That was
the easy part.

Beyond the border, the landscape looked as if it had been
unraveled, like a badly knitted sweater. The road had been
severed by a series of landslides, and the Chinese-owned vans

that were to take us the rest of the way—up through the mountains and across the Tibetan Plateau—were parked on the farther side. To reach them, we would have to climb up the landslides, going from about 5,000 feet to 7,500 feet—half a vertical mile—scrambling on foot over cascades of dirt and rubble.

We hired a gang of rag-clad, barefoot porters to carry our packs and duffels. As if the mountain slopes were city sidewalks, the porters trotted straight uphill, following a trail so narrow that only one person could negotiate it at a time and so steep that I thought it was a mistake.

I stopped every few minutes to rest, gasping for breath, blaming the altitude for a sudden, puzzling confusion and wondering why thrice-weekly aerobic workouts hadn't left me in better shape. Then a wave of fever and nausea broke over me, and I realized I was suffering, not from altitude, but from food poisoning. (I blamed it on my last meal in Kathmandu. Why, I kept thinking, had eating shrimp cocktail in the Himalayas seemed like a good idea?)

I remember the early part of the journey as a dimly lit, exotic movie—a dizzy blur of thirst and fatigue; of eerily treeless mountains; of roads so rough they made my teeth chatter; mountain passes so high I got headaches riding over them, and dry, dirty villages with unfamiliar names like Tingri and Xegar Dzong.

What I saw was filtered by illness and shrouded in whirling dust. It seemed not quite real. But it was what I had longed for: A present tense so consumingly difficult that I could not focus on anything but *now*.

Prevailing winds follow the same route we did, pushing clouds up and over the mountains. As they rise, the clouds lose their moisture, so Nepal is damp and green near the border, while Tibet lies in the rain shadow, its skies as clear as blue glass, its land as sere as sand.

The rain shadow makes the Himalayas different, too, from one side to the other. Glimpsed from Nepal, their great snowy peaks had shimmered like a white curtain in the sky, like a congregation of angels. When we met them again in Tibet, they had changed. Sturdier, plainer, more of the earth, they looked like the broad, tan backs of draft horses tossing distant white manes.

It was spring when we were there, but it was hard to tell. Winter commanded the peaks, so the higher we went, the colder it was, and the earlier the season. The lowest fields were already green with shoots of barley, Tibet's staple crop, and tiny lilacs were blooming in sheltered gardens. But on the high slopes, people hadn't finished plowing, and everywhere they were repairing irrigation canals or building new ones to lure trickles of water into their fields, sometimes from miles away.

The brightest spot in those first days was the town of Shigatse and the golden-roofed monastery of Tashilhunpo that appeared to float above it against Tibet's cobalt sky. I was still shaky and out of breath—Shigatse is at 12,800 feet—and I lagged behind Jim and the others in the group. So far behind that I was alone when I stepped through the great monastery gate.

The sun-blasted courtyard beyond could have been a medieval city or the setting for "Lost Horizon" if James Hilton had chosen to locate his fictional Himalayan paradise in a desert. Painted buildings rose around the courtyard like a complicated heap of blocks, white and salmon-pink, adorned with fluttering awnings and the golden figures of deer, the first creatures to whom the Buddha preached.

Needing a map of the monastery, I pulled out my guidebook and was instantly mobbed by Tibetans: first an old couple, then a clot of children, then a family. They were pilgrims, come from other parts of Tibet to pray at the Tashilhunpo shrines—all wearing black clothes made of thick wool, all beaming and nodding and holding out their hands, all murmuring the same unintelligible syllables over and over:

Dalampich, dalampich, dalampich . . . .

I could not have felt more alien on the plains of Mars. Then a man reached forward and touched my guidebook and looked earnestly up at me. At last I understood. They were speaking the one English phrase all Tibetans seemed to know:

Dalai Lama picture.

In other countries, the poor beg for money. No one we met in Tibet ever did. The only things they wanted from us were photographs of their exiled religious leader, and they knew that tourists' guidebooks often contained them.

Forewarned by other travelers, I had packed copies of a recent picture of the Dalai Lama, and now I passed out a few. The reaction was startling. The Tibetans looked transfigured. They grinned, bowed, clasped my hands, held the pictures to their chests, tapped them on their heads. One old lady wept. So did I, at the thought that something so small could be so important and that belief could persist so long and so intensely.

It has been five decades since the Dalai Lama and his family fled their country. By any standard but Tibet's, he should now be nothing more than a mildly interesting, half-forgotten institution, like the late Duke of Windsor or the former royalty of Montenegro.

But where those gentlemen were mere earthly rulers, the Dalai Lama has the force of heaven on his side. Tibet's devout

Buddhists believe that he is a manifestation of the Chenrezi, the Buddha of Compassion, who chose to reincarnate to help human beings. This Dalai Lama is the fourteenth in a series of such reincarnations. That makes him as much a god as he is a king.

He was a sixteen-year-old boy when China's troops seized Tibet in 1950 and, despite objections from around the world, kept it. Tibet was bigger then, covering all of the Tibetan Plateau, an area roughly the size of Europe. The Chinese redrew the borders, so today's Tibet comprises only about one-third of its old territory, and its eastern districts, Amdo and Kham, have been absorbed into neighboring Chinese provinces.

Well over a million Tibetans died as a direct result of the Chinese occupation, according to the Office of Tibet in New York—either during the fighting or later, from executions, suicide, illness and famine. And, I would add, from heartbreak. The cultural price was shocking. Tibet had had more than 6,200 functioning monasteries when the Chinese invaded. When I visited, there were perhaps fifteen.

At first, the Tibetan government tried to coexist peacefully with its new overlords. But tensions worsened as more and more of Tibet's traditions were undermined and more Chinese settlers moved in. The situation exploded in the spring of 1959, when Tibetans attempted to throw the Chinese out and failed. On a night that March, the Dalai Lama and his family put on peasants' clothing, slipped out of the Norbulinka, his summer palace, and escaped on horseback over the mountains to India. He was twenty-three.

Now he is middle-aged, the religious shepherd of a scattered flock, a Tibetan diaspora of more than a hundred thousand exiles. There are colonies of Tibetan refugees all over the globe—in Nepal, in Switzerland, even in Minnesota—and the once-cloistered Dalai Lama has had to become a world traveler to visit them from his exile in northern India.

Back in Tibet, two generations have grown to adulthood in his absence. His palaces in Lhasa—the thousand-roomed Potala and the smaller Norbulinka—have been turned into museums. And even he has suggested that the end of the re-incarnations may be approaching—that when the people of Tibet no longer need a Dalai Lama, he will cease to reappear.

But there are no signs that the Tibetans at home have stopped needing him. I saw his picture on every altar, in every active temple. In his palaces, the beds he slept in are littered with offerings from pilgrims—coins, crumpled bills, handfuls of barley and skeins of the gauzy white ceremonial scarves called *kata*. In the Norbulinka, pilgrims touch their heads to the wall that bears his portrait, and when they pass the Potala, they bow because it was his home.

One afternoon, as Jim and I lingered there, an aging monk hurried up to us, glanced around to see if any Chinese guards were watching and struck a defiant pose, head up, shoulders back.

"Take my picture!" he commanded in English. "The Chinese will kill me if they find out, but take it! Send it to the Dalai Lama in India. Tell him that his monk says, 'Come back!'" We obeyed and sent the picture.

You can always tell the losers in a culture clash. They're the ones running around in native dress, the ones selling trinkets to tourists, the ones who are bilingual. Winners never need to learn the other language. That makes Tibet feel a lot like an Indian reservation in the American Southwest. It felt worst in Lhasa, a city of 60,000. Lhasa is still Tibet's capital, but it was not a Tibetan city anymore—it was an outpost of modern China, where the newcomers outnumbered the natives three to one.

"Lhasa is a disappointment," I wrote in my journal on our second night there. Not that I wasn't enjoying my spotless room at the Lhasa Holiday Inn, with its abundant hot water and clean towels. The hotel even had piped-in oxygen, bubbling in bottles by the headboards—more than a courtesy, considering we were at 11,800 feet. But as I sprawled on the comfortable bed, drinking Coke and watching "Death on the Nile" on closed-circuit TV, I felt as if I were anywhere but Lhasa. And I could have been.

It was, I wrote, "a shell of a city, like Christmas morning after the gifts are opened and nothing is left but the wrappings. The Jokhang Cathedral looks as if it were restored by Walt Disney. There are better Tibetan souvenirs in Nepal than there are here. Better, healthier Tibetans, too. Cities of dreams ought to be left there. Without Shangri-La, what will I dream about?"

But Lhasa grew on me. Partly it was my improving health and increasing acclimatization: Each day meant I could walk farther and climb more stairs before the altitude stole my breath. The other reason I came to like Lhasa was the Tibetans themselves.

In Tibet, a tug on a camera strap meant curiosity, not threatened theft. I'd look around and discover a child, an old person, once even a monk, solemnly examining the peculiar block of metal and glass that swung from my shoulder. It was a little like trolling: I never knew what I'd find on the end of the line.

They would smile up at me, blameless as cherubs, and then

return to the camera, poking fingers and noses into the lens. I found I could make instant friends by directing their eyes to the viewfinder.

Innocent though it was, this invasive curiosity was disconcerting. So was their habit of close personal inspection. Old people were particularly given to it. Prayer wheels spinning, the great mantra of Buddhism moving on their lips—*Om mani padme hum*: O thou jewel in the heart of the lotus—they would stroll to within a few inches of my face and then just stand there, smiling benignly and eyeing me head to toe, even when I didn't have Dalai Lama pictures to offer.

At first, I thought they were addled. Jim agreed: "Think of this as a nation of outpatients," he said, equally unnerved. They seemed to be chronological relics, endearing mementos of another age, until one evening at the Jokhang Cathedral, when the tables turned.

The Jokhang is the pilgrims' ultimate goal, the religious center of Tibet, so important that the modern Western world offers no parallel. If Tibet were Europe, the Jokhang would be Chartres, Westminster Abbey and the Vatican, all rolled into one.

Pilgrims stream around it, nearly four thousand an hour (I counted) in a river of black robes and rakish hats—men with red tassels in their hair, women with nuggets of turquoise strung on their long black braids, some people wearing charm boxes, some with daggers at their belts, some carrying statues of the Buddha as tenderly as if they were living children.

Standing before that fantastical parade, in my blue jeans, denim shirt and pink sneakers, I suddenly felt idiotic—as if I'd been invited to the world's most elaborate costume party and had underdressed. The sensation made me laugh out loud. I was the real curiosity, the one that didn't fit. The Tibetans who saw me laughing kindly joined in and laughed too.

Most obvious at the Jokhang but true everywhere in Tibet: Prayers were in the very air, fluttering into heaven with each gust on a prayer flag, each spin of a prayer wheel. "Wheel" is a misnomer, by the way. The little machines look more like tin cans tacked loosely to the end of a stick. Twirl the stick to spin the can, and the written prayers inside it are wafted up to God.

Tibetans carry prayer wheels with them, so they can pray while doing other things, but prayer flags are a different matter: They pray by themselves, whenever the wind blows.

Prayer flags festoon the high passes, mark bridges, bless the corners of houses and fields, protect painstakingly tended irrigation ditches and adorn the backs of living yaks, Tibet's totem animal, as valuable here as oxen were on the American frontier.

Squares of colored cotton printed with Buddhist scripture, prayer flags are vivid when new—red, blue, yellow, green or snowy white—but they weather badly. The dyes fade, the blowing dust stains them, and the wind worries them rapidly into rags. A line of old prayer flags, fallen beside a mountain pass, looks like laundry hung by elves—poor elves, at that.

This means there is a constant need for new prayer flags. In Lhasa, you can buy them by the yard in the festive clutter of Barkhor Bazaar, the market street that encircles the Jokhang Cathedral. The market is there because the pilgrims are there, and the pilgrims are there because the Barkhor is one of three sacred ways that devout Buddhists must follow in Lhasa. It is by far the busiest, given that pilgrims must circle the cathedral, clockwise, at least three times; most do many more circumnambulations than that.

Leaning on walking sticks, swinging prayer wheels, keeping count of their progress on Buddhist rosaries, the pilgrims form an unending parade, while prayer flags whip and rustle on the long poles in front of the temple, and sacred juniper smoke rises like incense from its outdoor hearths.

Whole families walk together, the elderly leaning on younger arms, toddlers on foot until they get tired, babies in their mothers' arms. Young men go by in little gangs, kidding each other, clowning around, hoping to be noticed. Nearby in the crowd, as inevitable in Tibet as in Timbuktu or Tallahassee, cliques of young girls are walking, whispering to each other and managing to stay within eyeshot of the boys.

Some people prostrate themselves before they enter the Jokhang. Some prostrate themselves as they circle the temple. And a gaunt handful, their eyes wild by the time they arrive, make their entire pilgrimage this way, no matter how far they need to come. Starting upright, hands raised prayerfully over their heads, they bow, kneel, lie down, stretch out, arise, take a step forward, bow, kneel, lie down, stretch out, arise—over and over again, like pious inchworms, all in the name of God.

I liked to go to the Barkhor in the late afternoons, to watch the pilgrims and sometimes to join them for a turn or two around the temple. Their pace, I found, was not fast but relentless. Stop for any reason, and you get left behind. Linger too long, and the pilgrims you started out with will come around again, catch up with you and keep on going. They don't look back.

But they do shop. Lhasa's merchants recognized the market potential centuries ago, and the pilgrims' way is crowded with their booths. On one circuit, I discovered a man making refills for prayer wheels—rolling thick pads of paper scriptures into tight cylinders like stubby fireplace logs. He kept shop just beyond the guy with the performing monkeys and just before the man selling hand-carved home altars.

Around them were vendors of bread, yak cheese, charm boxes, hair ornaments, gold teeth, red felt boots, sheepskin cloaks, black wool dresses, Tibetan rugs, turquoise and coral jewelry, a lady with bolts of prayer flags and a group of novice monks, swathed in maroon robes, chanting for donations in the middle of the street.

The Jokhang was just as rich inside. Tibetan temples are as black as caves, lit only by the flames of butter lamps and their flickering reflections in the golden skin of the Buddhas.

Butter lamps look like goblets made of brass. They're usually brim-full with *ghee*—clarified butter made from yak milk—continually refueled by pilgrims who spoon the stuff out of jars they bring from home. Before it melts, it looks like whipped honey.

Sometimes the pilgrims are too generous, and the lamps overflow. There are splashes of butter on the temple floors, butter on the railings, butter on the wall hangings and buttery smudges on the figures of protective saints. The burning butter gives the temples a familiar smell, like the lobbies of old movie theaters.

At first, in the darkness of the temples, I kept mistaking saints for demons, fooled by their fangs, bugged-out eyes and multiple arms; the most fearsome even had cloth veils over their snarling faces, to protect worshipers from shock. Eventually, I understood: These were the good guys, showing off their powers against evil. Like He-Man, they are who you want on your side if times get tough.

Tibetan worshipers pressed together near the altars, concentrating on the figures they most revered, and there the buttery air was warm and full of human smells—old clothes, unwashed hair, the milky breath of babies. This gave the temples a cozy intimacy, despite their high ceilings and dark, drafty rooms.

Ultimately, they seemed not much different from medieval cathedrals in Europe: the same little flames glowing in front of holy figures, the same smells of oil and incense, the same transforming devotion. The saints were different, the demons more garish. But could Christian hell be any less horrible than Tibetan? Or its heaven any sweeter?

The blessings, too, are kin. That was clear as early as the first temple in Shigatse, when I glanced up at its huge statue of the Buddha and was jolted, as if physically hit, by the serenity of his face. It was like that every time, at Gyantse, at Drepung, at Sera, in monastery after monastery, until I came to treasure—to long for—that sudden relief, that inoculation of stillness.

As time and temples passed, so did my illness, and when it was time to leave Tibet, I was clear-headed again. We looped briefly north from Lhasa, through natural pastures where herds of yaks, looking like long-horned cattle under shag rugs, were grazing at the foot of snowy peaks. Then we cut south into a region of blowing sand, crossed the young Brahmaputra River by ferry and joined the main road to retrace our path through the dry valleys to Shigatse and the Nepalese border beyond.

The way out was the same as the way in. Dust devils were still whirling, even over irrigated fields, and yaks were still trudging, and Tibetan peasants, still wearing the black wool clothes they'd worn all winter, were still looking up when the vans went by, to smile and wave at tourists they had not met and would never see again. If Shangri-la exists, I thought, it is no nearer and no farther than the Tibetan soul.

At the border, we climbed back down the landslides, walked across the Friendship Bridge, went through Nepali customs in a roadside shack and were promptly picked up for the long ride back to Kathmandu. We were back on the other side of the rain shadow now, and it showed. New rice gleamed neon-green in the paddies, and the fields of ripening wheat fluttered like gold leaf in the sun. In the rich, slanting light of that afternoon, Nepal—poor, dirty, overcrowded Nepal—had been transformed. To my Tibet-accustomed eyes, it looked like a garden.

I had changed too. Grief was still with me and would be for a long time, but Tibet had dulled the edge of its blade; I felt I could bear it better now. I had come for escape and hoped for epiphany; I'd gotten dust and distraction. In the end, they were almost the same, and I was grateful.

Viking America

1988

O N A J U N E D A Y in Newfoundland, when the wind is cutting cold, a Viking longhouse is a not a cheery refuge: a
dark, damp, smoky place, more earthen cave than house, wind-
proof but not warm. Or so I was thinking, huddled in my raincoat and trying to keep from shivering, inside the longhouse at
a village called L'Anse aux Meadows, on the northernmost tip
of this huge Canadian island.

Outside lay an eerie landscape, little changed in a thousand
years: A low, jagged coastline of dark rocks and small islands
silhouetted against a gunmetal sea. Up here, the trees of Newfoundland lie low—dwarf birch and spruce no bigger than
shrubs, natural bonzais pruned into submission by the wind.
It can snow as late as June. And when I was there, it did.

June is iceberg season, when the pack ice melts around
Greenland and Baffin Island, and the Labrador Current carries
the fragments south along Canada's Atlantic coast. Winter's
last wild children, the icebergs are refugees from the harsh season just past, prophets of the season to come.

"We get a lot of things from Greenland," a local man told
me, "salmon, seals, ice. Because Greenland's not very far from

here, actually." Well, actually, it's about 620 miles if you fly, 1,300 if you follow the currents. But not far, I guessed, in Newfoundland terms.

Seen offshore through breaks in the frequent mist and rain, the summer icebergs loom like warships, as many as thirty visible at a time. Sometimes they get snared by eddies and drift too close to shore, stranding themselves on the cobblestone shoals. It takes them a long time to melt. The ice is so clean that even on sullen days, the bergs have a blue-green glow, as if they had turquoise lights inside.

Locals—mostly fishermen whose families have been here for generations—raid the stranded bergs for their fresh, pure ice. "You put it in drinks," a woman told me. "It crackles." So it did. I got a sample at my B & B; melting in my glass, it sounded like very cold Rice Krispies.

All this adds up to summer on the top of Newfoundland— a season when jackets can be unzipped but not necessarily taken off, and children can play outdoors without mittens and caps.

Winter is something else. Winter explains why every home in the frequent fishing villages has a house-sized pile of stove wood beside it. In winter, snow mounds up to the rooftops. Winter. Winter in Newfoundland. On a summer day when snow is drifting down, it is a grim prospect, impossible to imagine.

More impossible: This is where the Vikings landed. This is where they wintered over, ten centuries ago. This is where they built a handful of long, low sod houses and settled down to wait for spring.

Vikings were here—that much is known—but L'Anse aux Meadows isn't their famous Vinland. Not unless Leif Ericson was kidding when he called it a "land of wine." And he could have been: His family had a liking for geographic humor. Leif's father, Erik the Red, had named another uninviting place "Greenland" in an early attempt at public relations. People would be more apt to settle there, Erik maintained, if the place had an attractive name.

Or so the sagas say—those rollicking old Scandinavian texts that have kept scholars busy for generations, trying to establish how much is fact and how much fiction in Viking accounts of New World discoveries.

The sagas are vividly emphatic about America. When Leif's people sailed west from Greenland, the sagas say, they encountered three large islands: First, Helluland, a landscape of flat stones that may have been Baffin Island. Then Markland, a forested place that likely was Labrador. And finally Vinland, named for wild grapes, location now unknown.

"The weather was fine," goes one version of the Vikings' landfall. "There was dew on the grass, and the first thing they did was to get some of it on their hands and put it to their lips, and to them it seemed the sweetest thing they had ever tasted."

The sagas say the Norsemen made several trips from Greenland to Vinland, mostly to cut timber, though one time they went to establish a settlement, and several times, groups had to winter over there. It's been established that L'Anse aux Meadows was one of their wintering places. It is the only proven Viking settlement in the New World.

The surprise of the site lies in its humbleness. For all its significance, it is very small—just the rounded, overgrown foundations of three longhouses and five outbuildings—and so hard to see against the scrubby landscape that it's a wonder it was ever noticed.

What helped is that locals knew all along where—though not what—it was. So when a Scandinavian explorer came by in the late 1950s asking about ruins, L'Anse villagers—there are about 150 of them—showed him the low, sod-covered foundations near their homes.

"We all knew about it," said Clayton Colbourne, a middle-aged fisherman working as a summer guide at L'Anse aux Meadows National Historic Park. He and his friends played in the ruins as children. "To us, it was always 'the Indian camps.' We never had an inkling about the Norse."

After archaeological excavations in the 1960s and '70s, L'Anse was designated the first historic site on UNESCO's World Heritage List. One of the most significant archaeological sites in the world, it draws just under 20,000 visitors a year.

A few summers back, Colbourne was one of the local men hired to cut and pile peat sod to build the park's replica longhouse. They used the floor plan of one of the original foundations and copied the upper architecture from a Viking house that's been standing in Iceland since the 1100s. The doors and roof vents are on the side away from the sea, protected from the prevailing winds.

The building's contents, spread on low benches against the walls or hung from log beams, are modern copies of known Viking goods: Long-handled wrought-iron forks and griddles for cooking on open hearths; iron-bound wooden trunks for storage; a wooden churn; a few Viking-style sleeping bags made of sheepskin, with the wool turned inside for warmth, and small mountains of spruce logs, split and stacked for firewood.

With no fires burning in the hearths, the fine, dry snow was sifting through the vents, and the longhouse was so cold inside that I could see my breath. The thick peat walls deadened what sounds there were, and there weren't many—just the wind growling around the corners, the pulse of waves on the nearby shore and the murmuring of a tour guide in the next chamber.

On such a day, when the seasons seem reversed, it is easy to let your mind slip a little, easy to let go of time and fact. The past stepped closer, and the longhouse filled with Viking ghosts. How would it have been for these people, huddling by the firepits as ancient snows built up toward the rooflines? What did it feel like, facing a winter on the edge of vast America, with an unknown continent at their backs?

Lonely, no doubt. Frightening, sometimes. And almost certainly boring—even the sagas hint at bouts of cabin fever. Daily events become important history only in retrospect; most are ordinary enough in the living.

"All the artifacts found here were either misplaced or broken," said Debbie Penney, the head guide at the park. It meant that the Vikings took all their useful possessions away with them: "When they left, they left with the intention of leaving—as opposed to having been driven out in the middle of the night."

The three large dwellings would have held about twenty-five people apiece, Penney said, so archaeologists concluded that only seventy or eighty Norsemen lived here—a hundred, tops. "The amount of debris in the middens [the garbage heaps] indicates that they stayed no longer than three years"—either three in a row or three scattered over about a quarter century, the length of time that a sod longhouse lasts.

Only a few European-style items have been found here.

Most are displayed in a single glass case in the park's museum: A spindle weight, used to spin wool into yarn—a sign that women were present. A bronze pin, like ones the Vikings used to fasten their cloaks. Part of an iron rivet and a washer-like "rove," specialized gadgets that held the planks of Viking ships together.

But these alone wouldn't prove the site was Viking, Debbie Penney said. Native peoples had used the same site for 6,000 years, and the Norse items could have been brought in from farther east, through trade.

No, the proof that L'Anse aux Meadows was a Viking site lies in even plainer things: a multitude of wood chips and shavings found on the sloping beach, and a small pile of what look like ordinary rocks.

The wood chips were hewn with iron tools, which the native peoples didn't have. And those rocks turned out to be slag, a by-product found wherever Vikings smelted iron. Judging by the amount of slag, the Vikings made about five pounds of iron while they were at L'Anse aux Meadows. "It could not have been made by the native peoples," Penney said.

But where did the Vikings get the ore? Simple, she said. They used bog iron—hydrated ferric oxide—just as they did in Scandinavia. Bog iron forms in creeks and marshes where water percolates through spruce soils.

Outside, another guide dipped a hand into Black Duck Brook, a gutter-sized streamlet flowing along one side of the site, and brought up a brownish-black lump of what looked like hardened mud. It was about that friable. He offered it to a few visitors, and we crumbled it in our fingers. "Bog iron," he said firmly.

Viking iron. When you're standing on what feels like the edge of the earth, making a connection like that can send shivers up your spine.

Here's one more: Butternuts. Archaeologists found two of them at L'Anse aux Meadows, on the beach among the wood shavings. But butternuts don't grow here. They never have. The nearest source for them would have been New Brunswick.

The proof is slender, but it all points to one conclusion: "We think that L'Anse aux Meadows was the *entrance* to Vinland," Penney said. "They wintered here but did their exploring and gathered their grapes and lumber farther south."

So this was only a way station between Scandinavia and the real Vinland—just a convenient place where the Vikings stopped to repair their ships, before better weather and the long voyage home. The last of them could not have known it when they left, but it would be another five hundred years before any Europeans came back.

I wondered how the itinerant Vikings had felt about this place. Were they even a little attached to this edge of the New World? I mean, when they put their boats in the water and pushed off that final day, did any of them take a last nostalgic look at the alien shore that they briefly had called home?

Amazon Queen

1984

—

IT WAS ALREADY DARK when we arrived in Iquitos, but I headed for the river anyway. The Amazon was the point of this long journey, and I didn't want to wait until morning to see it.

The great river begins not far above Iquitos, capital of Peru's upper Amazon basin, where two great tributaries, the Marañon and the Ucayali, come together. From here, it sweeps 2,300 miles to the sea, pouring enough water into the Atlantic each day to supply New York City for nine years.

Or so I had read. Like so many things in this part of the world, statistics can't always be trusted.

Our map said the river was close by—at the end of our street, just past the door of our tiny hotel. I started walking toward it, but the street suddenly ended in mid-air. The river had undermined it, and the pavement had broken off, leaving a ragged edge, like a stick of chewing gum torn in half. Where the pavement ended, the riverbank began, but it sloped so far down into the darkness that light from the street lamps behind me never reached the water. The effect was like standing on a lighted stage, looking into a vast, darkened auditorium, over a distance so great that the stage lights didn't matter. There were no reflections in that blackness. No sounds, either. No lapping waves, no rocking boats, no water music. Only shadow and soft, warm silence. And a sense of enormous space.

For a moment, I thought I could feel the Amazon, even though I couldn't see it. What I was really feeling was fatigue. It was one of those moments I never plan on when I'm dreaming about a place I've never been. Adventurers aren't supposed to get tired. They never do in movies, right? Or in my wildest dreams. But home was thirty hours in the past, and I hadn't yet slept. Communing with the river would have to wait.

Just after dawn, I tried again. This time the river appeared: A lake-like swath of water glinting pink and gold in the early light, with a soft mist of trees on the far banks, resplendent sun and clouds overhead, and at my feet—garbage. Garbage and vultures.

Residents of Amazon towns—even ones like Iquitos, with roughly 200,000 people—have always dumped trash down the banks for the river to take away. When the trash settles too high, above the water's reach, it draws vultures, big bald-headed black birds whose feathers rustle like palm fronds when they quarrel over rotten banana peels, kitchen scraps and general crud. They were quarreling over them now—another image I'd left out of the fantasy.

This trip had had ceremonial beginnings: My friend Mary Ann had just been admitted to law school and wanted to celebrate. I had just turned 40 and had held my annual meditation on the meaning of life, which always turns into a list of places I intend to go someday. Someday, I decided, was now. We pooled our motivations and flew to Iquitos in mid-March, intending to spend a week in the neighborhood, most of it at one of the jungle lodges set up for tourists along the river. We scrapped our plans the very first morning, just because of a boat. We were walking along the Malecon, the once-elegant promenade that straggled above the tattered riverfront. Below us, a jumble of towboats, rotting barges and homemade canoes nuzzled the bank. One boat stood out.

She was the real thing—a genuine tropical river queen, twice the length of anything else and twice as tall, with a black smokestack, orange lifeboats on the roof and vestiges of elegance. A sign on her bow gave her name: "Huallaga," after another Amazon tributary.

"That looks like something out of the movie 'Fitzcarraldo,'" Mary Ann said. The film was about the turn-of-the-century rubber boom that brought brief prosperity to jungle-bound Amazon towns like Iquitos. The boom had brought the Huallaga here too.

We took a couple of pictures and continued up the dusty street, past the broken balustrades and crumbling blue-tiled house fronts—mementos of the long-gone rubber days. Ten feet farther on, we saw the sign that changed our plans—crude black letters hand-printed on a scrap of cardboard that shifted in the wind on the end of a crooked pole.

"The Huallaga," it read in Spanish, "departs today at 4 P.M. for Requena. Passengers and cargo accepted."

We'd never heard of Requena, but we only hesitated about three seconds. Then we were stumbling down the steep bank, stepping over garbage, negotiating a skinny gangplank and climbing aboard. Three men, lolling in hammocks slung on the Huallaga's cargo deck, eyed us tranquilly but didn't move.

"We want to go to Requena." More mild stares; no motion. "Do you have any cabins left?" The nearest crewman hoisted himself out of his hammock, hitched up his pants and went over to peer at a scribbled list. "Yes," he said.

Accustomed to Latin American hotel regulations, we offered our passports, but the crewman dismissed them with a wave, slowly wrote "Mary Ann y Catherine" beside No. 12, told us we could pay later and ambled back toward his hammock.

But first we wanted to see the room. Another man arose from another hammock and led us up the steps to the passenger deck. The brass stair treads were dated 1891, and the deck's centerpiece was a magnificent relic of that era: a huge black refectory table with a dozen antique club chairs bolted to the floor around it. The bases of the chairs were polished brass—Victorian originals, just like the boat. Mark Twain would have loved it.

Cabin 12 turned out to be locked, and the only available key, when located, didn't work. Another crewman sauntered upstairs with a pair of broken scissors and picked the lock. "So much for security," said Mary Ann.

At 3:30 that afternoon, we stumbled down the bank again, tossed a small bag of essentials—toothbrushes, spare T-shirts, undies, sun block, mosquito repellent and malaria pills—through the still-open door of Cabin 12 and took seats at the huge table. Four o'clock came and went, and nothing much happened. A handful of passengers straggled down the bank and strung their hammocks on the cargo deck. A crewman climbed the riverbank with a shovel and cut a few steps into the hardened mud at the top. Some men wrestled drums of gasoline aboard. We bought beers from the Huallaga's bar and waited. By 4:30, the pace had not quickened. A little more cargo trickled aboard, and a few more passengers joined us, including a family of three boys and their mother, aunt and grandmother, heading for a week-long vacation upstream in Requena. Now youngsters came aboard selling packs of gum and cookies, and a man and two little girls paddled up in a *lancha*, a long narrow canoe, hoping to sell us fresh fruit. One of the passengers bought a huge pod-like thing more than three feet long and shared it around. It had a sweet, white, foam-like pulp and black seeds the size of a thumb. "Only eat this," he advised, pointing to the pulp and spitting the black seeds overboard.

The weird fruit made everybody thirsty. We reached for our beers, but one crewman just tossed a bucket overboard, drew it up full of muddy river water and drank deep. The trip hadn't even started, and already we were getting a portrait of Amazon life.

Five o'clock brought subtle changes. There was more scuffling noise from below, and the few passengers still coming down the bank looked as if they were hurrying. Somebody tested the engine, a small diesel that long ago had replaced the Huallaga's original steam boilers. It sounded like popcorn popping, and blue plumes of oily exhaust filtered up through holes in the passenger deck floor.

Then, with no announcement or even a blast of the horn, the engine's popping evened into a steady throb, the crew pulled in the long gangplank, and almost imperceptibly, the Huallaga began backing away from the bank.

The Amazon makes a wide bend at Iquitos, and we churned out onto it, swung the bow upstream and began to fight the relentless current of one of the most powerful rivers on the planet. It was almost sunset. The sky was banded in coral and blue-gray, and the river looked like a sheet of pastel silk, dotted with floating patches of water hyacinth. Mary Ann and I dragged folding chairs up to the rail and settled down to savor the scene.

From here on, for the entire trip, the banks unrolled like painted scrolls—a solid wall of jungle, green by day, black by night, broken occasionally by a clearing with a thatched hut or two and, no matter what the hour, a small group of people huddled together, watching the boat go by.

The Amazon was in full spring flood, some forty feet higher than normal and so wide that it should have had tides. It looked kind of familiar—like an extra-wide version of the Mississippi. Mosquitoes completed the illusion—just like ours, except these carried malaria. They were weak fliers, though, and stuck close to land, so they bothered us only when the boat nosed into the muddy bank to drop off passengers or pick up a load of green cooking bananas, sacks of corn or a squealing pig for market.

The captain kept swinging the boat from one bank to the other, trying to position it where the current was weakest— and inadvertently giving us close-up glimpses of the thatched dwellings that dotted the banks. The dark backdrop of jungle made the houses look vulnerable, but at dusk, the orange glow of the kerosene lamps inside gave their rooms a look of cozy warmth. Not that we needed heat. The weather mimicked a Midwestern summer, with temperatures hovering around 98 degrees, and humidity at least that high.

Plenty of passengers, all poor, were traveling on the cargo deck, but only a few shared ours: A school administrator going to Requena to supervise a test for teachers in training; a young couple from Lima on their honeymoon; the vacationing family, and a few uncommunicative single men who immediately started a card game that lasted as long as the trip.

Requena lies about 130 miles upstream from Iquitos. The trip took something like twenty-two hours, cost about six dollars and was supposed to include two meals, but it became clear that one of those meals was not going to be supper. So we had another beer and split a package of cookies. The vacationing family took pity on us and shared their supplies: hard-boiled eggs squished between Saltine crackers.

The boat's purser came by to collect our fares and lingered to talk. The Huallaga, he said, had been built in Britain and shipped to Peru in 1906. It was so picturesque that it had even been in a movie. Which one?

"Fitzcarraldo," he said, and we grinned.

After supper, the vacationing children sat with us, and we took turns asking each other questions in Spanish: "Are there dogs like Lassie in Miami?" *What do you call that kind of boat?* "Are there lions in Miami?" And so on.

The children also pointed out scenic highlights: Houses. Boats. Sticks .... Sticks? Yes, that was the right translation, but it seemed an odd term for what looked, in the darkness, like floating Volkswagen vans. Then I understood: Not sticks, but logs—logs as big as cars. The familiar, Mississippi quality of the warm evening vanished. Trees that big haven't been logged along Old Man River in more than a century. The forest out there was jungle, jungle for real, and light-years distant from home.

We didn't sleep much that night. Cabin 12 was tiny, almost airless when the boat was moving, stifling when it wasn't. It was like trying to sleep on the worst night of a Minnesota summer. Without air conditioning. Under a blanket. In the attic.

Somewhere in this sweltering night, we left the Amazon itself and began to travel up the Ucayali. The change changed nothing. At dawn there were the same green riverbanks, thick with trees; the same thatched huts with brown water lapping at the thresholds; the same little kids waving at the boat, the way kids wave to trains at home.

Dawn was followed, mercifully fast, by breakfast: black coffee and two hard rolls apiece. When the caffeine had taken effect, we climbed up to the pilothouse to talk to the captain.

Agustin Manzanares was a gentle-voiced man from Iquitos, who had been a river pilot for forty years. His pilothouse was more basic than the ones Mark Twain described in "Life on the Mississippi." It had nothing but a wheel, a stool for Manzanares to perch on, a flashlight for signaling people on the banks at night and a single switch to communicate speed preferences to the engineer. The captain's uniform was also basic—just shorts, a baseball cap and bare feet.

Manzanares was piloting without depth-finder or measuring line—just by instinct and experience. On this morning, he was also doing what old river boatmen used to do when the Mississippi was in flood—taking short-cuts through temporary channels over normally dry land. Mark Twain called it "running the chutes." On the flooded Amazon, Captain Manzanares was steering us through the tree-tops.

Lunch, served at the big antique table, was a thin stew of rice boiled in river water, with tomato sauce to mask the Amazon's dead-fish taste. Food and bright sun made people sleepy; even the perpetual card game took a siesta break.

Those of us who stayed awake saw fresh-water dolphins, their pinkish-gray backs arching through the water near shore. They are air-breathing mammals, usually sea creatures, but the Amazon and its tributaries are large enough to sustain them. They swam in pods of three or four and leaped out of the water ahead of the rumbling boat, like rabbits fleeing an oncoming car. "They have skin just like ours," a passenger said, with a touch of awe.

The town of Requena appeared in late afternoon, a poor, tattered place of perhaps 10,000 people, up to its knees in flood waters. We said goodbye to our friends on the Huallaga and set out to see the town. There wasn't much to see, and what there was, was sad.

It was like all Upper Amazon towns, Requena's only doctor told us. He was young, just out of medical school, and spoke with fervor about his patients' chronic ills—malnutrition, malaria, tuberculosis, leprosy and many more. "The river is a textbook of parasitology," the doctor said. "Many people think boiled water has a bad taste" so they drink the unboiled Amazon and get sick. Babies often die of the resulting diarrhea.

In flood season, the problems worsen. Because there's more water, the fish spread out, so they're harder to catch, and the people have less to eat. Mosquitoes increase, which means more malaria. And snakes get driven onto higher ground. Snakebite is common, the doctor said, especially among children because they like to swim in the water rising around their homes.

Death from snakebite is common too: Antivenin serum wasn't available this far from Iquitos. "In the first ten days of this month," he said, his voice a mixture of sadness and disgust, "we had six deaths."

Night was coming, and we needed a place to stay. The Hotel Municipal was the best in Requena, people on the boat had told us. But the Municipal made Cabin 12 look like a Hilton. The Huallaga was still tied off at the dock, so we trooped back there, ready to pay anything. The crew took us in as if we were family and gave us our room back, free of charge.

The Huallaga was staying on for a while at Requena, so we had to find our own way back to Iquitos the next day. We took the competition, a brand-new freighter called the Ferrys that was tied up next door. It was made of steel—which meant the decks got hotter than the Huallaga's wooden ones—and it was very popular: Hammocks were strung so thickly on the passenger deck that it was easier to crawl under them than try to walk.

The Ferrys left on time, and it was faster than our now-beloved Huallaga. For one little girl, speed was a matter of life or death. She was what the doctor in Requena had predicted—a snakebite victim. Glassy-eyed and feverish, she lay listlessly in a hammock, surrounded by her worried family. They were taking her downriver to Iquitos for a shot of antivenin.

A priest we had been talking to shook his head. Even going downriver, with the current to push us, Iquitos was more than twelve hours away. The little girl would not live to get there. "Somebody dies all the time," he said, and turned back to the rail.

All through that night, as the Huallaga had done, the Ferrys pulled over and stopped wherever there was a light at the water's edge. Sometimes *lanchas* rowed out to meet us and guide us in; mostly, the captain just rammed the boat into the trees and held it there with the force of the engine, while pigs and bananas and people came aboard and passengers departed, trudging down the gangplank and off into the dark jungle, going home.

I woke when the sound of the engines suddenly stopped. It was six in the morning, just getting light. We were back in Iquitos, and deck passengers were taking their hammocks down. The family with the bitten child had already left; we never learned whether she lived.

Mary Ann and I joined the crowd pushing its way across the gangplank and up the steep dirt bank—back to where we'd started from, and into another of those travel moments I'm never prepared for.

Iquitos had been a jungle backwater when we first saw it. After Requena, though, it seemed part of the modern world, a place with hot showers and clean hotel rooms and decent places to eat. We'd left the real adventure behind us on the river, back with the mosquitoes and the heat, the flooding and the fitful nights.

Hearts to God

1993

—·—

THE MESSAGE WAS WHAT I'd been hoping for: "The family has decided to meet with you," it read. "Go to the front door of the Dwelling House at 10 A.M., and ring the bell." I did so, feeling nervous, as if I were about to visit an enclave of saints. Which was almost the truth.

The big red-brick Dwelling House stood on a tree-shaded country road in Maine, at a place called Sabbathday Lake. It was built in 1883 by one of America's most unusual religious communities—the United Society of Believers in Christ's Second Appearing, better known as the Shakers. If today's Americans know anything about them, it is likely to be two things: their elegantly plain (and highly collectible) furniture and a single song—"'Tis a Gift to Be Simple"—out of an estimated 10,000 Shaker hymns.

Indeed, nearly every friend I told said, "Shakers? I thought they were dead!" No, there are a handful left, and they are all at Sabbathday Lake. Once home to about seventy-five Shakers, the community now had only eight—six women and two men, ranging in age from about thirty to ninety. They had been written about, studied, criticized, defended and generally puz-

zled over by scholars and journalists for decades. Now they
had agreed to talk to one more reporter. I was amazed at that.
Glad, but amazed. And a little scared.

I waited for their spokesperson inside a plain front room in
the cool, spotless Dwelling House. Shaker things stood along
the walls, precious things, things so beautifully made that
they seemed sacred in themselves: A Shaker tall-case clock. A
wood-burning Shaker stove. A pair of those famously elegant
ladder-back Shaker chairs.

And the Shaker dog. A golden retriever shambled in, seized
my arm in his jaws, mouthed it gently for a moment and then
happily slumped to the floor at my feet, waving his paws in
the air, hoping to have his tummy scratched. I scratched him
and relaxed. The big, gentle golden had just de-mystified the
Shakers, proving to me what I hadn't believed: That the people
who live at Sabbathday Lake were a real family. Authentic.
Down-to-earth. And very human.

The golden was Jason, the family dog. One of two, plus
any number of cats. There was also a family car, a family TV
and a family swimming beach, to say nothing of the family's
microwave, dishwasher and three desktop computers. All of
which surprised me.

It shouldn't have, said the quiet man I had been waiting for.
A dark-bearded, well-spoken, young-looking guy in a blue polo
shirt and slacks (traditional Shaker dress has been optional
since 1900), Brother Arnold Hadd joined about ten years earlier, when he was twenty-one. He talked about his new family
and its remarkable history.

The Shakers at Sabbathday Lake are all that remain of a
movement that spanned 200 years. They were the most successful of the many communal religious groups founded in

America's youth. They call themselves Believers, as their prede-cessors did, and they do not believe they are the last.

"The great problem that we have to combat is the general misconception that we are gone," Brother Arnold said. "I'm not asking them [the world] to accept what we believe, just to know that we're here . . . . Even people who know, who are collectors . . . think we should have stopped."

At their peak, just before the Civil War, there were as many as 6,000 Believers, living in nearly twenty Shaker villages in New England, New York, Kentucky and Ohio. They were in-ventors, designers, efficiency experts and, until the 1960s, foster parents to thousands of orphaned or abandoned New England children, placed in their care by state welfare agencies.

Perhaps because their heyday was the 19th century, the Shakers are often confused with the Amish, who avoid the modern world and cling to old ways. But the Shakers always looked to the future, Brother Arnold said, and they still do. Shakers were not only on the cutting edge of current tech-nology, sometimes they sharpened it: Every time you sweep the floor, for example, or hang out a load of wash or plant a garden, you owe a debt to the Shakers. Among their many in-novations were the modern flat broom, the clothespin and the idea of selling seeds in packets. Also water-repellent cloth, a washing machine, swivel chairs and the circular saw.

That last one was the brainstorm of a Shaker sister, which illustrates another modern idea the Shakers embraced: equal rights for women. "Wherever a brother served in any capacity, there was always a female serving in the same capacity," said Sister Frances Carr, a strong, kindly woman with iron-gray hair and a hearty voice who has emerged as the family's leader.

Shakerism was founded by a woman, British-born Ann

Lee, who arrived in the United States with eight followers in 1774. Shakers are Christians, and they read the Christian Bible, but unlike others, they believe that the second appearing of Christ has already taken place—not in a cataclysmic way, but in the hearts of true Believers, beginning with Mother Ann. She preached that Christ would appear in everyone who lived a pure, Christ-like life.

The requirements of that life "can be summed up as the three Cs," Sister Frances said: "Community of goods. Celibacy. And confession." The world's curiosity has always zeroed in on that middle requirement. Questions about sex and celibacy are inevitable on the village tours that the Shakers sponsor. Visitors can't let the topic alone. "How do they make babes?" a woman with a heavy foreign accent asked. "They don't make babes," the young guide replied. The Shakers' survival still depends on new converts.

"Just as priests and nuns don't marry, we don't marry," Sister Frances explained to me. "Jesus did not marry, neither did he condemn marriage." The Shakers do likewise, because "we have to be able to love—not just one person of the opposite sex, but . . . all persons equally."

Their focus on purity—on living a Christ-like life in a perfect community—led to the Shakers' exquisitely plain, clean rooms; to their fine, unadorned furniture that museums and the wealthy now collect, and to their famous emphasis on efficiency.

"Put your hands to work," Mother Ann advised her flock of Believers long ago, "and give your hearts to God." It is the most quoted phrase of Shaker philosophy.

Also known as Chosen Land, Sabbathday Lake sits in the soft hills of south-central Maine, near the small town of Gray, about an hour's drive north of Portland. Chosen Land is physically smaller than it used to be and no longer fully peaceful: Many buildings had to be taken down as they fell into disuse and disrepair, and the road that runs through it has become a truck route so busy that the roar of passing semis sometimes drowns out conversation in the front rooms of the Dwelling House.

But eighteen buildings still stand along the road—small, white-frame structures except for the brick Dwelling House—and farther on are two small cemeteries, each with a single monument bearing a single word: "Shakers."

The most important building is the white, barn-roofed meeting house, built in 1794. Inside, its roof beams and peg rails still wear their original deep blue paint. Its formula is unknown (it is thought to contain blueberries), but the Shaker-made paint is so good that, in nearly two hundred years, the luminous blue has never needed repainting.

Early Shakers danced in meeting houses like this, intricate dances to their own inspired music, and the way they danced gave them their name. They invited the world to watch; non-Shakers sat on benches around the walls to watch the Believers shake off sin and receive blessings. They no longer dance, but the Sabbathday Lake community still invites the world to worship: Every Sunday morning at 10 A.M., anyone who wishes may join the family for a simple service and some Shaker hymns.

They are not cloistered here. "We have friends that visit us," Brother Arnold said. "We have guests. We have relatives who come for visits." The community also subscribes to two daily newspapers so "we're up on the affairs in the world," he said. They do business in the world's banks and shops. And they travel around the country—usually to attend gatherings where they are the subject but sometimes just on vacations together, like any family.

Mostly, though, the Shakers work together, keeping a flock of sixty sheep; tending a large orchard and vegetable garden, and packing and selling the herbs for cooking and for medicinal teas that traditionally have brought them income. They are fairly self-sufficient—"as much as our numbers will permit," Brother Arnold said—though they get help from the outside world to work their tree farm and manage the rest of their 1,900 acres.

Three of the current family were raised in Shaker communities like this. Sister Frances is one of them. In the days when the Shakers still took in needy children, "my little sister and I came here because we had been orphaned," she said. "I was just ten." The girls stayed till they reached "the age of decision," at which point her sister left, later to marry, have six children and now a flock of grandchildren. Sister Frances chose the other path.

"I was probably the last young person that they expected to become a Shaker," she said. At first, when she still felt the pain of losing her own home, "I didn't like it. I covered it up by being defiant." Then in her early teens, "I became very fortunate in having Sister Mildred [Barker, a beloved eldress of the church] become my mentor, my surrogate mother."

As they came of age, eight or ten of the other youngsters Sister Frances had grown up with decided to leave, drawn away to a changing post-war world. She realized that this must have hurt the Shakers "because they love you . . . . Many of the older sisters were just like grandmothers." She decided to stay "so I could at least give them back some of what they'd given me." She knew full well what she was giving up: "I had to take into consideration that I would not be married, I would not have my own family. But being a Shaker outweighed it."

Brother Arnold's story is quite different. When he was a teenager in the early 1970s, he wrote to the community with a question—he said he no longer remembers what it was—and got a long, warm letter back. After corresponding for two years, the family invited him for a visit.

"I worked, I worshipped, I fell in love with the people and the community," Brother Arnold said. During the next few years, he felt himself drawn closer and closer to Shaker life and finally joined the order in 1978. That made him the youngest in the family, and he had so much to learn, it was like "becoming a child all over again."

"You can't *read* Shakerism," he said. "You have to *live* Shakerism."

As in the past, the faith is lived in a daily round of work and prayer, ruled by the Great Bell, which hangs in a belfry atop the Dwelling House. It rings for breakfast at 7:30 and for morning prayers at 8, and it signals the halt of work for noon dinner, the Shakers' main meal.

On the day I was there, the Shakers and their guests sat down in the dining room of the Dwelling House and quietly partook of tuna hot dish, beef stew, home-grown spinach, homemade bread and two flavors of birthday cake, left over from recent family celebrations.

By Shaker tradition, the men sat at one table, the women at another, and except for the golden retriever, who was sprawled on the floor, and a wandering German shepherd, we sat in "Shaker squares"—eight people to a table, in two blocks of four, each block with its own salt and pepper, sugar bowl and napkins.

Shaker meals used to be silent occasions, and the self-contained Shaker squares meant that no one had to ask to have something passed. The rule of silence was dropped as the Shakers' numbers dwindled, but we still observed another Shaker maxim: "Shaker your plate!" Sister Frances advised. It means you eat all that you take, and it's the name she chose for her cookbook of Shaker recipes.

The community still accepts new members, and "in the last five or six years, we've had many, many more serious inquirers," Brother Arnold said—as many as forty or fifty a year. Mother Ann foresaw this: Shaker numbers would dwindle, she predicted, but then there would be a revival.

After noon dinner, I talked more with Sister Frances, back in the front room of the Dwelling House, amid the clean-lined furniture I'd seen before only in museums. Gauzy white curtains moved in and out with the summer breeze—the Shakers' interest in modern technology has not extended to air conditioning—and trucks rumbled by on the highway just outside the front door.

Sister Frances had a message to convey to the outside world: "I want people to know that while there's certainly a beauty in Shaker things—the furniture, the artifacts—there is still a group of people living in a place called Chosen Land where there have been Shakers for two hundred years, living the Shaker life."

Will the faith survive? I asked.

"Yes," she said firmly. "It has to. It's God's work." And then she added, with a confident smile, "Remember—there are as many people now as came over with Mother Ann—and look what happened!"

Lawrence Country

1999

———

THE FOUR-WHEEL-DRIVE jolted off the pavement and onto an expanse of pink sand. Ahead, a wide plain stretched out, studded with enormous outcroppings of rock. "*Now* are we in Wadi Rum?" I asked. I must have sounded like the middle-aged desert version of the proverbial impatient child.

"No," said the Bedouin at the wheel. "First, Seven Pillars of Wisdom. After, Wadi Rum."

"The Seven Pillars of Wisdom?" I echoed. "You mean they're *real?*"

Until that moment, I had thought of them only as a concept—like the Seven Deadly Sins or the Ten Commandments. Now the Seven Pillars of Wisdom were not only real, they were *right there.*

My guide, the jovial Abed-Allah Ali Salim, looking as regal as an Arabian prince in his sky-blue robe and black-and-white head cloth, gestured grandly at a lofty promontory of brown rock ahead of us. Without my knowing it, this rock was one of the reasons I'd come to the desert valley called Wadi Rum, in southwest Jordan. "The Seven Pillars of Wisdom" is the title of a book I admire, the memoirs of T.E. Lawrence, better known as Lawrence of Arabia.

The face of the giant bluff was indeed eroded into what looked like pillars. I counted them. I counted them again. Finally, I sketched them in my notebook and showed them to Abed-Allah, who nodded.

"But there are only six," I said. "See?"

I numbered the pillars in Arabic, immensely proud of the skill I'd picked up from reading bilingual license plates in a traffic jam in Beirut a few days before. I shouldn't have been so proud: After most of a month in the Middle East, all the Arabic I'd learned was how to count to seven. Big deal. But it came in handy now.

"Wahid," I said. One. "Nain. Talata. Arba. Hamsa. Sita." I still had another number—one-seventh of my entire Arabic vocabulary—left over.

"Short one!" Abed-Allah commanded, pointing. So I sketched in the squatty-looking rock crouched at one side of the massif, and he grinned in agreement.

When I got out of the vehicle to take a picture of the Six-and-a-Half Pillars of Wisdom, my feet sank ankle-deep into sand that felt like face powder. The sand didn't stretch to the horizon—that happens farther to the east and south—but it stretched impressively far, and it was empty. Wow, I thought, this is really *desert*.

It is really Lawrence country, too. During World War I, Lawrence had been all over this part of what would become Jordan, working to instigate an Arab revolt against the crumbling Turkish Empire.

The revolt not only succeeded, it made Lawrence a legend—with some help from American newsman Lowell Thomas, who promoted the romantic "Lawrence of Arabia" image far harder than Lawrence did himself.

We made a right turn just past the Seven Pillars of Wisdom, and a long canyon opened up, like a wide, waterless river. "*Now* Wadi Rum," Abed-Allah said.

The name means "Valley of the Moon," and it fit—a river of sand walled in by towering sandstone cliffs, their faces weathered dark with desert varnish, the sand beneath them warmly pink.

Lawrence compared it to an oversized boulevard where the bluffs were buildings; he could not shake the sense that it was a corridor leading somewhere. "Even the unsentimental Howeitat," he wrote, mentioning one of the Arab tribes, "had told me it was lovely."

It was also vast. We seemed to grow smaller the farther we went into Wadi Rum, as if a celestial camera lens were pulling back and back, shrinking us by comparison.

Abed-Allah stopped to show me some petroglyphs carved into the base of a cliff, and when he turned off the engine, the silence was so intense that I would have believed there were no other people in the world that morning except for the two of us.

But then we saw a herd of camels, standing around looking implausible, and my sense of aloneness evaporated. Like reindeer in Scandinavia, all camels belong to somebody, so their presence means a human being is somewhere nearby. Almost on cue, a boy soon appeared, sat down on a nearby crest of sand and regarded us from among the long-necked beasts.

The petroglyphs showed the unmistakable humped profiles of camels, with stick-figure people and huge birds: an ancient hunting scene. The birds weren't here any more, Abed-Allah hastened to explain: "Not now. *Before*. Now only Africa." He raised his elbows toward his ears, jutted his dignified head forward and did a good impression of an ostrich.

One of the camels walked gawkily up to the young herder who was watching us, bent its neck and nuzzled his face. It looked as if the camel were kissing him, and it was the friendliest thing I'd seen a camel do.

In this place where deadlines used to be a foreign concept, we now ran up against the clock. Abed-Allah placed a hand on his heart, gave me an overly angelic smile and said, with utmost humility, "I have no time."

He meant *I* had no time. He drove me to the ragged village of Rum—a place so dreary that it insulted its landscape—and turned me over to the tourist police. They, in turn, introduced me to the leader of my pre-arranged one-person camel caravan.

Selim Sabah Ateik, the camel-drover, was not what I expected. For starters, he was only eleven years old. This put my expedition-in-the-camel-tracks-of-Lawrence in the same league as a tractor ride through the family pasture with a Minnesota farm kid at the controls.

I'm blank on how I got up on my camel. It must have knelt down. I was once told that a camel doesn't "kneel" in Arabic; the literal translation is that the camel "demolishes its foundations." That's certainly how it looks. Once I was aboard, Selim mounted his own camel, and we set off. He led my camel by its reins, which gave me the odd sensation that I was being towed. I had nothing to do but sit there.

We rode down the sandy main street as if Rum village were

Dodge City and made an immediate stop at the general store. Selim dashed in to get himself a bottle of water and a can of Coke in a plastic bag—his pack, he called it—leaving me at the hitching post, stranded ten feet in the air, atop my camel. I felt stupid.

Camels look great by themselves and flat-out dramatic with kaffiyeh-clad Bedouins on their backs. But put a tourist up there, and the effect is ridiculous. I was like the village of Rum itself: Both the camel and the desert would have been more dignified without us.

I stopped feeling stupid as soon as we got going but only because I was too uncomfortable to care. We weren't out of sight of the village before I was actively hurting and wondering how long I could endure the ride. Selim was taking me to Small Bridge, an eroded sandstone arch near the top of a cliff. The round-trip would be four hours, perhaps ten miles in all. I could see where we were going from the beginning, but there was a sandy haze in the air, and it exaggerated the distances. Everything seemed both close and far away.

Camels pad silently, their feet like round sponges on the sand, and their shadows glide along as smoothly as ripples. I marveled at that. How could something that looked so serene and moved so smoothly feel so awful?

I blamed the camel saddle. Real ones aren't like the fancy gilded leather versions tourists buy. Those have cushions. Real ones are little more than a frame made from a few pieces of wood, like sections sawn from a broomstick, with high pommels front and back and a blanket or two tossed over them in a failed attempt at padding.

All the saddle does is level off the hump on the camel's back. It's the equivalent of a narrow, swaying, lumpy shelf, where you struggle to keep your balance. Every time the shelf rocks, your sitz bones grind over the wooden frame. At least mine did.

Selim, of course, was completely comfortable. He moved around on his saddle as if it were a hassock in front of the den TV. At one point, late in the day, he turned completely around and rode backward, staring at me.

I wished I'd thought of that one. I had tried every other position I could think of on my camel saddle—except for flinging myself across it belly-down—and never found anything I could stand for more than four minutes.

The most comfortable position was also the most precarious: Instead of hunching over and holding on tight, I let go of the saddle, crossed my legs loosely around the front pommel and tried to make my back—and backside—relax. That's how everybody rode in "Lawrence of Arabia," my all-time favorite movie, but while I appreciated the example, I still felt as if I were being pounded.

If Lawrence's saddle had hurt like this, I grumped to myself, Jordan would still belong to the Ottoman Turks.

My experience with camels isn't vast (and it's not going to be, thanks), but I became pretty sure that they aren't trained to carry stuff on their backs as much as tricked into it. It really ticks them off. And they let you know it. All the time. In wet, guttural voices that sound like a cross between Chewbacca in "Star Wars" and a cow trying to throw up.

They also bite each other in the butt, cough, chew cud, sneak nibbles of tough desert plants instead of walking, swivel their heads and wipe their noses on your socks, scratch their long faces by rubbing them on your leg and generally behave like . . . camels.

Despite my pain, I found them fascinating. The only things

more fascinating would be great white sharks and Siberian tigers. Which, now that I think about it, are probably easier to get along with.

"What's better," I asked Selim at one point on our endless, plodding journey, "a donkey or a camel?"

"Camel," he said. Donkeys, I thought, must be hell on earth.

Early on, we stopped to see Lawrence's Well, a spring where the Arab army had watered its camels. Now it's a cement water trough by the foot of a bluff just beyond Rum village.

"Camels drink," Selim said simply.

Selim said everything simply because, although he was studying English in school, his vocabulary was still small. This made him sound wiser than his years.

Now and then, I called out questions to Selim. Now and then, Selim sang long Arabic songs in a childish monotone. His favorites, he told me when I asked, were "Welcome Song for Prince" and a traveling ditty called "Come, Camel, Come."

Selim also shouted at birds to startle them into the air. Pointed out a dangerous snake: "Very bad," he said. And passed on bits of desert lore: "Snake catch on camel. Camel die. Seven days."

It was a reminder of how harsh this landscape could be. There was more proof after we reached Small Bridge, where I took one picture, mainly so I wouldn't hurt Selim's feelings, and we turned around and headed back toward the concrete-block haven of Rum.

Gazing down at the sand, wondering if I should finally accept a humiliating defeat and walk, I noticed a scattering of something white around us. Bones, white bones, dotted the pink sand—ribs here, a few vertebrae there, a long bone or two, a skull with protruding teeth. The skull looked as if it had belonged to a sheep. A very big sheep.

"What kind of bones are those?" I asked.

Selim turned around, looked, said simply, "camel."

"How did the camel die?"

"Camel very age."

Ah. The camel died of old age. It had lain down in the pink sand one day and never gotten up.

We rode in silence until, off to the right, I saw what looked like a white canvas tent, badly pitched and abandoned. It was partly covered with sand. That was odd. Who would leave a tent? Then I noticed that four rocks to one side of it weren't rocks but hooves. It was another animal corpse, lying on its side; the white "canvas" was its sun-bleached skin. But camels don't have hooves . . . .

"What's that one?" I asked.

"Horse," Selim said simply.

"How did the horse die?"

"Horse fast," Selim said.

That took me a second. Then I realized that he didn't mean "speedy," he meant "foodless." Fast, as in hunger strike. The horse had starved to death, and eventually the dry climate had turned its body into this semi-mummy. We lapsed into silence again.

On the sand, trash thickened. We were approaching civilization, closing in on Rum at last, passing the juice boxes and aluminum cans that announced its presence.

Slowly, we had been making a slight curve around a bluff, and now the gray profile of the village appeared in the distance. I was relieved to see it because it meant that I could finally get off the damn camel, and disappointed because it meant the adventure was over. Then, just as I was hoping our camels wouldn't speed up like saddle horses do when they see the barn, we stopped.

Selim was pulling hard on the reins and struggling to make both camels turn around. They finally submitted, backing up a few paces so Selim could show me something on the ground. It was the black circle of a cast-off tire.

"Car," he said simply, in the same deadpan way he'd identified the dead horse and the dead camel. He eyed me, waiting for a reaction, and I thought I saw a faint smile on his lips. His point was clear. I refrained from asking how the car died.

Over the Sea to Skye

1997

M Y WELL-USED SCOTTISH road map bears the usual il-legible scribbles—mileages, notes about which pictures I took where—and one startling exception, as easy to read as if it were neon: "This is where I'd want to live!"

I wrote that in a burst of enthusiasm one afternoon on the Duirinish Peninsula, the westernmost lobe of this amoeba-shaped island. But I could have written it about a dozen other places on Skye—any place with whitewashed cottages hiding from the wind in a small green valley near the shore, which is just about everywhere.

Maybe it was the rainbows, a byproduct of Skye's wild weather, that made me like it so much. Maybe it was the closeness of the sea. Maybe the island's blanketing sense of isolation, even though it's now connected to the mainland by a bridge. More likely, it was all those things and a few more. On Skye, the combination gave me the feeling that I associate with successful house-hunting: I not only knew where I'd like to live, I knew where I'd put the Christmas tree.

Skye was part of a grand plan to hit the highlights of the Highlands in a single week. I could tour Skye, I figured, zip on to the Isle of Mull, ferry back to the mainland, drive up to Loch Ness and look for the monster, and end up back in Glasgow with time to look around Scotland's second city.

Right. As any Scot could have told me, that itinerary was laughably ambitious. You don't zip anywhere in Scotland, certainly not in the Highlands and Islands. The land's too ragged, the roads too narrow, the lochs too long. And the scenery . . . well, at some points it was so far past breathtaking that I had to choose between pulling over to stare or driving off the road. I pulled over.

Instead of zipping, then, I stayed on Skye, taking long drives around peninsula after peninsula, while the weather changed so often that every day on the island was like a week anywhere else. The distances were deceptive too. Skye is only about twenty-five miles wide and fifty long, but there were no short jaunts. Most roads follow the coast, and the coastline is as intricate as lace.

An added catch was that, away from Broadford and Portree, Skye's two main towns, most of the roads were "single-track" with bump-outs called "passing places" every quarter-mile or so. Shoulders were nonexistent, when they weren't ditches. Passing-place etiquette called for me to flash my headlights and pull over into a passing place the moment I spotted an oncoming car. The on-comers were supposed to do the same for me.

Sometimes we both pulled over. Sometimes, most often on the frequent hills and curves where neither driver could see, neither of us pulled over, which meant one of us—usually me, taking no chances with a drive-on-the-left rental car—backed up a hundred yards to the previous passing place and waited.

While this was invariably a polite process—Skye etiquette

also calls for both drivers to give a slight wave as they finally pass each other—it took time. Add to that the spare, splendid scenery; flocks of traffic-stopping sheep; sudden squalls that fogged the vistas and flung raindrops onto the windshield as if they were buckshot—and a circle drive around little Skye became an all-day proposition.

The reward for laboriously exploring the island was its people. Scots are famously regarded as taciturn, but locals opened up when I asked about Skye. Many had long off-island histories: They'd either come home to Skye after full careers elsewhere, or they'd been almost magically drawn here, knowing—as soon as they rounded a particular curve in the road or gazed across a particular valley—that they'd found the place they were meant to live.

The guidebooks direct everybody north to Portree, the biggest town, packed around a little harbor midway up Skye's eastern shore. This meant the main tourist office in Portree was also packed, mostly with hikers smelling of damp wool and wet boots.

Down at the visitor's center in Broadford, a smaller, more spread-out town closer to the mainland bridge, a woman named Nan MacDonald had fewer tourists to please. I asked basic questions, then ventured one about Highland dancing—flings and sword dances and the like, which I've always loved. No luck, wrong season, but the question encouraged Nan, a slight woman of about sixty, with short reddish hair, to admit quietly that in her girlhood, she and her sister had won Skye's first trophies for Highland dancing.

Nan MacDonald is one of those who came back home to Skye after a career away—very far away. She had gone to sea, working as a children's nurse on international liners for twenty-five years, while the great ships carried her to South Africa, South America, Australia and most of the Pacific islands, until illness forced her to retire. Skye is home now, but so was the world: "I would do it all again," she said. "I've no regrets. I would do it now if I were fit enough."

I loved wandering her island. Its scenery changed with the weather—now grim, now lovely—and the weather changed constantly, producing light that reminded me of Paris. It was like being inside a watercolor, with vast washes of pearl, gray and charcoal on every horizon.

What struck me most about Skye, however—and the Highlands as a whole—is that so much of it was empty. There were long valleys, towering hillsides, vista upon vista of loch-riven land and lots of sheep, dotting the distant hills like handfuls of thrown rice. But almost no people.

That haunting, empty beauty was something I enjoyed, but the reasons behind it were ugly. Skye's best-known observer blamed it on sheep and greed. I'd been spending my evenings reading Skye history as I recovered from each day's drive, but the more I learned, the more I wanted to know. I was most interested in Scotland's saddest period: the Clearances. Most of what I read was written by one man, James Hunter, an island resident. Finally I phoned him, and one morning I drove out to his croft—a Highland term for a small farmstead—with an invitation for tea and answers.

Hunter, a light-haired, forty-ish man with glasses, was a student of Scottish history and culture, the former head of the Skye Crofters Union, a former journalist and professor and a prolific writer. His books were in every shop I saw, including a quick-stop at Broadford's biggest gas station.

We started with the Clearances. In simplest terms, Hunter

said, the Clearances swept ordinary peasants aside so that the clan chiefs could raise sheep on clan lands and make money. The Clearances began in the mid-1700s and continued, in various forms, until the 1880s, when protests on Skye led to legal reform for the Highlands.

If the chiefs hadn't been involved, he said, "a lot of people would have left the Highlands anyway," the way people left the west coast of Norway—"more voluntarily and under slightly better circumstances." The countryside might even have looked different: "Sheep have had a very devastating effect on the environment, especially in terms of deforestation."

You mean, all that bald scenery . . . ?

Yes, Hunter said, "that archetypal Highland landscape is, in large part, a human creation."

What the Highland exiles left behind weren't the tidy, story-and-a-half whitewashed cottages that grace Skye today. Back then, people lived in "black houses"—more huts than buildings, with thatched roofs riding low on their thick, gray stone walls. Fewer than a dozen black houses still stand, preserved at outdoor museums around the island. The largest group—seven of them—is at Kilmuir, on Trotternish Peninsula. I saw them in a wind so fierce I had to lean against it to walk. Their walls blocked the wind, but that was about all. The black houses were cold even with a fire in the parlor grate—and the grate itself was a modern innovation. The originals got their nickname because they had no chimneys; smoke from the hearth just seeped out through the roof, blackening the building—and the residents' lungs—on the way.

Not everybody lived like that on Skye, though, and for a glimpse of the other extreme, I drove to the polar extremes of the island. I went north to Skye's best-known tourist attraction, picture-perfect Dunvegan Castle, the still-occupied ancestral home of the chief of the MacLeods: a medieval castle with Victorian touches set amid gardens on an inlet where seals lazed on the rocky shore.

And I went south to Armadale, where the MacLeods' archrivals, the MacDonalds—formerly titled the Lords of the Isles—once had their stronghold. Their castle is in ruins now, but the High Chief of the MacDonalds and his wife run a respected country hotel nearby. Called Kinloch Lodge, it is renowned for its food, the specialty of Lady MacDonald, an award-winning cookbook author. I stayed there one night, in a room that was small, rather ordinary and very expensive, but the dinner they served was a highlight of the trip.

Just after the best paté I'd ever tasted and just before the mushroom-leek soup, a dapper man of about fifty, casually but impeccably dressed in a navy blue sweater and tan slacks, bounded into the dining room and up to my table.

"Godfrey MacDonald," he announced, shaking my hand. "Everything all right? You're enjoying your trip to Skye? How long have you been in Scotland? Well, then, you've had a few good days and a few bad, but if you'd come to Scotland and hadn't seen a bit of rain, you'd have wondered what was wrong!"

Then Lord MacDonald dashed off to visit the rest of his dining room's eleven tables, shaking hands and greeting guests at all of them. I was so startled—and awed—that he had bounded out of the room before I recovered. I wished I'd told him what had been on my mind. "Why didn't your ancestor send troops to help Bonnie Prince Charlie at Culloden?" I wanted to call after him. "That could have changed history! And what about the Clearances?"

Too late. I swallowed my historical curiosity with the last bite of that excellent paté.

My last afternoon on Skye, trying to reach the ruins of Borreraig, a "cleared" village far out on the Duirinish Peninsula, I stopped for directions at the local post office, started talking to the postmistress and never got any farther.

A lean woman with gray hair and a sharp gaze, she was Audrey Manwaring-Spencer, a craftswoman who runs a tiny shop filled with the work of neighborhood knitters, including her own designs, along with yarns and knitting tools. Her husband tends a flock of sheep, selling the lambs and the wool. I picked up a pair of hand-made wooden knitting needles, more than a foot long and almost too beautiful to use, and held them so long I knew I was going to take them home.

The couple is typical of the island's crofters. By one definition I'd heard, crofts are "small pieces of land entirely surrounded by regulations." Crofts aren't on the best land, either—that went for sheep pasture in the Clearances—and they usually aren't big enough to support a family.

Manwaring-Spencer said that was true. "I don't know anybody who's making a living out of the land—who has [only] one income," she said. "Crofting basically means you do various things—as a way of life—and somehow you get by."

She sounded like an island native, but she wasn't Skye-born. She and her husband had come to the island from Blackpool, well to the south in England, in search of a saner life: "It was not so much a decision to come to Skye as to get out of city-style living—to slow down." They'd arrived on Skye "twelve years ago with four kids and ten pounds," she said, and now they could boast "five kids and fifteen pounds." During all those years, she'd only been off the island a handful of times, for a couple of hospital stays and two funerals. There had been no other need to leave.

I understood why she preferred to stay put; I would too, I thought, given the view. From her cottage door, I could see how sweetly the land sloped down, green and empty, toward the sea. With twilight coming on, the place was beautifully peaceful, almost enchanted.

"There's a pace of life goes with islands," she said, following my gaze. "Doesn't matter the island."

Into the Country of Memory

1995

―――

"YOU CAN'T GO HOME AGAIN." Thomas Wolfe said it, and so did countless others, including me, and before that, my high school German teacher, who had the grace to add, "Yes, but the heart always tries."

Sometimes the heart succeeds, if two recent experiences are any proof. Both involved time travel, the kind you get in a French Quarter cemetery on a cloudy day or the Tower of London at closing time, when the frontier blurs between then and now. It's the same when the place you're visiting is your own past. My excursions there, twice in the same year, were simultaneously troublesome and reassuring.

The first was in August, at a home-town reunion. It was an odd home town: Fort Snelling, a long-time military base that was a Veterans Administration center after the war. My father worked for the VA, and part of the deal was being able to live in one of the former officers' quarters. But the VA left the fort in the early 1970s, and everybody had to move away, my folks and all our neighbors. Our houses have stood empty ever since, their windows boarded up, their interiors vandalized.

Since there is no town anymore, we held our reunion on

the front lawns. And afterward—after the guests had finished their barbeque, and one of my brothers had led a flock of children in a remarkably messy egg toss—a few of us adults sneaked off to see if we could get into my family's old house.

Vandals had left a good-sized entrance via a basement window. One by one, we eased ourselves through and dropped down into a dim pool of light and broken glass beside our ancient asbestos-clad furnace. Beyond that, we could see nothing. I mean *nothing*. All the other windows were covered with sheets of plywood, and the darkness was absolute—the blinding black that makes your eyes widen and stare in hope of light. There was none.

It was like spelunking, only we went up instead of down. Up the back stairs, into the kitchen, through the dining room, across the living room, into the front foyer where we always put the Christmas tree, up the front stairs to our bedrooms, and finally up into the attic, where the summer heat and the scent of bat droppings were instantly familiar and perfectly normal.

You know how it feels to close your eyes and imagine yourself in a home you used to love? Your grandmother's, say, or the one you lived in when you started grade school? How you can picture every room, every piece of furniture, every knick-knack in its proper place? Going through our house was like that. But it wasn't imagination, it was real. And it bent time for me.

I knew the house was empty. But it was so dark, I couldn't *see* that it was empty. As we explored, relying on memory and the touch of familiar woodwork, the cave-dark house filled up again, furnishing itself as it had been when we lived there.

Everything came back—chairs, tables, pictures on the walls, china in the cupboards. In this imagined house, I couldn't tell past from present. The darkness seemed a thin curtain, with the real house behind it, just as it used to be, living its old life, maybe with all of us in it, little again, and my parents still alive. It made me think of Emily, in "Our Town," come back from the dead. But the past saddened her. For me, it was a kind of reassurance—a place I'd longed for, reachable and still the same.

When we finally crawled back out the basement window and into our own era—and were met by puzzled little children wondering where the grown-ups had gone—we admitted that we'd all felt like children ourselves in that house. It was the kind of adventure that we'd have envied at about age ten. And I felt as if I'd really been home.

The second episode happened in Germany that December. I'd flown into Frankfurt, picked up a car and was heading south toward Heidelberg—right past the turnoff for a place I once lived. I made a sudden, unplanned detour and went, well, home—though I didn't expect it to feel like that. I went back to the boarding school where I'd been a sixteen-year-old exchange student—the Odenwaldschule, which stood near a tiny village in a forest. I hadn't seen it in thirty-four years.

As usual on these spur-of-the-moment expeditions, I had no map. As usual, I figured I could guess my way. As often usual, it didn't work.

I left the autobahn at Heppenheim and was quickly lost. Crisp new houses stood where there should have been fields, and I had to ask directions for the village of Unterhambach; I remembered only that it lay in a narrow valley, and the school would have stood a mile or so farther upstream.

Unterhambach had doubled in size, running along its single street like a true town, instead of the hamlet I had known. I recognized nothing in it or beyond it—until I came around a wooded curve, where a green field opened on one side and a gnarled apple tree leaned drunkenly away from the road.

I knew that apple tree. I'd taken its picture once, a lifetime ago. I looked up, and there, in the distance, were the big brown-shingled cottages of the school, arrayed across the hillside like their own village.

Wandering the campus, I was surprised at how familiar it felt. Nothing had changed—except me. I found my way to Humboldt Haus, where I'd lived for a semester, and knocked on the door of my old room. A young teacher let me in, so I could gaze out my old window at what was once my favorite view—a wedge of green pasture below a wall of black trees, silhouetted against winter sky. I'd last seen it in another December, and it looked the same now, a living flashback.

Driving away that evening, I realized I owed the Odenwaldschule a debt. I became a traveler while I was there—not least because I learned to cut classes and sneak off to wander around Heidelberg, in an early experiment with freedom.

When I got back to Minneapolis, I dug out the journal I'd kept that winter at the school and was as startled as if I'd met myself in our Fort Snelling attic. At the time I wrote it, I remember feeling that my journal was a letter to someone in the distant future; I didn't know the reader would be me.

"Winter is coming down on our hillside," one entry read, "in criss-cross patterns of snow, which melts on our windowsills, pads one side of the black lilac branches and the trunks of the trees, fills in the cracks and rills of the ground . . . . The grass was still green yesterday, and the ivy will stay green all year."

The description still matched, and the writer's voice was

disturbingly familiar. My sixteen-year-old self was already preoccupied with the geography of time, with feeling and not feeling enough, with the difficulty of translating a place into words, of nailing experience onto paper—*for someone else to read.*

I'd even offered helpful travel tips ("the trick is, never unpack until you get where you're going" and "there is only one antidote for homesickness—hard work"), as well as some embarrassing descriptions of people and a great deal of fretting.

"Perhaps this whole diary-keeping idea is only an affectation," one entry lamented. "I will probably remember just as much without my record, as I do with it." Oh, no, the adult reader thought, you're wrong there, kid. The record will matter.

And then this: "I wish my dreams could be real . . . . I wish I could be what I want!"

Which was? A writer, a photographer, a traveler. I stared at that page for a long time before I closed the old journal. How odd to know how the story would turn out. And how early in life we start to be ourselves.

So. Two journeys. Two places where past and present tangled. There are such junctions for everyone, whether the path to them lies in a German village or a Minnesota attic. And when you come to one, you know that Thomas Wolfe was wrong. You *can* go home again. But only as a tourist: In the landscape of your life, you do not get to stay.

Chez Nous

1986

WHEN I CAME BACK from Paris last time, friends asked me if it had rained while I was there, and I was surprised that I couldn't remember. It must have, I decided, because it always rains in Paris sooner or later, and because I recalled sitting in a cafe one afternoon and sipping hot chocolate while my raincoat dried out.

The point is that the rain didn't matter. Paris is its own climate. The city always looks about the same, no matter the weather or the time of year. The buildings are always the same soft shade of pewter-gray. The sky is always wan and changeable and slightly hazy, as if a pale, shimmering veil lay over it, like one of Schiaparelli's famous scarves. And at all seasons, being out in the city's intimate gray streets is almost like being indoors somewhere else.

If I were lucky enough to live in Paris for the rest of my life, I think I'd remain a tourist at heart. Could I ever walk past Notre Dame without looking up at the great facade? Or stroll past the fountains of the Trocadero and not be transfixed by the Eiffel Tower across the river? Or drive to work every day on the clogged riverside boulevards and concentrate more on traffic than on the Seine? I can't imagine it.

That's why I'm always saddened to meet Americans who haven't liked the city. There are a lot of them, and they tend to say the same things about it: *Loved the architecture, didn't care much for the people . . . .*

I understand that—I used to feel that way myself—but then a neighborhood changed my mind. And changed me. What turned me around was a series of visits to a friend who was living in Auteuil, a quiet residential enclave on the western edge of the city, next door to the Bois de Boulogne.

It may be that every tourist has to start in the brusque and busy center of the city—a trial by ire, perhaps?—just as every tourist has to track down the Venus de Milo and the Mona Lisa before seeing the rest of the Louvre, ride the elevator to the top of the Eiffel Tower, and join the crowds of shoppers at the *grands magazins,* the city's vast department stores.

But you only need to do those things once. Then you can head for a neighborhood and turn it into your temporary home. Neighborhoods are the key to understanding this city—maybe any city—and to liking its residents.

Real neighborhoods, I mean. Americans always yearn to see "the real Paris," but we make the mistake of looking for it only in the places we've heard of—along the Champs-Elysées or around Notre Dame or along the Boulevard St. Michel. Those are all interesting, but I don't think "the real Paris" is there. The real Paris is out in the neighborhoods where the real people live. Though Auteuil is more affluent than most, it remains the best example I know.

Parisians like to think of their city as a collection of villages, and to a great extent that's true. Even touristy Montmartre retains a village spirit. But unlike most of the others, Auteuil (pronounced more or less "O-toy") actually *was* a village—a legally separate small town—until the city of Paris annexed it in 1860. Its main artery, the Rue d'Auteuil, still looks like the main street of a country village, and residents enjoy perpetuating the distinction: They still talk about "going to the city" when they're heading for central Paris.

I'd been in Paris several times before, but I didn't begin to understand about neighborhoods until my first visit to Auteuil. My friend was working nights on the International Herald Tribune, so I spent a lot of time wandering on my own. One afternoon, I was browsing through the bargain bins outside an old bookstore on Auteuil's central square when I spotted a little hand-lettered sign in the bookshop window. It announced what I thought would be a concert of Gregorian chant in the neighborhood church, Notre Dame d'Auteuil.

I love Gregorian chant. But when I went there on concert night, the main doors of the church were locked. I found a side door that was open, heard singing and followed the sound to a small basement room, where eleven people were sitting around with song sheets.

"Come in, come in," the director said in French, "we need another voice!" No, no, I protested, I can't sing—I just came to listen.

Nonsense, he said, handing me a song sheet and waving me toward the group. The singers made room for me, told me I spoke good French (not true) and inquired politely whether I knew any of the Americans they knew. I didn't. What a pity, they said, and they seemed to mean it.

They were rehearsing, I learned between chants, so that

they could perform during a church service a few weeks hence. Before that first practice session ended, they had made me part of their team—tin ear and all. One of the women, whose family turned out to own the bookshop, insisted on driving me home, even though it was out of her way.

I rehearsed with the group three more times after that, and when the designated Sunday came, I joined them in the choir stalls, singing Gregorian chants at morning mass. I can't remember the words or the music, but I have loved the French—and Auteuil—ever since.

Neighborhoods like Auteuil help keep Paris the same, their habits and patterns acting like flywheels on the engines of change. Whenever I am in Auteuil, for example, I can count on the neighborhood farmers' market taking place on Wednesday and Saturday mornings and turning Place Jean-Lorrain into a carnival of fresh vegetables, fruits and flowers.

I also know that Le Village d'Auteuil, the cafe that overlooks that little triangular plaza, will never have croissants on hand when you order them. I know the waiter will always dash out to fetch them from the bakery next door. That way they'll be fresh.

Some things do change in Auteuil. In the nearly ten years since I first stayed there, a new consulate has gone up on Rue d'Auteuil, the only modern building on the street; the owner of the neighborhood's best Chinese restaurant has turned it over to his children, and Les Marronniers, a grubby little ma-and-pa eatery near the west end of Rue d'Auteuil, has at last changed hands.

Its name—The Chestnut Trees—was the nicest thing about it. A hold-over from pre-war Paris, it was more a diner than a restaurant, a narrow room with dingy chartreuse walls and long oil-cloth-covered tables flanked by benches that customers shared. The elderly man who owned it—who used to spend his afternoons sitting in the doorway, personally arranging the sliced plums on the evening's desserts—finally sold the place.

The new owner is a dapper middle-aged Algerian, whose wife is the hostess and whose teenage son is in training at the bar. ("He wants my job!" the owner told me proudly.) Now the walls are covered in pale gray linen, the worn picnic-table seating has been replaced by café tables and tiny chairs, and the menu—once a not-very-good bargain that attracted impoverished students and pensioners—has become scrumptious.

But the dishes are still cheaper than the same good food would be in the heart of the city. Other things in Auteuil are cheaper too: hotel rooms, for example, and even the great tourist staple, French perfume. The last time I was there, it was slightly cheaper in a pretty boutique in Auteuil than in the tourist-clogged department stores downtown.

True, it wasn't much cheaper—only a couple of francs a bottle—but I didn't have to fight my way past other shoppers to buy it. And the elegant older woman who waited on me took time to explain how the precious bottle should be stored: somewhere cool, always in its box, away from the light.

She added that her shop was going to start some makeup classes for people who lived in the neighborhood, and would I be interested in attending? I had to say no, but I loved being included.

That was another clue to how Paris neighborhoods tick: The proprietors of the small shops—including every bakery and grocery and *charcuterie* (a French deli)—take pains to build relationships with their clients. They have to. Paris is full of wonderful bakeries and groceries and delis. To survive such stiff competition, the small shops depend on personal bonds. If you're in a neighborhood long enough to develop shopping patterns, the shopkeepers will claim you, too. And they *do* remember.

During my first stay, the charcuterie I went to most often on Rue d'Auteuil was Carlier's. I shopped there four or five times a week for supper items, in particular their green beans with garlic butter. The proprietress and I never had a real conversation, but she must have decided I was a regular.

Six months elapsed between that stay and my next. When I finally got back to see my friend in Auteuil again, I picked up where I'd left off. Hungry for those green beans, I stopped in at Carlier's to get some for supper the first night.

The proprietress spotted me at the door and gave me a huge smile. "Ah!" she said, recognizing one of her prodigals. "You're *back!* You went to America for a visit, but now you are *back home!*" The warmth of her greeting made me feel I truly was.

A Suzdal Spring

1979

—·—

"GUTEN TAG!" an old voice rasps from a yard, and the tourist swings around. German again; you hear so much German here—a godsend, since I don't speak Russian. The speaker is an old man, down to three unsteady teeth in bare gums that show when he grins. He is grinning now. Dressed in a dark-blue smock and the high black boots of the Russian peasant, he leans on his cane, taking the sun by the side of his house and wanting to talk.

"I am by Berlin," he says in German, grinning and nodding. "Thirty years."

It takes a second to translate. He means not *for* 30 years, but more than 30 years *ago*. The war again, and the war's long aftermath. He was an officer, the old man says, stationed in the East Zone of the German capital. He was there long enough to pick up a vocabulary that has survived unused till now.

"Spaziergang?" he asks. Taking a stroll? Yes, I say, I'm just looking around, and he nods, grinning. "Kein Mann?" he wonders. No husband? Ah, too bad. The grin fades. Tourist? Ah! The grin returns.

His German is beginning to falter now, but there is enough

left to outline his life. Suzdal was home, he says, and after he got out of the army, he came back here and did farm work. That is no surprise, judging by his clothes and the work-thickened hands knotted over his cane.

"Russian? You speak?" Ah, too bad, too bad. His German is used up. The conversation ends in a small flurry of waves and nods and smiles. A friendly moment in a not-always-friendly country.

But that is how Suzdal is, if you can judge a town by a two-day visit. I hope you can, because Suzdal seems to be, as its old name says, a "sweet valley"—as far away from the bureaucratic grimness of Moscow as it may be possible to get without leaving the Soviet Union.

To walk its quiet streets on a warm spring afternoon, when the ice has mostly melted from the fields and the soft air smells of mud, is almost to be free, to forget where you are. People smile. It is possible to stroll for hours, stopping to photograph a carved window on a cottage or a cat sleeping in the sun or an old couple resting near the tranquil Kamenka River, without being hassled. Nobody appears in a doorway to shake a warning finger at the camera. Nobody orders you to desist before you push the shutter. *Nobody hassles you.*

And it is beautiful here. When the communist presence lifts, the Russian countryside remains. The countryside—and the Russian past.

Suzdal is a town of churches, a horizon of spires. Dozens of them—big ones, little ones, white ones, red. The town was settled in the ninth century, and by medieval times, it had become a powerful religious center. One look proves it: At first glance, there seem to be more churches than houses.

Three dozen major religious structures—churches, monastic

buildings, bell towers—and many lesser ones still stand, and that is only part of what the town once had. It was so beautiful, my government-assigned guide intoned before turning me loose to wander on my own, that people believed Suzdal was favored by God: "Only God could create such a miracle."

The masonry churches, old by American standards, are relatively new from Suzdal's perspective. Most date from the 17th and 18th centuries, though parts of the blue-domed Cathedral of Our Lady date back to 1225. The cathedral is the centerpiece of Suzdal's old Kremlin, the fortified city center overlooking the river.

At the end of the 11th century, Suzdal was larger than London or Paris, and in the 16th century, the town had fifteen flourishing monasteries. Gradually, the town's power declined, until by the 19th century, Suzdal was just a large village. Its merchants turned down a chance for a rail spur, and that preserved its architecture, because modern industry passed it by.

So many historical buildings survive that Suzdal has been designated a museum town. Sometimes, it's even billed as "the Soviet equivalent of Colonial Williamsburg"—I find political irony in that—and it is being positioned to become a major tourist attraction. Old walls are being patched and whitewashed, belfries shored up, and the picturesque log cabins that had served as cells for cloistered nuns are being replaced. A new hotel—well-designed and low-roofed, so it does not intrude on Suzdal's gentle skyline—has been built on the edge of town, and tourism is visibly on the increase.

I am part of that tourism but not by choice. I didn't ask to go to Suzdal when I sent my visa request to Inturist, the U.S.S.R.'s travel administration, but when I got my final itinerary, there it was. Clearly, they wanted to show it off. They carved time for this side trip out of the days I'd requested to spend in Moscow. Suzdal lies to the southeast, a six-hour drive away, so the round-trip alone will eat up two days, and with two days here, I will have almost no time in the capital. I tried pointing that out, but there is no arguing with Inturist.

Now I am glad they hijacked me. I'd rather be in a village than a city, anywhere, any day. And this village is a gem. Eleven thousand people live here now—quietly. On this afternoon at the end of April, with townspeople bustling to get ready for May Day celebrations, Suzdal feels as peaceful as the setting of a Chekov short story.

A team of men is installing a huge pink and red placard of Lenin's face beside Market Square, the old commercial heart of town. Another team works on a new log house, putting the notched and numbered timbers together exactly as if they were giant Lincoln Logs.

Elderly women in black—black coats, black scarves, black felt boots with rubber-coated soles, necessities on Suzdal's mud-clogged streets—are queued up to buy sweet rolls near a bus stop on the main boulevard.

Young mothers push perambulators along Traders' Row, a white-columned block of shops built about 1810 on Market Square, and they tuck their parcels in beside their sober, red-cheeked babies.

Primary-school children, buoyant after classes, climb in the small trees in Market Square, teasing each other. Older children, obviously on a work project, rake the riverbank, gathering up last fall's leaves and snow-buried trash, exposed by the spring thaw.

And three little girls, armed with bits of white chalk, draw complicated patterns on the pavement by the Archbishop's

Palace in the Kremlin, scattering like rabbits when I approach with my camera. Their progress through town is marked by murals of kings and queens and hopscotch squares chalked on streets and sidewalks.

For all the activity, there is almost no noise. From the voices of the children to the grating gears of the buses, Suzdal's sounds seem to be sponged up by the soft spring sky. Only one sound stands out in memory—the steady cawing of rooks, a European edition of crows, from treetops crowded with their nests. No, two sounds: the cawing of rooks and the intermittent clang of church bells from one or another old tower, striking the hours.

If I were in Moscow this afternoon, listening near Moscow's Kremlin, I'd hear something quite different marking the hours. I'd hear the grim, steady thump of goose-stepping soldiers, striding out into Red Square to relieve the guards at Lenin's Tomb. But here in Suzdal, even the soldiers have a gentler side.

As dusk comes on and the mild air begins to chill, I duck into a restaurant at the end of Traders' Row, hoping for hot tea and a snack. Its looks deceive. Outside, it has been restored to its antique charm, but inside, it is like so many other public spaces across the U.S.S.R.—bleak and boring.

At least the mood is cheerful: A wedding party is gathering, a small rock band is warming up, and friends of the bride are arranging food on a long table, adding apples and pickles, brought from home, to the meager spread that the restaurant has provided.

When the table is finished, one of the young women brings out a small bouquet of flowers—three red tulips and a calla lily. It is too early in the year for these to be home-grown—they have to be hot-house flowers, rare and therefore expensive. Almost reverently, the women arrange them in a glass and stand back, beaming at the results.

There are only two other people in the restaurant, a uniformed soldier in red-trimmed khaki, an officer, I think, eating alone in one corner, and me, alone in another. Because of us, a different drama unfolds.

The soldier calls to the women with the wedding party, and one of them goes over to him. They whisper back and forth, he sounding insistent, she stubborn. Finally she goes back to the carefully arranged table, takes one of the red tulips out of the vase and gives it to the soldier. He immediately sends it over to me.

When I look up, startled and worried, the soldier stands, bows gallantly to me and strides out, leaving me stunned. He sent me the flower purely as a gesture, no modern strings attached, and it was as out of place in rough-edged Russia as anywhere else in the late-20th-century world. But it wasn't out of place in Suzdal.

I hold the tulip reverently until the door closes behind the soldier and then give the precious flower back to the wedding party; it brings smiles back to their faces. When the bride and groom arrive, I linger for a few of the wedding toasts and then step out into the cool spring evening, where the air is still full of church bells and rooks.

Every Which Way But Dry

1988

———

"SUCK RUBBER!" the boatman roars from the back of the raft over the noise of the approaching rapids, and those of us riding the front tubes obey. We hunch down, press our faces close to the raft's wet rubber skin and clench our hands on the safety ropes. And then we're in it.

The big raft slides sickeningly off the smooth tongue of the rapids, plows at an angle into the foaming side waves, rises up on one edge until it's nearly on end and crashes down into the wave trough beyond.

Water the color of coffee ice cream—just as opaque and about as cold—slams into us, and people shriek with the shock—me included. I can't help it; neither can anybody else.

"Here comes another one!" somebody screams, and the raft rises again on another wave. And another. And . . . .

And suddenly we are through, riding gently into the eddy below. Hands relax on the ropes, and giggles of relief replace the screams. We drain the Colorado River out of our shoes and sleeves and dab its silt off our glasses with shreds of water-soaked Kleenex.

"Wow!"

"That was a good one!"

"That was great!"

Then we look up, and the giggles die. "Omigod," somebody groans. "Look at *that* one!"

Ahead, the smooth brown water is churning into another boil. Creamy foam spews into the air, and the growl of the rapids rises above the noise of the raft's 30-horsepower motor.

"Suck r-u-u-u-b-ber-r-r-r!" the boatman hollers again, and we grab the ropes and duck, doing what one passenger calls our rendition of "crossing the North Atlantic in an open boat." We're getting good at it.

This is Rapids Day in the Grand Canyon, the third and wettest day of a six-day trip. There are rapids on all the other days too, but on today's stretch of the river, there are more than thirty. Rapids are what I came for, but I am never fully ready for the shock. It feels like being on the inside of a giant washing machine, doing the world's dirtiest laundry. Only we never get to the rinse cycle.

The "we" are thirty-seven people divided between two giant gray rubber rafts. Each raft is thirty-three feet long; each is piloted by a boatman and his assistant, called a swamper, and each is mounded with waterproof duffel bags, coolers packed with food and ice, sturdy chests containing cooking gear, spare motors and, finally, us. Fully loaded, the rafts weigh about four tons apiece.

Our flotilla is traveling 180 miles downstream from Lee's Ferry, just below Glen Canyon Dam, to Whitmore Wash, where the rafts will nose onto the sandy river bank for the last time. From there, we'll be airlifted out of the canyon by helicopter, a ride so hair-raising—we've been warned—that it can compete with the rapids for thrills.

And the rapids are nothing to sneeze at. If someone had forced me to raft this river—and get bashed by icy waves and baked by blazing August sun—I'd be thinking lawsuit. But doing it by choice makes the Colorado the best thrill ride in the country. And it's real.

"This isn't Disneyland," one passenger says with satisfaction. "Anything can happen."

Surprisingly, what does happen is a combination of fear and tranquility, spectacular beauty and mud. And while it helps to be in good shape—especially if you want to hike into the Colorado's exquisite side canyons—you don't have to be young and rugged for this trip. More than half the passengers on my raft are over fifty.

Our days start about 5:30, not with sunrise but with first light. There are no true sunrises or sunsets in Grand Canyon. You need a horizon for those, and the horizon is nearly a mile above our heads. Nevertheless, a simple dawn—nothing more than fading stars and the canyon walls brightening to gold—can take your breath away. If it were music, dawn in the Grand Canyon would be a single, high, clear note, sustained until it echoed off the rocky cliffs.

Between night and morning—in the final, almost colorless light before full day—tiny bats skitter overhead, silhouetted like fat moths on a screen of bright air. And then the voices start in, and camp comes alive with the grating sound of sleeping-bag zippers and the clink of cooking pots.

The rapids, big and small, are the heartbeat of our life on the river. Our days pass in a rhythm of tensing up for rapids, drying off after rapids, waiting for more rapids. In the lulls between rapids, we try to separate the river facts from the river jokes the young boatmen yell at us. These, they allege, are the three most-asked questions on the river:

How high are the canyon walls?

How deep is the river?

When's lunch?

And these, according to boatman Rayn Hunt, 28, are the three most-common answers:

Pretty high.

Pretty deep.

Pretty soon.

Jokes aside, the canyon is a constant geology lesson, and the lesson is a mile deep and complicated. The easiest rocks to keep straight are at the very top and the very bottom: the cream-colored Kaibab Formation lies at the surface, where we started out. Five thousand feet below, where we are, is jet-black Vishnu schist, which glistens like coal and is estimated to be 1.7 billion years old.

I feel almost that ancient when we put into shore in the late afternoons. Canyon evenings always sneak up on us there and get lost in the shuffle of making camp: Unload the rafts. Ditch the life vests and raingear. Dig into our duffels and trade wet sneakers and T-shirts for (we hope) dry ones. Spread our ground cloths on the sand, unroll our mattress pads and sleeping bags. Find our plates, cups and silverware. Head for the chow line.

And then, somewhere between the grilled steaks and the bananas flambé (the boatmen are brilliant cooks), night falls. It always feels sudden, and people look up, startled, and stumble for bed.

The first night, overtaken by darkness on a wild, isolated

river bank, I had been scared. I lay there on the sand, trying to doze off and telling myself that rattlesnakes and tarantulas were no more likely to pick on me than on anybody else in the group. Then something crawled along my arm, and I made a panicky grab for my flashlight. It was just a red ant, but I had to start that whole not-very-reassuring monologue all over again.

Now sleeping outside has become a spiritual joy. The canyon's towering walls create a sense of safety. It's like being in a vast black fortress, roofed with sky. One night I counted ten shooting stars.

During the nights, the river rises—an artificial tide created by Glen Canyon Dam, built upstream in the early 1960s despite nation-wide environmental protests. The cause of the nightly tide is "peaking power"—a fluctuation in demand for the electricity that the dam produces.

"You guys had a good run through Crystal because the air conditioners were on in Phoenix," says trip leader Bill Skinner, 32, a river veteran. Crystal is the worst of the Grand Canyon rapids—so fiercely memorable that one young couple announces they are going to name their baby after it, if the baby turns out to be a girl. They are positive they conceived her the night before—or will the night after.

When we ran Crystal, midway through Rapids Day, the river was eight feet higher than it was the next morning, and it was flowing at 22,000 cubic feet per second—the summer's record volume. While it makes for good rides, that kind of rise and fall is bad for the canyon. The falling water rips sand away from the beaches every day.

In the decade that he's been running the river, Skinner says, five of every ten beaches in the Grand Canyon have been washed away. There's just not enough dirt left in the rising river to replace what's lost: Most of the silt settles out in Lake Powell, above Glen Canyon Dam, long before it gets to us.

Spanish explorers named this river for its reddish color, and even now—despite the silt-collecting dam—the Colorado's water is still muddy enough to dye my white socks and canvas sneakers a permanent rosy tan. The water gets even muddier after the Little Colorado comes in. In late summer, the small river is running as brown as paint. People who elect to jump into the Little C. come out looking like mud men.

But the river isn't the only water down here. Sometimes it rains. It dumps a skyful over us on Rapids Day. At first, nobody cares because we're so wet anyway, and the rapids command our complete attention. "It isn't as cold as yesterday," people assure each other all afternoon, through the constant parade of rapids.

But when it rains on into the evening, we care. Without the sun to dry us or the excitement of the rapids to keep us anaesthetized, it's cold in the canyon. I stand with the others on a damp beach that evening, shivering in our raingear while the boatmen get the stove going. You're not allowed to cook with wood in the canyon any more; in the absence of a campfire, we huddle around the propane.

Rafting the big river day after day, we get used to its silt on our bodies and in our hair. We get used to sand in our clothes and our sleeping bags. We even get used to grit in our lemonade—it's made from river water laced with a little chlorine. "Sand happens," one passenger says cheerfully. And it does. All the time. Everywhere. *Everywhere.*

Eventually, I quit caring about the sand. And about a lot of other things. Though I still keep hold of the safety ropes when we plow into a rapids, I've been able to let go of a lot of personal civilization, at least for a little while:

You're cold? Wait—you'll warm up.

You're wet? The wind will dry you.

Your hair's dirty? Live with it.

Somewhere between the discomforts and the thrills, you find out how much you can adapt to and how little it takes to feel content. The key is knowing that the river is still there, powerful and unbowed, despite the dams. And that there will be stars to sleep under. And good food to eat. And new friends to share it with. That's worth all the frigid water a rapids can throw at you.

Italy? Not Exactly

1993

— —

O KAY, I KNEW THIS was Italy. But it didn't feel like Italy.
And suddenly, on a Trieste sidestreet, in what felt like
an Eastern European downpour, it didn't smell like Italy, either. From a tiny storefront with steamed-up windows wafted
a mouth-watering scent that belonged a couple of countries
away: Sauerkraut. *Sauerkraut!* After a week of pasta, it smelled
like heaven.

The little restaurant was packed wall to wall with locals
waiting for heaping platters of sauerkraut topped with *wurst*
and boiled ham. Waiters pushed through the crowd, holding
mugs of good pale beer overhead. There wasn't a drop of tomato sauce in the place.

This wasn't just a German restaurant in an Italian town. It
was a *Trieste* restaurant, one of many such, and it was living,
breathing, eating proof of the city's dramatic history.

Trieste is a mapmaker's anomaly—a little pouch of territory at the top of the Adriatic Sea, two hours by train east of
Venice. Once it was a valuable port of the Austro-Hungarian
Empire. Now it's a European scrapbook, a Cliff's Notes edition of the rest of the continent.

Trieste's traffic is orderly—how could this be Italy?—and the streets are Germanically clean. The bakeries offer Austrian *Sachertorte* and apple strudel along with the *biscotti* and *pannetone*. The outdoor cafes could have come straight from Paris, and the indoor cafes have smoky counterparts in Berlin, Budapest and Prague. The imposing architecture downtown is pure Vienna, but the city's Roman ruins, hilltop fortress, 14th-century cathedral and pleasantly seedy medieval quarter evoke monuments from Sicily to Spain.

You can take the Cliff's Notes thing too far, though. "Trieste could be its own country," I said to one of its citizens and was puzzled when he looked crestfallen. That's because Trieste used to *be* its own country, and people still miss what they call their lost "hinterland."

That is also why guidebook authors can't resist mentioning the city's sad, romantic aura. I wouldn't label it sadness, exactly—how can a whole city of 250,000 people be sad?—but Trieste does have a definite pre-World War II ambiance. Even today, coming into Trieste for the first time, you half-expect Peter Lorre look-alikes to be lurking around the corners in its movie-set atmosphere.

In reality, I found a sedate city—so sedate that the tourist office even apologizes for Trieste's low-key nightlife. (The modern insurance industry is supposed to have been born here, which tells you something.)

From Roman times onward, Trieste was claimed and reclaimed and claimed again, bouncing in and out of the hands of Venice, Austria, France, Austria again and finally Italy, its episodes of occupation alternating with bouts of independence. The Hapsburgs had it longest: Trieste turned to them for protection in 1382, and in 1719, the Austro-Hungarian emperor designated the city as an imperial free port.

"Trieste was a little Vienna!" said Paolo de Gavardo, the tall, handsome man who directs the city's tourist office. Because it was a free port, Trieste drew sailors and merchants from all over Europe—English, French, Spanish, Swiss, Hungarian, Romanian, Greek, Turkish, Albanian—and they brought their cultures, cuisines and religions with them. The largest synagogue in Italy is here, for example, along with a mosque and an array of churches, Catholic and Eastern Orthodox and (one) Evangelical Lutheran.

"They were very free," de Gavardo said. "There was no opposition. They lived together without problems."

World War I ended the Austro-Hungarian Empire, and World War II left Trieste fully independent—a free territory, essentially a mini nation. In a different age, the city might have been able to go it alone, becoming another Andorra or a San Marino—a political potsherd, not a political football.

But Trieste was both noticeable and useful, and its freedom didn't last. When you're the crossroads of Europe, everybody's going your way. And everybody wants you.

Trieste was annexed to Italy in 1954 and had to cede about 200 square miles of itself to what used to be Yugoslavia. Today, the only open land it has left is a scrap along the top of its embracing cliffs. This relic of its old hinterland is called the Carso, because the limestone cliffs are known as *karst* formations, which are characterized by caves and underground watercourses.

(One of Trieste's caves, the Grotto Gigante, is said to be the largest tourable cavern in the world. You have to climb

500-plus steps down to see it, a vertical chamber big enough to hold a football stadium, and then climb 500-plus steps back up. My knees shook when it was over.)

Riding up to the Carso in a trolley that turns into a funicular, I could see why Triestines are so fascinated by it. The Carso really is a peculiar place: It starts out as a vertical suburb, with villas perched on the cliff walls, then flattens out on the cliff tops and becomes a green counterpane dotted with tiny villages, twisting streets, old stone church towers, low forests and vineyards open to the sky.

The Carso is also famous for a violent, tearing wind: the Boro. It isn't supposed to blow in the summer, locals said, but the Boro wasn't following the rules. "You," one Triestine assured me, as the wicked wind whipped flags, tangled my hair and roughed up the local pigeons, "are a lucky woman."

The city's free-wheeling reputation meant that lots of people washed up here over Trieste's long history, some of them famous. Irish author James Joyce and his wife, for example, spent twelve years in the safe haven of Trieste, mostly before World War I. This is where Joyce wrote much of "Ulysses," his masterpiece, while teaching English to support his family. His two children were born in Trieste, and his sister and brother both immigrated here and married Trieste citizens.

There aren't so many expatriates now—Trieste today is no more of a refuge than any other place in Italy. There weren't many tourists, either, while I was there. Tourism dropped with the outbreak of hostilities in Yugoslavia, because most of the tourists were just passing through on their way to the Dalmatian coast or to Greece and Turkey beyond; the city hadn't yet rebounded.

Very few of the tourists were fellow Americans; I encoun-

tered precisely one. A lack of our countrymen always gives me
the illusion that I've discovered someplace new, someplace off
the beaten track, which was another reason I liked Trieste. But
mostly what I liked was the very sedateness that the tourist
office apologized for. This was a place where a sedate Midwest-
erner could feel instantly at ease.

Two hours away, Venice was sweltering hot and crowded
with summer tourists. But in Trieste, the wild wind was blowing
chill rain down from the Carso, and there were so few people
in the streets, I'd have mistaken the place for East Berlin in late
fall, before the Wall came down.

I strolled around in the soft gray light, took deep breaths of
cool air and peacefully read the paper over coffee at the Caffe
degli Specchi in the main square. There were plenty of free
chairs under the umbrellas out front, and no rush from the
waiters. Relaxing there, I felt as if I'd been in town much longer
than I had—just one more exile washed up on Trieste's shores.
Lucky, indeed.

To the Not-So-Bitter End

1989

WALKING NORTH ON one of Alice Town's three parallel roads, I asked a passing Bimini citzen for directions. "How far to the end of the island?"

She was about eight years old and looked puzzled at the question. "That not the end of the island," she said solemnly. "End of the island *that* way," and she pointed back the way I'd come.

But what if I keep walking *this* way?

"That the *other* end of the island," she said firmly and marched off.

Whichever end you walk to, it isn't very far. North Bimini, the largest island in this tiny cluster between Florida and the Bahamas, is only about seven miles long. It's a hook-shaped scrap of sand and palm trees with little cottages, a handful of shops, restaurants and bars, and a great many friendly people sprinkled along its narrow roads.

Labeling the residents of any foreign country "friendly" is a cliché, and it's worse if the place is tropical. It sounds condescending and comes perilously close to talking about "the natives" instead of "the people."

But on North Bimini, home to about half of the archipelago's 1,500 citizens, people really *were* friendly—though "confident" and "curious" would be equally accurate.

I stopped to photograph a whitewashed church, for example, because with its white roof and white cross framed against a billowing white cloud, it looked as if it were made of seven-minute cake frosting. A local man paused to watch, said "Isn't it pretty?" and walked on.

At a house farther up the road, a hand-written sign was advertising "souse" for sale. "Excuse me," I said to a couple of kids playing in the road, "what's souse?" Two minutes later, I'd been invited inside, and the lady of the house was trying to get her baby grandson to coo at me while she explained how to make this local stew.

Even the drunk who accosted me, yet farther up the road, was friendly. What was I taking a picture of, he wanted to know, while his buddies stood around chuckling. And why was I taking pictures? And who was I, anyway, and what was my name?

"What's yours?" I asked.

"I am," he introduced himself with great dignity, "Under The Influence Of Alcohol!"

Everyone laughed, and I went on walking north to the other end of the island. I felt as if I had Under The Influence's permission.

That night I ate crispy conch fritters at the Red Lion Pub, a little restaurant in Alice Town. Except for the deep red paint on the walls, the place could have been a Formica-clad roadhouse in any small town in the American South or West: The food was good and abundant, and the waitresses were—cliché, cliché—friendly.

After dinner, I did what practically everybody, tourist or local, did that night on North Bimini. I went dancing. There had been a wedding that afternoon—the bride and groom were driven back and forth through Alice Town on a flower-bedecked float—and everybody they'd met along the way got invited to their reception at the Bimini Big Game Fishing Club.

The club is one of many reminders of Bimini's greatest claim to fame—the huge blue-fin tuna, blue marlin, swordfish and sailfish that thrive in the waters of the Gulf Stream, just offshore. Everywhere, there was evidence of game fishing, from the club names to the big power boats tied up at the marinas. Much of Alice Town had the seedy look of an active boatyard, with bits of rusting hardware and old fishing line lying about, in case it came in handy. On the docks, the day's catch was hung up by its tails for display, after the boats came back in late afternoon.

The most famous person to fish Bimini waters was Ernest Hemingway, who may have written part of "To Have and Have Not" here—though that's the Caribbean equivalent of New England inns' claiming that "Washington Slept Here." Hemingway's interest in game fishing helped put Bimini on sportsmen's maps in the mid-1930s. But another Hemingway helped keep it there: For many years, the late writer's younger brother, Leicester, published a fishing newspaper out of these islands.

At the extreme south end of Alice Town—that's the end of the island, not the other end—was a tiny bar with an extremely final name: The End of the World, reputed to have been the Bimini watering place that New York Congressman Adam Clayton Powell liked best. The floor was sand, and the walls and ceiling were decorated with women's panties—a large collection in an astonishing range of sizes, all of them covered with Magic Marker-ed graffiti.

When the bar pales, you can go out into the soft, mild air and loll on the beach and listen to the rustling palm trees and the gentle surf, glittering black and white under the bright night sky.

And that is about all there is to do in North Bimini—unless you're nursing sore muscles from a day's deep-sea struggle with a fish, or resting up because you're going after blue-fin or tarpon tomorrow, out on the deep blue Stream.

Wait, there *is* one more thing. Off a place called Paradise Point, large rocks are visible beneath the clear turquoise water. Some say the rocks are remains of the Lost Continent of Atlantis. But I can't confirm that because I didn't get that far north. I followed the advice of my first little guide and went back to the end of the island. Not the other end. The *other* other end.

Daunted by the Rock

1985

—◦—

IT MAY LOOK LIKE a radiant éclair when you see it from a distance—a long mound on the horizon, glowing orange or rust or lavender, depending on the time of day—but Ayers Rock is no creampuff to climb. That's about as metaphorical as I feel like getting about it.

A few teenagers of mixed nationalities, downward bound as my group struggled up, averred that it was easy. (One Japanese youth had even made the climb in beach flip-flops.) After only fifteen minutes on the rock, however, our ad-hoc group—aged mid-twenties to mid-fifties—already knew better.

What nobody tells you is that this thing is almost smooth.

Ayers Rock rises more than a thousand feet above the paprika-colored sands and gray-green vegetation of Australia's central desert. As mountains go, that isn't much height, so it doesn't look hard. But the rock's sides are nearly sheer. Even on the west face, where the climbing route has been etched—presumably the easiest route—the rock is dizzyingly steep.

So why bother? The old mountaineering cliché—"because it's there"—isn't the answer. I think it's because the rock is *all* that's there.

Like so much in Australia's Outback, Ayers Rock has an eerie, almost otherworldly appeal. How much of that is due to simple contrast with its horizontal surroundings, and how much to the strangeness of the rock itself, is hard to say. But it's strange enough to draw several thousand pilgrims a day, making it one of Australia's top tourist attractions.

Geologically speaking, it is the world's largest monolith— the biggest boulder on earth—more than two miles long, a mile and a half wide and 1,142 feet high, and that's only the part you can see. Like an iceberg in water, most of Ayers Rock lies below the surface; by one estimate, it may extend three miles under the ground. It's not completely alone, but almost: Its nearest competitors are the Olgas, a collection of pretty but less impressive lumps of reddish stone about eighteen miles away.

The Aborigines, to whom the rock belongs, call it Uluru, meaning "place of the howling dingo." To them, it has always been sacred. For something like 40,000 years, they have populated its cracks and niches with gods and legends, and on certain nights, the Aborigines who live near the base of the rock still gather to dance and sing their ancient stories.

But you don't see the Aborigines *climbing* Ayers Rock. As I worked my way upward one February morning, I guessed at reasons why.

The side of the rock is so steep that my ankles and calves hurt from the sharp angle, the way they do if you walk on your heels for more than few rounds of a gym floor. When any of us took rest breaks, we turned around and faced outward, allowing our feet the relief of slanting the other way.

Climbing Ayers Rock, I decided during one of those breaks, is more than a little dangerous anytime, and this was the middle of the Australian summer, when the surrounding desert is baking hot.

We'd been warned about the dangers several times, first by the driver of the air-conditioned tour bus that brought us—fifty tourists, on a variety of itineraries—from Alice Springs the day before. We'd also been warned by exhibits in the national park visitors center. And by signs posted at the base of the official climbing route. This is what the warnings boiled down to:

Wear sturdy shoes with textured soles. (I was already wishing for my hiking boots.) Carry juice or bottled water because you can get dehydrated climbing the rock, even though the round trip averages only about two hours. Pace yourself—don't try to prove anything. Travel light. (Too late—I'd brought two cameras and an extra lens.) And if you have any doubts about your physical condition, let alone something major like a heart condition, don't even attempt it.

We'd seen proof of the danger. The evening before, the bus driver had taken everyone to the west face so that any potential climbers could see what we'd be up against. I was duly sobered by the memorial plaques riveted to the rock by families of climbers who died in the attempt. All but one had died in falls, the driver said; that one—a 63-year-old man whose life's ambition was to climb Ayers Rock—had made it to the top before he collapsed of a heart attack. It was something to think about, all right, and I thought about it, as I panted for breath halfway up.

We did have several things in our favor that morning: It was early—we had arrived at the west face about 7:15, before the day heated up. It was cloudy. And it was fairly cool—only about 80 degrees.

But even so, several people in our group gave up after only a few minutes and perhaps fifteen vertical yards. One woman froze with fear as she turned to go back; she finally sat down on the rock and scooted her way over to an outcropping of boulders where she could find some handholds.

The first goal of the climb was reaching the chain—a heavy iron chain that started part way up and was attached to stanchions driven into the stone.

Once you reach the start of the chain, the next goal becomes reaching the end. It was like reverse rappelling: Grab the chain, lean back till you're nearly horizontal and walk up; move your grip, lean back, walk some more.

Nearing the end of the chain, I passed another solo climber, a man in his 50s, who was sitting on an outcropping to one side of the trail and staring off into infinity. I asked how he was, and he mumbled something like "this is it for me." He just meant that he had decided to quit climbing, not—as I'd instantly concluded—that he was about to drop dead.

The big chain ran out at a room-sized dent in the rock where even teenagers tend to take a break. There's another stretch of maybe ten feet that is also chain-assisted, and then you're near the top and on your own.

That's when the painted path begins—a white dotted line like something from the middle of a country road, only this one leads across the corrugated top of Ayers Rock to a distant cairn with a geodetic marker. The base of the cairn holds a battered guest book. To say we'd climbed Ayers Rock, we had to get that far and sign that book.

The only good thing about crossing the top of the rock was that you couldn't fall very far. Otherwise, it was the hardest part of all. The rock is an enormous chunk of layered sandstone, somehow turned on edge, and erosion has worn down its softer layers so the top is a series of up-and-down ridges, many of which are steeper than the west face itself. And because it's sandstone, it's slippery. Trying to walk up and down the ridges was a matter of controlled skidding.

Because the sky was overcast, there were almost no shadows, and people—including me—complained of being surprised by ridges and hollows that you couldn't see until you slid or stumbled into them. My predilection for short cuts didn't help. The few times I attempted to trim a curve or two off the route by deviating from the painted path, I ended up with scraped elbows or bruised knees and still had to retrace my steps to do it the path's way.

The cairn was an anticlimax. You wait your turn to sign the book. You take turns taking pictures of each other signing the book. You share leftover juice and water. You look out over the rock's expanse toward the other, barely visible outcroppings that break the desert's flat surface. Then you start back, over the same tedious, sand-slippery, hard-to-see ridges.

Once we reached the chain, though, the climb down was easier. Maybe that was what the teenagers had meant. As long as you weren't afraid of heights, you could grab hold of the chain, face outward and practically skip down, as if Ayers Rock were a giant staircase.

At the bottom—hot, sweaty and more relieved than triumphant—we made a bee-line for the bus, where the driver was dispensing paper cups of cold, sweet water. From that distance, Ayers Rock looked the way it always does—maddeningly easy. "What gets me," said a young woman from Illinois, "is that nobody at home is going to believe it was hard."

Cheechakos on the Road

1998

M Y BROTHER STEVE AND I turned the most dangerous corner of our Alaska trip two months before we left, over supper at Ruby Tuesday's. We were going to rent a recreational vehicle in Anchorage and drive through Alaska and the Canadian Yukon, but first, Steve said, we needed to plan. We hadn't traveled together in thirty-two years—not since our last family camping trip as kids—and he didn't want anything to go wrong. Neither did I.

I usually wing it on trips. For me, that's the surest path to serendipity. But I'm not against planning, if it's in a good cause. So I brought a road atlas to dinner that night, and we looked at it before the hamburgers arrived.

Alaska is twice as big as Texas, and Canada's Yukon Territory, next door, is one-and-a-half times as big as Montana. We wanted to cover them both. In two weeks. Alaskans have a name for people like us: *Cheechakos.* Greenhorns.

The sights we most wanted to see had to do with the Gold Rush of 1898. Skagway, Alaska, and Dawson City, Yukon, topped the list. Bent over the atlas, we traced out a route, heading for the Yukon first and leaving the crowded stretch from Fairbanks to Anchorage for the end. It took us about ten minutes.

"Sounds good to me," I said, closing the atlas and reaching for a French fry. I thought we were done planning.

"No," my brother said. "I meant like this."

He took a sheet of paper, wrote down the date of every day we'd be gone, divided our route into 250-mile chunks—the distance we could realistically drive each day—and filled in the name of each town where we would need to stay the night. The result was beautiful—and to me, totally alien.

Astonished, I stopped chewing. Steve and I are only two years apart. We grew up in the same household. We took the same family trips—all over the country, first in tents, then a travel trailer, then a camper truck—and we shared the same travel mishaps and travel joys.

But I don't plan, and he does. How had this happened?

The answer lay in those family trips. We'd shared the same experiences, all right—but we'd drawn utterly opposite conclusions.

I had liked not knowing where we were going to stop at night. I admired the way my father would drive until long after dark and find imaginative places to set up camp—maybe behind a closed gas station or in a roadside picnic area or on the front lawn of an abandoned farm. I especially loved the nights we spent in schoolyards on the Great Plains, when I could listen to the prairie wind whipping around the trailer as I fell asleep in my bunk.

But what I called adventure, Steve saw as near-fatal disorganization. It had driven him crazy and taught him, indelibly, the need for planning.

"Remember Joplin, Missouri?" he said now.

Well, yeah, there *was* Joplin. But I always make an exception for Joplin. Steve doesn't.

Joplin is family code for an obscure park where we spent our all-time nastiest summer night. As usual, Dad figured to drive until he "found somewhere." That didn't happen until it was so long after midnight, and we were all so tired, that we didn't even bother setting up camp. We just unfolded the cots on a patch of open ground and crashed in our clothes. No tent. No mosquito netting. No covers.

Near dawn, it must have started to rain, and my father roused himself long enough to throw a ground cloth over his sleeping children—a dirty, dark-brown, canvas ground cloth. It must have weighed a hundred pounds.

When the sun came up, the humid air under the canvas started to steam. I woke up in panic, trying to fight my way out of the stifling darkness, unable to stand up or push the heavy canvas away. It felt like being smothered.

Yes, I said, I remember Joplin, but . . . .

That wouldn't have happened, Steve said, if Dad had done proper planning.

"But Dad planned," I protested. "He started planning in March!"

"Dad started planning *the route* in March," Steve corrected. *"But he never made a single reservation!"*

Oh.

Chastened, I took our trip outline home and bought a copy of "The Milepost." It's the bible of Alaskan road travelers, a highly detailed, flimsy-paged, ad-crammed, fine-print paperback the size of a J.C. Penney catalog. The options seemed infinite.

I spent most of two days and several evenings calling

campgrounds and RV parks on our route through the Far North and requesting "a full hookup" for the night we'd be there. ("Full" meant electricity, water and sewer; we'd have had even more campground choices if we'd settled for electricity alone.)

This task was incredibly . . . tedious. I completely understood why my father would have outlined a route and skipped the details. The details were boring. And all the campgrounds sounded alike.

At first I tried to be systematic, writing down important things like the quality of the view and the proximity to points of interest, stores and washing machines. Soon, I was ranking them by the tone of voice of the person who answered the phone.

Finally, I gave up on having a system and just chose campgrounds on the basis of name alone: If it sounded cute or referred to the Gold Rush, I booked it. Which is why we stayed at the Golden Bear RV Park in Tok, Alaska; the Route of '98 RV Park in Whitehorse, Yukon, and the Gold Rush RV Park in Dawson City, in the heart of the famous Klondike.

Separately, Steve and I had confided to friends that we were uneasy about how this trip was going to go. But once we were on the road, our attitudes changed. In fact, we kind of swapped attitudes. I discovered that I liked knowing that we had a home for the night. It gave us something to shoot for. Steve, who had insisted on nightly reservations, turned out to be perfectly comfortable with unstructured days, which left plenty of room for serendipity.

In the course of the next two weeks, we logged more than 2,000 miles, got so close to moose that we could hear them chewing, clambered across the slippery face of the Matanuska

Glacier, explored old gold camps, were informed by locals that winters in Tok "are so dry that you can't even make a snowball," and discovered that you can tee off at the Whitehorse golf course at 11:30 P.M. and still have enough daylight to play 18 holes.

We also laughed—a lot, the way we had when we were growing up. What we didn't do was argue.

Arguments, involving a revolving cast of characters, had been a staple on our family trips. But on this one, despite cramped quarters and virtually constant companionship—every mealtime, every moment of driving, every evening—Steve and I never exchanged a harsh word. Our late parents wouldn't have believed it. We almost didn't, either. Had to be all that advance planning.

Safari

1998

—·—

W HEN I WAS GROWING UP, one of my father's favorite conversational gambits was this question: If you
could see any moment in history, what would it be? I always
wished for a glimpse of the Great Plains, before the Europeans
arrived—when the land was still carpeted with grass and buffalo, before the plows, before the killing.

My old wish came true half a world away, on a safari in
East Africa, when the Land Rover I was riding in got separated for an hour from the rest of the vehicles on our so-called
"game drive." (Even though most tourists shoot with cameras
these days, safari culture preserves the antiquated lingo of the
"great white hunters.")

We were in Ngorongoro Crater, a flat-bottomed bowl of
national park land that covers nearly a hundred square miles
of Tanzania and shelters thousands of animals. For once,
there was no other Land Rover in sight. There were only the
dark lumps of wildebeest dotting the plain, interspersed with
zebras, gazelles and antelope, all quiet, all cropping grass together. The purple-shadowed walls of the crater rose behind
them like distant mountains.

Protected there, the animals paid us no heed. They knew they were safe. Even a hyena, ambling past, did not ruffle them; it was daytime, and they knew the hyena wasn't hunting.

Like nearly everybody, I'd been conditioned by zoos, where animals are always segregated by species. Seeing them mingled together like this was like gazing at a garden. Or a painting of Eden. Or the Great Plains, long ago, when wild animals like these stretched contentedly to the horizon.

"That's how it would have looked!" I thought, choking up as I recognized it. "That's how it would have been!" The scene was so beautiful that it called for background music—some rising symphony, some chorus of angels—but there was only the ragged churning of the engine.

East Africa is everything it is reputed to be—beautiful, compelling, exciting, heart-rending, addicting. More than anything, though, it is animals. They are what tourists go to East Africa for, what engenders the greatest awe, what provides the greatest joy. Animals are what you take away, banked in photos or entrusted to memory.

I loved the gangly grace of giraffes, sailing like schooners across the Serengeti Plain. Loved the elephant babies, sleeping on the ground like little gray balloons, under their mothers' eyes. Loved the lions, majestic even at rest in the afternoon shade. Loved the hair-raising cough of a cheetah at night. And loved, everywhere, the flocks of gazelles springing out of the paths of vehicles like summer grasshoppers on a prairie at home.

Those are the riches I carried away from the national parks of northern Tanzania, where I spent a dozen days with a dozen people in March, on a classic safari complete with Land Rovers and game spotters, good food and comfortable lodges.

A safari, even a plush one, is not like any other group trip I've taken. If you go to Paris on a bus tour, for instance, you can always skip a guided walk through the Louvre or a group dinner at a too-popular restaurant and strike off on your own. A safari is more like being marooned on a moving desert island.

The lodges are isolated, self-contained fortresses in the middle of nowhere. Ground transportation is limited to the vehicles your group brings in. And you can't hike off on your own because the wild animals you've come to see really *are* wild animals. You can't even get out of the car.

Another down side is that you can't predict what you'll see or when you'll see it. You may drive for hours and see "nothing." Standards for "nothing" can change fast. On our first afternoon, people insisted that the vehicles stop for pictures of *dik-dik,* cute puppy-sized antelope typically seen in pairs. Next morning, dik-dik were passé. We had graduated to stopping for baboons and zebras. Then those grew familiar. Next, the giraffes were old hat—and then hyenas and ostriches and Cape buffalo too.

What we never got used to were the most dangerous things—lions, cheetahs, elephants—the creatures that can kill you. There must be a lesson in that.

Our safari did not have its own naturalist, so nearly all information about what we were seeing came from the drivers. Some of them were great talkers, some weren't. Some knew a lot, some didn't.

The results could be funny—like the time we saw a cheetah rolling around in the grass exactly like a housecat on carpet. "Female," our driver said. "Pregnant." True, it had a huge belly. But a few moments later, when the cheetah raised its hind leg and scent-marked a tree, the driver revised his assessment: It was a male that had just finished the meal of a lifetime.

Sometimes, the information—or lack of it—was exasperating. In Ngorongoro Crater, for example, our driver eased the Land Rover to a stop beside a herd of zebras and their brown-and-white colts. I leaned forward, expecting to hear something on, perhaps, zebra gestation and parenting. Or why zebras frequently stand in pairs with their heads resting on each other's backs. Or why human beings never managed to domesticate them.

The driver indicated the herd. "Zebras," he said. That was all.

I complained to our group leader. She wasn't sympathetic: "Well, what did you expect him to say?" she wanted to know. More, I said. Given that zebras can be identified by any American three-year-old with access to a TV set, I expected *more*.

Fortunately, the tour organizer had recommended a fine book, "The Safari Companion" by Richard Estes, and a few copies were drifting around the group. At night, I borrowed one and looked up the answers on my own. Zebra gestation is similar to that of horses, I read. Twins are rare. Adults stand around in pairs—or even trios—with their heads on each other's backs because it lets them rest while watching for danger in different directions.

I never did find out why nobody except circus riders has managed to train zebras or—maybe more interesting—why nobody has come up with a horse/zebra cross. What would that be? A zorse? A zule?

The Companion also explained an encounter with a female

lion that our driver did not interpret and that otherwise I'd have misunderstood. The lioness was alone when we spotted her, sleeping on a patch of sunny grass beside the road in Ngorongoro Crater. She barely stirred as our vehicle pulled up, allowing us get so close that we could count the flies crawling on her face.

Then a second Land Rover joined us. That's standard Land Rover behavior: They flock to another parked vehicle like vultures, hoping to catch sight of what the first vehicle has found. Sometimes there were half a dozen Land Rovers, bristling with tourist cameras, around a single animal.

When the second vehicle came, the lioness opened her eyes, slowly shifted position, rolled onto her back, stretched casually, sat up, looked around—but never at us—and finally rose and ambled nonchalantly toward a clump of shrubbery, looking as aloof as a bored queen. Her calm arrogance was impressive. Lions, I thought, sure do know that they're at the top of the food chain.

Later I found out the truth. A lot of the aloofness attributed to lions is part of their defense strategy, the Companion said. When disturbed, a lion sizes up the situation, and if it thinks it can't win, it acts very cool, avoids looking at its challenger and slowly eases itself away to safety.

Wow, I thought, that's just what our lioness did—she felt outnumbered by the Land Rovers! For a moment, I was as excited as if I'd done the feline behavioral research myself.

Late in the trip, my roommate, Mary, a veterinarian from New England, asked why I often included the circling Land Rovers when I took a picture of an animal. I said I wanted to remember how it really was—one wild creature in the distance and four or five or six mechanical ones raising dust clouds as they raced across the landscape to reach it.

Mary was doing just the opposite—deliberately cropping out the Land Rovers. "I want to remember it wrong," she said.

Without the Land Rovers, we'd never have gotten so close to so many magnificent creatures. That should have made me fonder of those sturdy vehicles. But jouncing along in one for hours at a crack, with the wind blowing dust into my face and hair, I longed to get out and walk.

Our last lodge offered that option, and Mary and I leapt at it. For an extra fee, a silent park ranger with a semiautomatic rifle strolled with us for an hour or so on the salty margin of a drying lake. The only wildlife we saw was ex-wildlife—big dung beetles by the thousands and the husks of scorpions, dead and dried where the water should have been.

But we were out in the world again, on foot in Africa, under our own power. We could sift dirt through our fingers, reach out to examine a leaf or feel the splinters of an elephant-ravaged tree. It was great.

Some of the best wildlife viewing—I mean the closest—was off the front porch of Ndutu Lodge, our last stop. Many waterholes in the region had gone dry, and that sent a couple of elephant herds storming daily toward a still-wet pond in full view of the lodge veranda—twenty to fifty elephants at a time, once about two hundred.

Knowing this, lodge staff had posted a row of "danger" signs about fifty feet from the building. Strung with cameras, I walked to the sign nearest the pond, stood on its safe side and started taking pictures.

Elephant youngsters were frolicking in the water, the moisture turning their dusty gray skins to glistening charcoal. Adult elephants took turns on guard, alternating their own bathing and drinking with anxious watching. Occasionally, a big elephant would lay its trunk affectionately on a little one's head or reach out and stroke a baby's shoulder.

At the first sound of the shutter, one of the biggest adults wheeled and stared full at me, head up, ears flared, tusks glinting. Magnificent, I thought, and no problem—I'm behind the danger signs—I'm safe. I kept on shooting.

Then another big adult wheeled and faced me, trunk swinging like the tail of an angry cat. I checked to be sure I hadn't strayed. Nope—still safely behind the signs. Click. Click. Cli . . . .

Then, just as a couple more good-sized elephants began to stare my way, one of the lodge staff came rushing toward me across the lawn, crouching as he ran. "Please!" he said, in a fierce whisper, "very dangerous! They have their children with them!"

It was his look of genuine fear that made the truth dawn. The signs I was relying on wouldn't give me any more protection than the cardboard they were made of—for one single, idiotically obvious reason: *Elephants can't read.*

Thankfully, they chose not to charge. I backed away very slowly, coached by the staffer, and did the rest of my shooting from the questionable shelter of the porch. Elephants had already knocked the porch down a couple of times, accomplishing its destruction as easily as they pushed over acacia trees to snack on their leaves.

Sometimes—the best times—the animals materialized right beneath our noses. One image, one moment, summarized all the others and made me feel peaceful even as it happened and for long while after.

Partway across a vast, grassy flatness, we stopped at Naabi Hill Gate—one of the entrances to Serengeti National Park—to wait among other vehicles and trucks for entry permits. In the couple of hours we'd spent getting there that day, I'd grown used to squinting into bright distance at a horizon as level as a kitchen counter, trying to distinguish between the black dots that were animals and the black dots that were shrubs or rocks.

"Lions," the driver announced quietly, and passengers' heads swiveled, eyes searching.

Where? "There—by that truck."

But I was so used to looking far away that I couldn't pull my eyes in close enough to see them. Our driver, pointing, was amused.

And then suddenly I *saw*. The lions were dozing under a tree only one vehicle away, mere feet from us—three lionesses and at least three cubs, sleeping in a fuzzy, golden heap. At the first shutter click, one cub stirred and woke and raised his head, gazing sleepily but steadily back at me. He looked almost as if he were smiling, and it filled my heart with peace.

It touched the others too. Voices softened to whispers, picture-taking slowed. Almost without noticing, we lowered our cameras, lapsed into silence and gazed back into the cub's innocent eyes. We sat there, not moving, for perhaps fifteen minutes, a long time to stare at a single thing. All I know is, it wasn't long enough. It could never have been long enough.

Without a Sob

1986

————

WE WERE HALF-WAY across the dark, soggy moor when I heard a cry that made the hair prickle on the back of my neck. A faint, ghostly voice was calling "Cathy . . . Caaaaaathy . . . ."

I whirled around and caught my mother with her hands cupped by her mouth, about to call my name again. She was paused on the path twenty feet behind me, looking happily sheepish. "I always wanted to do that," she said.

Of course she had. Calling out that name on the Yorkshire moors is something Heathcliff does in "Wuthering Heights," my mother's favorite book and, by default, one of mine as well. She had named me for its heroine, Catherine Earnshaw, Heathcliff's lost love. So when the two of us headed for England on a long-awaited trip, our itinerary had to include Haworth, the Yorkshire village where the author, Emily Brontë, had lived with her sisters, also writers, in the middle 1800s.

The Brontës' lives had all the elements of the romance novel, a genre the sisters helped create: the isolated village, the strong-willed parson father, the storm-wracked moors.

But theirs were lives of extraordinary sadness, which they faced with ordinary—by which I mean magnificent—human courage.

As good Brontë fans would, my mother and I had pictured Haworth as a lonely island in a sea of bleak and empty moorland. An island it is, but the sea is smokestacks, factories and workers' houses spilling over the encircling hills. Another shock was the Brontë industry that thrived everywhere in town: the Brontë Cafe, the Brontë Inn, Brontëland Menswear, Heathcliff Apartments. The shops were full of Brontë souvenirs, from Brontë tea-towels to Brontë liqueur.

No doubt it would have embarrassed the Rev. Brontë's three reclusive daughters—Charlotte, best-known for "Jane Eyre"; Emily, who produced some striking poetry as well as "Wuthering Heights," and the gentle Anne, whose books, less famous than her sisters', also featured strong heroines and the same elements of vain hope and tormented love.

As we wandered through Haworth, a gray stone village that tumbles down a steep central street, it was the three sisters' lives, not their books, that came to tug most at our hearts. For them, there were no happy endings. They encountered no Mr. Rochesters. No Heathcliffs swept them off their feet on the wild moors.

The three Brontë girls grew up clinging to home and to each other, and—except for brief and homesick interludes away at school and, later, while they were working as governesses—home was where they stayed.

Home was the Haworth parsonage, which still stands behind its church on a rise at one end of town. The front windows of the house look out on stone-lidded tombs and crooked headstones jostling for space in the churchyard—a little tenement of the dead that stretches almost to the front door. Overhead, a colony of rooks—loud crow-like black birds—sends up a constant, screeching ruckus.

Behind the house, the moor begins, a landscape as alien as anything in fiction. I'd always pictured heather as something pretty, but it looked more like dark-brown seaweed strewn over the hilltops. I found it threatening. It made me feel that something was going to happen, and it would be nothing good.

Graves in front, the moor behind: No wonder the Brontë children turned inward. The sisters—along with their only brother, Branwell—took refuge in a fantasy kingdom they invented together, a place called Gondal, whose elaborate sagas helped hone their writing skills. The rest of their days were stitched as precisely as their own needlework, circumscribed by the endless round of Victorian domesticity: cooking, baking, washing, cleaning, sewing, mending and getting up next morning to start it all over again.

The real theme that runs through their lives is endurance, not romance, and my mother could identify with it more than I could: She too had grown up poor and knew the strength it takes to survive grief and hardship. Charlotte described how it felt in a searing paragraph that I first read in Haworth and have never been able to forget:

> "*You held out your hand for an egg, and Fate put into it a scorpion. Show no consternation; close your fingers firmly upon the gift; let it sting through your palm. Never mind; in time, after your hand and arm have swelled and quivered long with torture, the squeezed scorpion will die, and you*

*will have learned the great lesson—how to endure without
a sob."*

One by one, like their mother and two older sisters, the Brontës succumbed to the family disease—tuberculosis. Emily died first, aged thirty, in 1848. "Never in all her life had she lingered over any task that lay before her," Charlotte wrote, "and she did not linger now .... She made haste to leave us."

Anne, twenty-nine, died the next year. Charlotte survived the longest, until 1855, when she was nearly forty. She lived to see her books become successful and to have a tantalizing glimpse of a brighter future: She had gotten married—to a clergyman like her father—and was expecting her first child when death overtook her.

Before my mother and I left the Brontës' small realm, we had a final pilgrimage to make. On our last afternoon, we set out across a moor near town, following a narrow path toward an old farmstead called Far Withens, thought to be Emily's model for "Wuthering Heights."

The moor was as treacherous to walk on as a frozen swamp, full of hummocks and pitted with soppy places just big enough to trap a shoe or twist an ankle. The coarse heather kept catching at our clothes and scratching our legs. No one could run lightly over something like this even if, like Emily Brontë, she knew it by heart.

As we trudged, gloomy clouds thickened overhead, and in the sinister light, distances warped. We could see the roof of the dark, squat farmhouse in the distance, but it never seemed to get any closer.

We struggled toward it for two hours before we gave up.

By then, dusk and a storm were coming on together, and the moor had worn us out. Perhaps that was how it should be, we decided. Far Withens, like Wuthering Heights, like Gondal, is more than anything a place of the imagination. We left it there and turned back to Haworth, ahead of the rain.

'Be Content'

2000

—•—

A MONTH BEFORE CHRISTMAS—and less than a day after a long trip, while I was still jet-lagged, still mentally on the road—I made the mistake of venturing out to replenish household supplies. Usually I don't run errands so soon after a trip. Usually I just sleep a lot and sort the mail until my soul catches up with my body. I should have done that this time, too.

The easiest destination was Target. Bad move: I was immediately dazzled—by the lights, by the bright packages on the shelves, by all the people and the red carts and the aisles that stretched to infinity. It was like stepping into the world's best bazaar, a better *souk* than any I've seen from Tangier to Istanbul. So colorful. So alluring. So *American*.

Thus happily mesmerized, I walked too near the cosmetics department and became ensnared. Suddenly, I absolutely needed nail polish—even though I never wear it. An hour later, I emerged as if from a trance, sixty bucks lighter but with enough equipment to start my own manicure salon. I didn't even buy what I went in for. I think it was going to be Comet cleanser.

Apparently, I'd been traveling so long that my protective shopping shell had worn off. This was dangerous so close to Christmas. I needed to re-grow that shell, and fast, or local retailers would have a holiday season that surpassed their wildest dreams. Time to bring out the big guns of memory and remind myself of a lesson I keep needing to relearn.

It had happened in Churchill, Manitoba, a town on Hudson Bay, where I'd gone to watch polar bears. The bears congregate there in October, waiting for the bay to freeze so they can get out on the ice and hunt seals.

My lesson didn't come from polar bears, though. It came from the Inuit, the northern people whom we used to call Eskimo, and a local museum with a fine collection of old Inuit carvings. These sculptures were smaller than the big, dramatic Inuit statues of dancing bears and defiant musk oxen now sold in Native American art galleries. Very much smaller, but they packed as big a wallop.

From ancient times until well into the twentieth century, the Inuit traveled by boat and sled, so any art they made had to be small enough to carry. Some of their portable carvings were no bigger than a piece of jewelry or even a single bead. Most were graceful miniatures of animals, and they weren't dancing, they were teaching.

I went through the museum slowly, charmed by the little sculptures, and then one leaped into my heart.

It was a disc of dark stone about three inches across. On it stood five tiny figures—a bird and three smaller birds with what looked like a rabbit at their feet. A typed card explained that the big bird was teaching the little birds a lesson that the Inuit wanted their own little ones to live by.

Once, the parable said, a young owl went out to hunt Arctic

hares. These hares are much bigger and stronger than ordinary rabbits, but the young bird was lucky enough to swoop down and catch one.

Then greed overtook him. He saw a second Arctic hare, and with the talons of his other foot, he caught that one, too. Now the young owl had two Arctic hares, one in each foot, and both were fighting desperately to get away. The owl wasn't wise enough to let go, and the hares fought so hard that they finally tore him apart. He lost both his catch and his life. This was the moral:

"Be content with enough."

I read that sentence with a mental gasp. Sometimes, travel hands you exactly what you need to hear. Living by it is a different matter.

I repeat that simple Inuit truth to myself every time I buy something that, instead of satisfying, whets my appetite for more; every time I try to make something perfect and go too far and make it worse; every time I crave too much.

Usually I don't remember to *be content with enough* until after I've craved and paid. But now that I've dusted off the lesson again, maybe this time it will stick. Or at least get me safely through December.

CRETE

Enchanted Isle

1994

—

IT WAS AFTERNOON when I sat down at home to write about Crete. A quarter of the way around the globe—across half the United States, one ocean, most of a continent and part of another sea—it was already twilight there. In Khania, blue dusk was deepening over the centuries-old buildings around the harbor, and the street lamps were coming on, painting the dark water with wavering bands of color—emerald, amber, aquamarine, ruby, opal, amethyst, jade—like an Impressionist painting rendered in jewels.

The evening's promenade was gathering while I typed— nothing special, nothing organized, just the relaxed strolls that people take around the harbor every night, whether they are tourists or locals. I could picture it all again: Lovers, with their arms around each others' waists. White-haired couples fondly holding hands. Young parents with toddlers and babies in arms and little kids dashing ahead as the adults pause to read the menus outside the waterfront restaurants.

I could hear it again too, Khania's normal evening cho- rus: Bouzouki music, flooding like light from every doorway.

Eager waiters pleading, "Please, my restaurant! Please!" The gentle clink of silverware and glasses. A blur of voices, like a party, overheard.

Delicious smells waft out on that music—roast lamb, grilled shrimp and red mullet, fried calamari, souvlaki on skewers, sizzling cheese. Drawn by the scent of food, Khania's street cats slink under the restaurant tables—pregnant cats, wounded cats, skinny cats, meek ones, bullies—all of them brushing back and forth against the diners' legs, purring for fish heads or a morsel of squid.

There is more to say about Khania, just as there is about all of Crete, given that its history extends nearly 4,000 years, from the ancient Minoans through four centuries of rule by Venice and eventually to a brutal occupation by the Nazis in World War II.

But those soft evenings in Khania are the first thing I think of when I remember Crete, and I remember it often. It is the largest of the Greek islands, but it's still small. Crete measures only about 160 miles east to west and, on average, 25 miles north to south. Its mountain ranges, steep valleys and sinuous roads connive to slow the driving, making it seem much bigger. A friend and I spent two weeks exploring it by car and still weren't done.

At first, it was like being in Europe's Mexico—off-beat, accessible, attractive, sunny and cheap—so we were following waves of Germans and Britons wherever we went. But there were very few Americans. We had trouble finding a copy of the International Herald Tribune, for example, but we had a daily choice of the London Times, the Manchester Guardian, the Frankfurter Allgemeine and the Suddeutsche Zeitung. At least, when we tired of moussaka, calamari and stuffed grape leaves, we could get a good English fry-up or a decent Wiener schnitzel.

Most of the European tourists flocked to Crete's north coast, where white-stuccoed hotels, houses, rental villas and condo-apartments flanked both sides of the main highway for miles out of Heraklion, the island's capital. There appeared to be no zoning. If you owned a bit of beach, you could build what you thought tourists would want, and the rising developments were beginning to block everybody's views.

The rest of the island more than made up for that. In the west, we drove till the road stopped and caught a glimpse of the sea from a mountainside where there were no man-made sounds beyond the tinkle of bells around the necks of grazing sheep.

The human fabric also loosened in Crete's eastern lobe, what we dubbed the Wild East. It reminded me of the Scottish Highlands but without the rain: These mostly treeless slopes were sun-washed and dotted with miniature snow-white chapels, their sanctuaries not much bigger than closets.

People were generous here, accommodating, even when we didn't ask. Over and over on Crete, local people waved from the roadsides as we passed, mostly just being pleasant, sometimes hoping we'd buy their fresh oranges or home-packed jars of thick, dark, wildflower honey. (I'd always hated honey until I tasted Crete's. It had the color and consistency of heavy motor oil, with a tang to its sweetness, like mountain air. Poured over a dish of thick Cretan yogurt, it was a breakfast delight that I haven't been able to duplicate at home.)

One villager stopped the donkey he was leading long enough for me to get its picture—it was his idea—then gave me a courtly nod and went on his way. In another village, an older woman in black trudged straight toward my lens and said hello as I focused.

And in more than one town—after dozens of other tourists must have aimed cameras at them that day—the old men sitting outside the cafe still straightened their sweaters, struck poses for us, grinned and waved goodbye. Amazing.

We liked Crete so much that we started reminiscing about it while we were still there, counting off the highlights like prayer beads.

There was the Lasithi Plain, a garden-like oval of rich green in a ring of mountains, where the flowering fruit trees looked like pink and white clouds drifting over the fields. Goats were grazing there, belly-deep in grass so lush you wanted to taste it too.

And the village of Lastros, riding the spine of a mountain east of Gournia, where we were the only tourists one afternoon. The town's tiny lanes, its streets of steps, its miniature patios and sugar-cube houses were the modern extensions of the same things we kept seeing at Crete's Minoan archaeological sites. "So this is what it would have looked like!" I thought, on a day when we'd just come from one of those 3,500-year-old stone puzzles.

And Agia Galini, where we spent Easter—a seaside resort wedged in a valley so narrow that geography makes heavy development impossible. Small, cheap, cliff-hanging hotels overlooked the harbor, like balconies. Our rooms opened onto a patio framed in hot-pink bougainvillea, with a view over the bright blue sea. I sat out there and tried to paint it; I could get the color of the flowers right, but nobody—certainly not me—has ever caught the intensity of that water.

It would have been perfect there, except for the bombs. All right, *firecrackers*—part of the celebrations for Holy Week. Local teenagers set off so many on Easter eve that it sounded like a war zone.

Oh, yes, and there was that crazy restaurant in Zakros where what you ate was what the owner felt like giving you. The place was just a few oilcloth-covered tables on one side of a triangular plaza so small that I had to work to turn the car around. By the time I got to our table, the rotund, bright-eyed owner had just bustled away, leaving my companion weeping tears of laughter.

The owner had announced that he didn't speak English and had then asked, in perfect English, "What do you want?"

"What do you have?" my friend said.

"Nothing!" the owner countered and scampered off.

He changed his mind quickly and bounced back with platters of fried rabbit. Eventually he also brought fried potatoes, veal stew, tomato salad and tall plastic tumblers filled to the brim with strong red Cretan wine.

"No fork," he commanded. "Eat with fingers!"

And there was Elounda. I list it last, but it was the first place we stayed and the one where I most fervently vowed to return. There were drawbacks to the others—too many tourists in Khania, a dismal hotel in Zakros, those firecrackers—but Elounda was a solid delight. (We weren't the only Americans to be impressed, by the way: Walt Disney's "The Moonspinners" was filmed there in the 1960s.)

Elounda was a one-street village on a long bay in northeastern Crete, a few miles beyond the tourist metropolis of Agios Nikolaos, which we rejected as too crowded. I was at the wheel, and I can't resist side roads, so I took one that rose suddenly above the sea, leaped over a mountain ridge and dropped down beside a long bay. It led straight into Elounda, population 1,600.

It was the perfect template for the ultimate seaside village—vest-pocket harbor, bobbing fishing boats, sandy beach, clever shops, restaurants by the water and heaps of bougainvillea, spilling over doorways and patio walls, in every shade of pink.

We were there pre-season, but shopkeepers were already setting out racks of sun hats and sunscreen for the coming summer crush, and a harbor-front grocery was selling potted shrubs to dress up rental patios. I almost mistook them for roses, but their fragrance gave them away. The otherwise ordinary grocery was selling gardenia bushes.

Where I live, gardenias are only for corsages; the shrubs are too delicate to survive our winters. But here on Crete, they were thriving—thick with dark, glossy leaves and whipped-cream flowers, their luscious scent calling out to passersby, calling me. I wanted gardenias of my own like that and a sun-bathed patio in Elounda to grow them on.

Perhaps a Haunting?

2000

———

I DON'T STAY IN HAUNTED HOUSES—not if I can help it, anyway. I do not find it amusing to hear, after a long day's drive into night, that Room No. 1 in that evening's bed-and-breakfast has, um, *happenings*. Or to be shown a proud innkeeper's snapshot of a pale shape in a place it shouldn't be, like right next to my bedroom door.

B & B owners tend to regard their uninvited guests as just another amenity, like plush bathrobes in the closet or blueberry crumble on the dining-room buffet. But as much as I love bed-and-breakfasts, a convincing ghost story makes me want to run screaming to a Motel 6.

Sometimes escape is impossible, a risk I take whenever I drive too long after dark. I start getting tired; towns start looking sinister, and pretty soon all the B & Bs—so homey by daylight—look as creepy as the Adams Family's manse. If nearby motels are seedy or nonexistent, I cross my fingers, ask no ghost-friendly questions and stay in the manse anyway.

But those weren't the circumstances of my night in Helena, Arkansas, on a solitary trip down the Mississippi in September. I had quit driving while the sun was still up and sought out Magnolia Hill, an 1895 Queen Anne-style bed-and-breakfast that a friend had recommended. Innkeeper Jane Insco—friendly, dark-haired, middle-aged—told me I could have the pick of her upstairs rooms.

There were no other guests (uh-oh, I thought), but Jane said I wouldn't be alone because her own quarters were in the back of the house (whew). I chose the Emerald Room, a big square bedroom with dark green walls and flowered borders. Or it chose me: "That's my room," I thought instantly, even though the others Jane showed me were equally pretty.

At breakfast next morning, just as I was digging into fresh fruit salad with mango cream, Jane asked quietly if I'd noticed anything the previous night.

No, I said, guessing what was coming, I'd slept fine. Why?

Sometimes, she said, speaking a little too carefully, sometimes, especially in that room, guests notice . . . *things*. They hear . . . things. She'd heard things herself.

What kind of things, I asked, not wanting to know.

Footsteps hurrying up and down the stairs. The sound of a door shutting. A baby crying in some other part of the house, when there are no babies around. Once one of Jane's grandkids looked at the empty staircase and asked cheerfully, "Who's that?" and couldn't understand why no one else saw the lady standing there.

The oddest thing, Jane said, is that guests' stories match: "Sometimes they have the same dream."

I hadn't dreamt at all in the Emerald Room. But her words were enough to freeze me in place, my teaspoon of mango cream stopped half-way to my lips.

The dream, she said, is always of a pale woman in white. The woman does no harm—just stands by the bed—though once a man reported that the lady got in bed with him, and another time a girl said that she'd felt her hair being stroked. Another man, a devout Christian who insisted in advance that there's no such thing as ghosts, announced next morning that the beautiful pale woman was a test. "Once again," he boasted, "I chose my wife!"

No one knows who the pale lady might be. There is no murder in the house's history, though a medium once said that the lady may be the ghost of the original owner—a woman who had lived in the house for forty years.

I was immensely grateful that I hadn't learned any of this the night before. I don't officially believe in ghosts, but I wouldn't have dared to sleep, just in case.

Then Jane went back to the kitchen to fetch a cheese souffle, and a baffling thing happened. No white mist appeared, no cold breeze fanned across my forehead, but suddenly an intense sadness pierced my heart—a sadness so profound that I broke down and cried.

But it wasn't *my* sadness. It was someone else's.

"It's so *clear*," I thought, sitting alone in the empty dining room and sobbing miserably. If you loved a house—loved it dearly, I mean—loved it so much that its walls felt like your own skin, and it was taken from you, for whatever reason, wouldn't you want to stay close by? Wouldn't you *linger*?

I have loved a few houses that way, loved them enough to believe they had souls, and it tore my heart to leave them. If it had been death that separated me from them, instead of ordinary life choices—then *yes*.

Yes, I would have haunted them. I would haunt them still. At that thought, the sadness vanished as suddenly as it came. I'd blotted my tears and gotten back to normal before Jane reappeared with the souffle, which, by the way, was delicious. I told her what had happened—"it was the strangest thing"—and she wasn't a bit surprised.

Britain in the South Atlantic

1994

D URING THE 1982 FALKLANDS WAR (yes, it was that long ago), the rest of the world speculated about why Britain didn't just let Argentina keep these bare and distant islands. When I saw them, though—when I walked the hillsides and watched wild geese poke their heads above the grass, or when I strolled the compact streets of Stanley, the only town, and smelled the lingering peat smoke that is a symbol of life here—I understood why Britain fought so hard to keep them.

The Falkland Islands are British, pure and simple. As British as Orkney or the Shetlands or the Hebrides. They're just at the other end of the earth.

They are a British crown colony, one of the few left. The islands' motto: "Desire the Right."

They issue their own stamps and coins, "with our own little critters on them," said a local woman who moonlights as a guide.

And they maintain their own very British traditions. For a time, because most people still burn peat for heating and cooking, the islands even celebrated a quaint national holiday: Peat Cutting Monday.

I arrived in early February, the equivalent of August in the States, and was immediately slapped with my first dose of Falklands weather. One 19th-century visitor, evidently an optimist, described the climate as "boisterous but exhilarating."

Still true: In my first five minutes on the ground—I timed it—we endured rain, strong wind, hail and more wind, with a rare burst of sunshine showing up a bit later. At least the volatile weather is mild: It can frost in any season, the guide said, but Falkland temperatures aren't known to drop below 10 degrees Fahrenheit or rise above 80. Summer temps hover around 50, and cloudy skies are the year-round norm. In sum, it felt like Scotland.

The road from the airport to Stanley wound through wind-combed hills and stretches of stringy tussock grass, past flocks of sheep, stacks of drying peat and occasional "stone runs"— weird boulder-filled ribbons that resemble rocky riverbeds but aren't. And then more sheep and more wind and more grass and more peat.

Charles Darwin labeled this landscape "desolate and wretched." But I found it serene, like a miniature version of the American prairies. It was at least that treeless. The Falklands have no native trees—no trees of any sort, except stunted cypress and a few other imports around Stanley and on the lee sides of farms. They look like large shrubs; the endless wind prunes every attempt at height.

There are two main islands—East Falkland, where Stanley is, and West Falkland. They're surrounded by about three hundred smaller ones, though some residents say there are as many as seven hundred, if you count the odd rock.

In total area, the Falklands add up to 4,700 square miles— larger than Hawaii, a little smaller than Connecticut. And yes, they're far away—300 miles east of Argentina, at the southern tip of South America, and 1,000 miles north of Antarctica.

This isolation caused Falklanders to develop their own culture, their own lore, their own jargon, and it isn't just something hauled out for tourists—you hear it in everyday use: Native-born islanders are known as "kelpers"—a reference to the abundant local seaweed. A farm is a "settlement." A coffee break is a "smoko," and it's for tea.

"Town" means Stanley, no place else. All the countryside outside of Stanley, no matter which island it's on, is lumped under a single word: "Camp." The word comes from *campo*, Spanish for *field*. All told, only about eight hundred people live in Camp, and out there, life still revolves around raising sheep. That has been the Falklands' only real industry, so kelpers divide the year according to the flocks: sheep-breeding season, lambing time, shearing.

"It's just a miniature world," said another long-time resident, describing the whole archipelago. "It's a small village. It has its politics. It has its big business. It has its people who are seeking power."

Despite being on the far side of the Atlantic, "Town" turned out to be an English classic, as English as St. Pierre and Miquelon are French: Rows of neat, chimneyed cottages of stucco and brick, on slight terraces above an inlet. They couldn't have looked more English if they'd had thatched roofs.

I kicked around Stanley for a day, while I waited for a cruise ship to Antarctica, and would happily have stayed longer, poking into tiny shops, wandering along the seafront and pondering the stranded hulks of sailing ships that once limped into port and never left.

For all its British familiarity, though, there was something disorienting about Stanley.

It's a small town—only about 1,500 people—small enough that the residents already know where everything is, so they don't need to put up street signs or house numbers, and I had to keep asking for directions. But it wasn't that.

And it wasn't just that Stanley's tidy houses face *north* to take advantage of the sun's rays, the way ours might face south.

What unsettled me was the light itself. Perhaps because of the islands' exquisitely clean, clear air, the light was peculiar. This was summer in the Falklands, but the light was blue and cold, the way it is on a winter morning at home, so 3:30 on a Stanley afternoon looked like no time I'd ever seen before.

If you come from the northern hemisphere, sunlight in the southern one seems to slant the "wrong" way. That meant I could never *feel* north, even when I was facing it. It was like being in a Kodachrome slide that somebody stuck into the projector backward. If Stanley had been any bigger, I'd have lost my way.

The islands produce nothing but wool for export and mutton for local consumption—plus a few home-knitted sweaters and jars of jam, made from wild "diddle-dee" berries, that are sold to tourists and homeward-bound British soldiers as souvenirs. Everything else, from groceries to diesel fuel, has to be shipped or flown in.

The pace of this subdued lifestyle picked up after the Argentine war, when a Royal Air Force garrison was established on East Falkland; its detachment of nearly 2,000 isn't counted in local population figures.

The war grew out of history (what else?). As usual in the

New World, big colonial powers—Spain, France and Britain—wrestled for control of the Falklands in the 18th and early 19th centuries. Britain ended up with them in 1832 and has held them ever since—except for two and a half months in the spring of 1982 when Argentine forces took over.

Kelpers still tell painful stories about the occupation—about families having to sleep in bug-infested cellars while Argentine soldiers bedded down in their comfortable homes and about the local dairy being wiped out because Argentine soldiers ate all the cows.

Before the war, people said, many Argentines hoped the islanders might choose to join them of their own accord. Contact was encouraged, since Argentina was relatively close, and a number of Falklanders even sent their older children to school there.

That backfired, one native told me, using her own case as an example. She was sent to school in Argentina in the mid-1970s, when that country was in political turmoil, and armed soldiers were stalking the streets of Buenos Aires. "We saw their lifestyle," she said, her lips grim. "We didn't want to live like that."

British Prime Minister Margaret Thatcher ordered the military action that got the islands back, making her a local heroine and giving the Falklanders a new holiday. They may have lost Peat Cutting Monday, but they gained Liberation Day, June 14, the day of the Argentine surrender.

The war killed more than 250 Britons and 1,200 Argentines. It also severed the Falklands' diplomatic relations with Argentina. To get to the islands, I had to fly from Chile, right over Argentina, on the once-weekly mail run. To get there from

Britain, I'd have had to take a military plane—an 8,000-mile flight, with a stop at Ascension Island to refuel.

More than a decade after the war, Argentine anti-personnel mines still littered the countryside. Posters at the airport showed stomach-turning photos of shrapnel wounds and gave stern warnings to tourists against random hiking, especially near Stanley and the settlement of Goose Green, where fighting had been heavy.

"Camp" fared better than Town, because so much of it is on the outer islands. I got a glimpse of it on my Antarctic cruise ship's first stop—New Island, an overnight sail to the west of Stanley. New Island resembled two great camel humps, covered in grass, with a small beach on one side and cliffs that dropped sheer to the ocean on the other. Falklands wind had scoured away the clouds, and the combination of deep blue sky and tawny tussock grass made it look like an autumn day in Minnesota; the air was about that crisp too.

We came ashore on a tiny crescent of creamy sand, the color of light brown sugar and about as clingy. A ruined stone hut from whaling days stood on the beach, with a rusting iron try-pot beside it. The pot had been used for boiling the oil out of whale blubber, back when there were still enough whales to hunt.

On top of the cliffs was a rookery of rockhopper penguins, with black-browed albatrosses nesting among them. The albatross nests looked like top hats made of mud, nearly a foot tall, each holding a single chick. The penguins nested on the ground, among rocks and stones.

The chicks of penguins and albatrosses alike were covered with fluffy gray down, and the older penguins were beginning to molt—avian teenagers, caught between chickdom and adulthood. The albatross youngsters were not that far along, but they were already stretching their great wings; when they unfurled them, they looked like broken umbrellas—all fuzzy struts, no fabric.

It was a busy, noisy place, and to my eyes, it was seething with penguins. But to a man named Ian Strange, the lanky, gray-haired Briton who counts them every year, the rookery had been decimated, just like the whales a century before.

Normally, there would have been 60,000 nesting pairs of rockhoppers here, Strange said, as we talked in the kitchen of his small farmhouse on the grassy slopes nearby. But for the past two years there had been only 6,000. He blamed the shocking decline on a burgeoning international industry—commercial fishing for squid—mostly by boats from Korea, Taiwan and Japan. Squid was the penguins' main food, so the birds now had to compete with human appetites.

Things were better for the albatrosses, he said. Their numbers, normally around 12,000 breeding pairs, had actually risen: They'd been seen following the squid-fishing boats, feeding on castoffs.

Ian Strange had come to the Falklands thirty years before, to look into raising mink but quickly nixed the idea. "I liked the islands," he said, "and I felt there was something I could do here."

There was: As an artist-naturalist, he designed Falklands postage stamps and wrote half a dozen books about the islands. Now he was turning his farmland—he owned half of New Island's 10,000 acres—into a wildlife refuge, one of a growing number in the Falklands.

It was a gesture of hope: Though the Falklands had suffered

terrible losses—in past centuries, hunters killed thousands of seals and penguins here—"a lot of land is still in its original state," Strange said, quickly adding that "you can't really talk about that when you've got a very big international fishery, which is scooping up the very lifeline of what we have."

The problem was that revenue from international fishing licenses helped pay for such improvements as Stanley's new school and new swimming pool and the new airport road. "We should have been more careful in the beginning," he said. Once the licenses were given out, "it's very difficult to say, 'hang on, chaps, let's cut our licenses by half' because it'll reduce the standard of living."

Another threat—oil exploration—was looming, but Strange was optimistic about that. He thought there was still time to put protections in place. "You know the saying, 'you can't see the woods for the trees'? Well, here you can see the trees."

As I listened, I tried to keep my mind on the fluffy penguin chicks toddling around the rookery and the albatross infants stretching their wings atop their mud nests. But I kept picturing that abandoned whaling station on the pretty half-moon beach. International greed has always had long arms, reaching even here. I hoped Ian Strange was right. I hoped the Falklands still had time.

[*In 2002, Great Britain officially relabeled its colonies. The Falklands and 13 others around the world are now "British Overseas Territories."*]

Aboard the Orient Express

1993

M EN SHOULD BE ISSUED tuxedos at birth.
I'm not going anywhere with that thought—I was
just reminiscing about the after-dinner scene in the club car
of the Venice Simplon-Orient-Express. It was midnight, and
we were crossing France—sipping champagne, listening to
the soft tinklings of the baby grand and basking in the retro
glow of polished wood, plush armchairs and discreetly shaded
lamps.

The passengers were glowing too. Women were shimmering in pearls and satin, and the men, even the dumpy ones,
were looking sophisticated and suave in black tie, but the real
head-turner was a Scotsman in formal clan regalia, something
you usually don't see in real life, just in the movies. He wore
a red velvet jacket, lace at throat and cuffs, knee socks, patent
leather shoes with buckles and the mandatory plaid kilt. This
was the kind of crowd that didn't ask him what he was wearing underneath.

Those of us who weren't actually rich were pretending
to be. And in that sumptuous setting—shades of Hercule
Poirot—pretending came pretty naturally. But then, the mood

was always "let's pretend" in the first-class cars of the Orient-Express. *Let's pretend the great wars aren't coming. Let's pretend there are no poor wretches outside these windows. Let's pretend we can ride forever . . . .*

The Orient-Express was created for the international elite at the end of the nineteenth century and became the best-known luxury train in Europe. Its maiden run on October 4, 1883, established the route from Paris to Budapest, and in 1889 it added Istanbul, its most famous destination.

Today, its past is as checkered as Europe's. The Orient-Express survived World War I but suffered badly in World War II—so badly that the history of its carriages makes them sound like refugees. One of the exquisite dining cars received a direct hit in an air raid at London's Victoria Station in 1940. Two of the sleeping cars were used as war-time hotels in Lyons, France. A third was a brothel in Limoges.

After the war, the cars were repaired and put back into service, but luxury was giving way to mass travel. Second-class cars and stripped-down versions of first-class ones replaced the hand-polished marquetry walls and brass fixtures of the originals. The old train, the one made famous by such writers as Agatha Christie and Ian Fleming, stopped luxury service in 1962, when its beautiful carriages were sold or trashed for lack of demand.

By then, the Orient-Express had rolled into the realm of dreams, becoming a kind of Everest for train buffs like me. One winter night in the late 1970s, I took what was left of the Orient-Express across Europe, riding in a coldly modern steel-and-plastic sleeper, just because of its name. The glamour was all gone by then, and even the name vanished soon after.

Then in 1977, an American hotelier began tracking down

old Orient-Express carriages and having them restored, ultimately spending about sixteen million dollars on thirty-five original cars. Operated since 1982 as a private enterprise, the revived train is a railroad phoenix, a pre-war relic risen from its ashes. In short, the real thing.

I have ridden trains all over the globe—across Australia, through the Rockies, through the Andes and from Moscow to the Pacific on the Trans-Siberian, the longest train ride in the world. But none of them have the romantic aura of this one.

Riding it from London to Venice in summer, I was more aware of the train than the trip—trying to see and savor every detail of the antique carriages and the luxurious service—and simultaneously aware of myself in it, as if I were watching an actor on a moving stage. We went through five countries and the heart-stopping scenery of the Brenner Pass, but on this trip, Europe was just the backdrop.

Boarding at Victoria Station, we were ushered straight into the dining cars, as if this were a glorified dinner train. There were high-backed plush armchairs at tables set with pink-shaded lamps, fresh carnations, heavy crystal stemware, Wedgwood china and French silverware. In this mansion on wheels, the sense of the past was stronger than the present—a Victorian time warp so pretty, so perfect, that it brought a split second of tears to my eyes. For the rest of that afternoon, it also made the drab back yards of London tenements less ugly, the litter of aluminum cans and plastic cups by the tracks less noticeable, the rainy English day less drear.

We changed trains at Folkestone, leaving the English version behind, crossed the Channel by boat, and picked up the Continental train for the rest of the ride. The whole trip ran

1,065 miles and lasted roughly thirty-two hours, encompassing lunch and a formal dinner one day, and breakfast, lunch and tea the next: Geography measured off in mealtimes. I dressed for dinner at Amiens. Paris arrived as I finished my second helping of chocolate mousse with raspberry sauce. Lake Constance slid by with the morning croissants. If this is lunch, it had to be Innsbruck. And it was.

I am left now with a succession of cameos: Sculptured glass panels by Rene Lalique glowing in a dining car; beds made up with white damask sheets while we were away at dinner; the gray mountain walls and misty forests of the Alps; the way the grain in the wood paneling shown gold in the afternoon sun, when we were coming down into Italy. If I were rich, I thought, I would never fly again. I would travel this way for the rest of my life.

But it wasn't perfect. The Venice-Simplon-Orient Express— VSOE, for short—is still a train, and like any train, it has flaws. It doesn't even go through the Simplon Tunnel anymore, the great shortcut that opened in 1906; it goes through the Arlberg Tunnel instead. At a few hundred dollars a ticket, none of its flaws would matter. But my tab was $1,525 a person for a day and a half's ride, and for that much money, you expect perfection—which is the one thing you can't have on the road, no matter how much you choose to spend.

Things that go wrong have always been part of the deal, even between the two world wars, in luxury travel's so-called golden age. Like any train, this one can—and did—run late. Like any train, it jolted and shuddered over the tracks, making walking difficult for the sober and impossible for those who'd had too much champagne. And like any train, it stopped a lot, not only at scheduled stations but whenever it had to pull over to let a high-speed freight or regular passenger train zoom by.

Sleep shattered against the unpredictable stops and the bright station lights and the swaying ride—despite those immaculate damask sheets and the only comfortable mattress I've ever encountered on a railroad.

Even so, it is still the best train in the world, and it is rightly famous. Charisma and romance still swirl around it like perfumed smoke. Whenever the Orient-Express pulled into a station, people waiting for ordinary trains would notice the golden emblems on its dark-blue flanks and then look up at the gleaming windows and pink lampshades in the dining cars. Usually they just stared; a couple of times, I saw jaws drop.

Only once did the train's shock effect ricochet. As we took on midnight passengers at the Gare de l'Est in Paris, the glamorous crowd in the club car became aware of yips and hoots from outside.

"What's that noise?" someone asked, and coifed heads swiveled to see a regular passenger train pulling out past us, with young students at the windows, jeering and making obscene gestures. The incident was dismissed as soon as it happened, and the VSOE passengers turned back to the business at hand—champagne and small talk and the gentle tinkling of the piano.

Except for that one formal evening, however, the Orient-Express was not a very social experience. Cruise ships seem to have nearly as many lounges as passengers, but the train's only gathering places were three dining cars (used only at mealtime) and the club car. Most of the time, most passengers stayed in their compartments, usually with the doors shut.

The train grew slightly more social—and much less

classy—when we came down from the chilly mountains into sweltering Italy. The air-conditioning couldn't cope. Passengers, sweating in the steamy heat, left their compartment doors open in hopes of catching a breeze. Which meant anyone going by in the corridors could see how they dressed in real life—mostly in shorts and T-shirts, like the rest of us common folk.

Perhaps the relative dearth of gathering spaces wasn't such a bad thing, given that even on a luxury train, you can't choose your companions. On this trip, they included the ugliest American I'd encountered in thirty years of foreign travel, a 69-year-old man I'll call Bob. He was so stereotypically offensive that, at first, I had trouble believing he was for real. Everyone else had no doubts.

"Ah nevah been outta Loo-siana in mah life!" Bob boasted to everyone within earshot at the formal-dress dinner.

And why is that? a British gentleman, seated across from him, murmured with exquisite politeness over the meal Bob was ruining for him.

"Ah got ever' thing ah need in Loo-siana!" Bob boomed back. "Why'd ah want to leave hit?"

But leave it he had. How lucky for us. Bob became as much a topic of conversation as the food and the alpine scenery, and he stayed that way to the end of the line.

It was a good thing the trip lasted only a day and a half, a Canadian woman mused aloud as we pulled into Venice. "Any longer," she said, "and there really would have been a murder on the Orient-Express."

Unceasing Grace

2000

———

I DIDN'T INTEND TO GET A DOG; I knew I was gone too much. But on impulse, fifteen years ago, my sister and I did exactly what the Animal Humane Society advises you not to do: We bought a dog for someone else as a present. As a surprise.

Our choice was a lively, twenty-pound mixed-breed rescue named Lucky. He was two years old, had fluffy reddish-gold fur and looked like a baby golden retriever. We gave the dog to our father, hoping to rouse him from a post-retirement depression. It didn't work.

Dad, predictably, didn't want him. My sister couldn't take him because her children were too young for a pet, and I was traveling for my newspaper three to four months a year.

I polled my colleagues on what to do: Keep the dog despite my traveling lifestyle or take him back to the Humane Society and an uncertain future?

Everybody said the same thing: "Take him back—you're gone too much." I kept Lucky anyway.

I expected having a dog would be pretty much like having a cat had been: easy. I thought, since the dog was an adult, it would sort of live its own life in my house, the way my old cat had—as if we were roommates. I was wrong.

You don't have to walk a cat morning and night. Cats don't have barking fits and throw themselves at the door every time the mail carrier comes. And very few cats are able to provoke the guilt that dogs can when they want you to play get-the-stick.

In return for the unexpected hassles, I got a flood of comfort. Lucky greeted me every night by running in joyous circles around the dining room table, barking on the turns. His sharp ears picked up scary sounds better than mine, so if he wasn't worried about something I heard in the middle of the night, I didn't have to be, either. And he steadied my life.

Dogs are the very essence of normal—regular little monitors of sameness. Pleasant, unvarying days are just fine with dogs. And that was what Lucky gave me: sweet, ordinary days at home, where nothing changed.

My traveling life didn't change, either, though now when I went out of town, I detoured to the boarding kennel to drop Lucky off before I caught my plane. I thought it was working well until the dog began freaking out at the sight of luggage. He paced and panted, he lay in doorways so I couldn't leave without stepping over him, and once—in a rare show of temper—he trotted up to a packed suitcase in the living room and left a neat pile of poop beside it. There was no missing his point.

Then the kennel gave me a dismaying tally: In the first three years I'd had him, Lucky had been kenneled nearly twenty times. Everyone had been right: I *was* gone too much.

Al Sicherman—columnist, colleague and dearest friend— came to our rescue, and Lucky began staying with Al when

I was on the road. It was a nice solution for all three of us, though Lucky never did get used to suitcases. (Just taking out the recycling bags made him nervous.)

Al wrote about conversations they had. Lucky was always quite sarcastic. Al helpfully did Lucky's voice for him, a high-pitched nasally voice suitable for a small, barky dog. Dogs are experts at interpreting context, and Lucky figured out that the silly dog-voice of Al's referred, somehow, to him.

Gentle and gentlemanly, Lucky arrived with a built-in code of honor: He never chewed anything that wasn't his, never snitched hors-d'oeuvres off the coffee table (even when we weren't looking), never raided the kitchen wastebasket. (Well, once, in the first year I had him: He looked so mortified at being caught with a corncob in his mouth that I barely scolded him. He never did it again.)

When I got him, my mother was dying of cancer. An on-duty mother to the last, she warned me not to get too attached: "Dogs don't last very long," she said. (Neither do moms, I thought sadly.)

But Lucky lasted. He lasted through her death and other family deaths, he lasted through a marriage, he lasted through life in five houses (six if you count the family cabin). He lasted so long that I grew complacent. Fifteen years of steady companionship can make you expect forever.

Through nearly all that time, Lucky himself seemed change-less. Even in his old age, when taking him for a walk was more like standing still, passersby would remark on how pretty, how soft, how well-behaved the *puppy* was.

He also lasted through five life-threatening episodes of his own, rallying miraculously each time. This fall we ran out of miracles.

Lucky died on the first of September, after a short illness, while I was—where else?—on a trip. Al held him and petted him as he slipped away. He was 17 ½.

I thought I knew how interwoven Lucky was in my life, but I didn't feel the extent of it until I came home from that trip and walked into the empty house.

Death had reversed our roles: Lucky had waited for me at home through all my trips, but now I was the one left at home, and he was the one who had gone away—a small dog-soul journeying onward, alone.

Friends have been asking if I'll get another dog. I'm not sure, I tell them; I am still gone too much. And I doubt if any dog but Lucky could put up with it.

[Epilogue: By Christmas that year, I had been claimed by another rescue dog, a small fellow named Teddy, half Lucky's size but with all his love and loyalty.]

All Good Thoughts to Tigers

1996

E LEPHANT TREKS START before dawn, and at first all
you can hear is the creak of the square wooden saddles
and the rustle of Gore-Tex jackets. Then a dove calls in the distance. Then the "ty-ooo" note of an oriole chimes in, a teardrop
of sound. Then a nearby bush explodes with bird chatter, loud
as a crate of squeaky toys. And then, as if a curtain has gone up
on a vast green stage, it's day.

Every morning began like this at Karnali Lodge, a wilderness camp inside Nepal's westernmost national park, in the
tropical lowlands called the Terai. A friend and I had just come
off a rafting trip on the Bheri River and were spending a
few days here, going tiger-hunting on elephant-back. Tiger-
seeking was more accurate.

Each morning, we woke before 6 and dressed in the damp
and surprisingly chill darkness, then joined other tourists mill-
ing about the lodge, sipping tea and waiting to board the elephants assigned to us. Ours was Raj Kali—Royal Lady in
Hindi, a title almost as elegant as our quarry's: Sher Khan—
Sher for Tiger, Khan for King or Lord. Yes, as in Genghis.

Raj Kali was about thirty years old and going a bit pink in

the face, as Asian elephants do later in life. The camp had four other Kalis, all younger and all female, because females are easier to handle than males.

To get onto our Kali, we had to climb a ladder-like mounting platform and step from that into an open wooden box strapped to her back; inside, we sat sideways, with our legs sticking out over her ribs and our backs braced against each other.

By the time all five Kalis were loaded—each with two tourists, a driver and a naturalist—the forest was light enough to see shapes but not colors. As we creaked and swayed down the first path, the light gathered, and the world changed. A turquoise baseball cap emerged from the gloom; somebody's down vest turned from matte black to bright navy; tree trunks grew brown, leaves a dull khaki.

Then full day broke above the treetops, and the forest was rainbowed in greens. Dewdrops spangled every leaf, every blade of grass, every spider web—and the spider webs were the size of dinner plates. Only the elephants stayed gray.

Under the trees, Raj Kali startled clouds of black butterflies into flight, and once we frightened a spotted-deer buck: Fawn-sized, fawn-colored, he froze for a moment, watching us from under antlers like tiny spikes, trying to decide whether to bolt. Then he bolted—but not very far, because he wasn't very scared: Wildlife perceives only the elephant, our naturalist said, not the people on its back.

But elephants make so much noise crashing through the forest that any tiger who lingered in our vicinity would have to be old, deaf and stupid. In the distance, an elephant on the move sounds like popcorn popping; up close, it's a mobile demolition project. Their feet are padded, like hassocks, so their footsteps are soundless. But they crash their bodies through the forest as loudly—and as resolutely—as a Sherman tank going through a wooden fence.

The only things Raj Kali bothered to avoid were the biggest trees. Everything else, she vanquished. Saplings bent before her bulk, branches broke, ordinary trees splintered. She snaked out her long gray trunk to wrestle shrubs to earth, stomped them flat and plodded on, ripping up snootfuls of tall elephant grass or tasty fern to munch on as she walked.

She walked loosely, like all the Kalis. From the back, they looked like aging chorus girls still trying to be sexy. With each step, they threw one huge hip up and out, then the other, almost gracefully, in a giant gray bump-and-grind. Raj Kali's saunter made us lurch forward, backward and sideways. Riding her always left me slightly dizzy, as if I'd been too long in a small boat on a choppy lake.

The flat land by the river held great stretches of elephant grass that rose twelve, fifteen, even twenty feet high. When Raj Kali pushed through it, its reddish plumes shook off drifts of pollen, like smoke. Too bad it isn't corn, I thought, as I swayed woozily on her back. Saying "the *grass* is as high as an elephant's eye," while true, just didn't have the same ring.

One morning in the grass, Raj Kali flushed a rhinoceros out of cover. He trotted off in a huff, snorting and annoyed, and kept looking back suspiciously over his shoulder as he went.

Everyone shot pictures of him, but after he disappeared into the tall grass again, a man on another elephant shouted, "If it's a rhino, don't call out!" Nepal has perhaps 300 tigers, compared with about 500 rhinos, so his unspoken meaning was clear: Call out *only* if you see a tiger—they're harder to find.

I tried to do better than that, sending a mental call to the great cats themselves: "*Come, Sher Khan. Come, Sher Khan. All good thoughts to tigers . . . .*" I sent this message over and over, every time we went out on Raj Kali, but it didn't work. All through our stay, tigers remained nothing more than an orange and black rumor.

My friend and I had done this kind of tiger hunt once before, a decade earlier in another part of Nepal. That time we had success but only because of an inhumane practice called "tiger-baiting." Each evening, the camp staff tied a water-buffalo calf to a stake in the jungle and put a bell around its neck. If a tiger attacked it, the calf would struggle, the bell would ring, and the guests would tiptoe out to a blind in the jungle and watch the tiger feast. One night, a tigress killed the calf for her two nearly grown sons, and we got to see the youngsters squabble over their dinner.

Tiger-baiting has been stopped in Nepal, but that has made tiger sightings even more unlikely. At Karnali, only seven tigers had been identified as regulars in the twenty-five-square-kilometer area we were searching, and the great cats don't wear striped camouflage for nothing.

On a hike with our naturalist, a handsome, well-educated young man named Darshand Singh, he told us, in crisp British English, how just a few days earlier, he'd seen a tigress sitting beside the road we were walking on.

Monkeys had alerted him to her presence. "You know how langurs are, when they see a tiger," he said, the off-hand way we might say, "You know how raccoons are around garbage cans." I didn't, but I admired how casually he said it.

Langurs—big gray monkeys with black faces and white beards—post sentries whenever their troop is busy feeding.

If a sentry spots a tiger, Darshand said, it goes hysterical, and then so do all the other langurs—shrieking, chattering and carrying on until the whole forest knows a big cat is on the prowl.

Despite the monkey ruckus, this tigress kept sitting calmly near the trail—just over there, Darshand said, gesturing with his hiking stick. She patrolled this area regularly, so another sighting was bound to happen. And sure enough—"look there," he said, pointing again—there were the she-tiger's paw prints, clear and fresh in the white dust of the road, proof of her living, breathing reality. But that was as close as we got.

You can't ride elephants all day—though we tried, putting in more than six hours on Raj Kali's back each day. In the afternoons, we waded into the murky river shallows and helped her trainer bathe her, and sometimes we got to feed her snacks—softball-sized green packages made of leaves tightly wrapped around a handful of grain.

And we took guided nature walks. The park around us— Royal Bardia National Park—is wilderness but not the wilderness Americans are used to. It's more like a wilderness *island*, with a growing sea of human beings surging around its shores. Once we went to visit them. Once, in the form of a corpse, one of them visited us.

The people who live in this part of Nepal's lowlands use every bit of land they can, farming right up to the park boundaries. There was no transition. On one side of a low, fragile-looking wire fence, there were small farms and bright yellow fields. On the other side of the wire, there was shadowy green jungle. I thought the juxtaposition was shocking until I remembered the garish tourist attractions that jam the gateways of our own national parks.

In the nearest village, everything was made of mud—mud houses, mud storage bins, mud granaries, mud floors, mud patios—and the result looked like adobe sculpture. White cattle fed at their troughs, and rows of villagers were moving through the yellow fields, harvesting ripe mustard seed, grown for its oil. At one farmstead, women in dresses as beautiful as evening gowns were weaving baskets in the shade. At another, a potter hurried into his workroom to demonstrate his craft for us, kicking a stone-weighted wheel to give it momentum before he slapped down a lump of clay and whirled it into a vase as his tiny daughters looked shyly on. It was all as peaceful as a painting.

The corpse was far less attractive. We were walking along a park trail on the lip of the river bank when Darshand Singh pointed it out. If he hadn't, we wouldn't have noticed it, let alone thought it was human.

It was what was left of a drowning victim, identity unknown, whose body had washed into the bank during the last monsoon. When the river level dropped, as it does every year, the body stayed there, tangled in a treetop. Now it hung, folded at the hips, over a long, jutting branch. It looked like a limp curtain or a big dishrag, the same weathered gray as the driftwood on the bank. The head was gone, and you had to stare a long time to notice that it still had a ribcage and feet.

Perhaps I shouldn't admit this, but the only thing that chilled me about this corpse was how little I reacted. I cared more about the living tigers I couldn't see than I did about the dead person before my eyes. There are a lot of us humans, and we're the reason there aren't many tigers left. Or rhinos, for that matter. They're both being poached because they're worth so much on the black market, Darshand and the other naturalists said.

Across the border in China, a rhino horn could bring more than $10,000, they said, and a dead tiger was worth $20,000 to $30,000. It's because many Chinese still believe that tigers and rhinos have medicinal power—most often as sexual stimulants—and the demand for tiger bone wine, tiger penis soup and other tiger concoctions is depleting the supply.

In other words, tigers are being killed so that a lot of people can make even more people. I found that reason about as repulsive as the corpse, and I knew that sending all good thoughts to tigers wasn't going to be enough to save them.

Taking Refuge, Finding Home

2006

I HAVE LEARNED TO BELIEVE in a mystical connection between people and places. It has come to me most often on trips—come in inklings, in waves, in glimpses. At its strongest, it is what I think of as "home." It always starts with a kind of recognition—not déjà-vu exactly, but a deep, heart-felt relief. I have sensed it in only a few places. Roshan is the one that still surprises me. Roshan, a place I never heard of and knew even at the time I would never see again.

Roshan was a gift. It came at the end of a long journey through Eastern Europe, before the Iron Curtain fell. By that point, my body was tired, and my mind was refusing to be open, not even to the new experiences that usually cure it. Roshan changed that.

Roshan is a tiny monastery in the extreme south of Bulgaria, a place so small, in a country then so remote, that no one in my world had heard of it, or ever needed to. I had climbed up there from Perlik, another small, barely known village, with a guide and the guide's mother, a woman my own age.

To say the young guide could have been my son was true, but he was leading me, and I felt as beholden and helpless as his child. His real mother was flitting around like some kind of gypsy, dancing through pastures full of daisies, bobbing like a human kite in the day's hot breezes. She didn't need (or wouldn't take) much leading.

I remember the dry pastures of late summer; a donkey munching placidly under a tree; the backdrop of white chalk mountains, dusted with green. From the hilltops, you could see across the border into Greece.

The monastery, when we reached it at last, was a little doughnut-shaped fortress with white stuccoed walls. In its round courtyard, Bulgarian school children were scampering and laughing, and a group of German tourists in short-shorts were crowding into the dimness of the miniature chapel. My guide pulled me and his mother inside, too, and began pointing out paintings of saints on walls and ceiling.

I had seen them all—saints and tourists and school-kids— all before on this trip. And I suddenly felt that if I had to stay a second longer in that dark, crowded, officially holy place, I would panic. "No," I said to him, "no more," fighting the urge to scream it.

I rushed out so fast that the startled guide could not catch up. I took the first staircase I came to, a narrow flight of wooden steps that ran up to a balcony encircling the courtyard, just above the heads of the crowd.

Grapevines stretched across the courtyard, like a green roof, and their leaves shielded the balcony: No one could see me from below, but I needed a better haven. I ducked into the first room I came to and found it blessedly empty. It looked like an abandoned schoolroom, no people, no desks, nothing—just some signs in Cyrillic on the walls and a large and grainy photograph of a man with a musket, posted on a board.

I had been seeing such pictures all day. From the man's rough clothes and shaggy beard, and from the clear age of the photo, I knew that he was one of a string of 19th-century Bulgarian revolutionaries. My guide had been giving me a crash course in revolutionaries, and I had been dutifully trying to pay attention—memorizing the faces of these distant men, asking the guide to translate the details of their individual heroics, decoding the letters of their names, writing down dates. But not this time. I took no notes. I left my camera in its case. I did not care who this revolutionary was or why he was connected with this place.

Then I heard someone coming and sought cover. There was a low doorway near the far corner. Quickly, I ducked my head and stepped through it—and into a tiny room so closed and quiet that it felt like a secret.

There was no other door to the room, only a small window filtering dusty light over plain furnishings—a bed and a couch, a hearth, a ewer and basin, a pine table. And peace. A sense of peace so deep, I caught my breath and almost wept.

As surely as if I had lived it, I knew how it would feel to fall asleep in that small safe bed, knew how the room would look flooded with light in the morning. I knew how it would feel to wake up here and how good the simplest tasks of life would be—washing my face in cool water, putting on clean coarse-woven clothes, tasting local bread and strong black coffee. I knew without being told that the man in the photograph had taken refuge here, had come in need of help and had received it. He had left healed. I knew it because the healing was still in the room.

I imagined no love affair for him here—life, after all, is not a movie. But someone had cared for him in this room, and he had dropped his guard and let himself be cared for. That made it a place of trust, a place of peace, and I realized that peace was part of the home I longed for and the few I'd found. Peace in all its meanings: An absence of chaos, a moment in which to breathe, time to remember who you are, to regain yourself.

I learned later that my revolutionary went away from Roshan and was killed somewhere else. I wrote his name down then, but I cannot find that notebook, and I had not looked long enough at the old photo to remember his face.

But I knew him nonetheless. I knew him because I knew the place where he took refuge. I knew the place where he found home.

Mush, You Huskies

1990

———

THE DOGS ARE SILENT when they run. All you hear is
the soft rush of sled on snow and the steady *huh-huh-huh*
of their panting. If the wind is blowing hard, you cannot hear
even that.

At such moments—on the blinding white of a frozen lake,
with ice forming on your eyelashes and the wind whipping
snow crystals against your face like stinging fog—driving a
dog sled is as much real adventure as anyone could want.

"Fantasy Island!" one of my companions called it.

For me, it was Sgt. Preston of the Yukon. Or Amundson
going for the Pole. Or . . . .

Except if you start fantasizing like that while you're on the
sled, it's a dead certainty that the dogs will do something unpredictable—like suddenly turning to check out an ice-fishing
shanty or veering onto a snowmobile track because it's clearer
than the trail you want them to follow or (worst) just plain
quitting.

That's what mine did. Right when I was deepest into playing Jack London, the leaders suddenly stopped, and the whole
team—Lightning, Gonzo, Eddie, Jasper, Yassir and Schultz—

just stood there looking over their shoulders at me like confused and not particularly forgiving children.

"They're not stupid," Doug Seim, the dog musher who owns them, explained later. The dogs were waiting for direction. The blowing snow had obliterated the trail, and they didn't know which way to go.

That happened several times in our mile-long run across Bearskin Lake near Ely, Minnesota, one January afternoon. Each time, my partner on the sled—a California man named Pat who was also a novice at dog mushing—would leap out of the sled basket, run up to the leaders, grab their collars and yank them forward. Then I'd yell, "Straight ahead!" and the dogs would throw their weight against the lines, the sled would shoot forward, and Pat would jump back in the basket as the sled flew past.

People watching from a nearby island said we looked like we knew what we were doing. We were pretty impressed with ourselves, too—until we reached the opposite shore and cut too close to a tree. The sled got caught on one side of the trunk, the dogs were on the other, and it took a lot of wrestling to sort it all out.

By then, we'd had perhaps three hours' experience with sled dogs. It was remarkable that we could be out with them at all—let alone trying to get somewhere on our own, like across a lake in thirty-below wind chill. It was also proof of the trust that Wilderness Inquiry, a Minnesota-based outdoor education program, places in its participants—all of its participants, whether seniors or children, whether disabled or able-bodied, whether moving on their feet, using a walker or propelling themselves in a wheelchair. On WI trips, it's differences that matter, not disabilities. It was a given that all of us would help each other.

In our group of fourteen, there was a British family with a three-year-old boy and an eight-year-old girl, who had just moved to Wisconsin from Thailand; a suburban homemaker, age 61, who had raised eleven children; two adults with mobility impairments; one man with epilepsy, and six other adults in various stages of middle age. Our careers ranged from poet to professor of engineering, from garage supervisor to clergywoman.

In addition, there were three young Wilderness Inquiry leaders, plus two staff members from Camp Menogyn on Bearskin Lake in the Superior National Forest, plus our indispensable dog musher, Doug Seim.

At 38, Seim was a red-bearded, tobacco-chewing giant who had gotten into raising and racing dogs about seven years before, who had run the John Beargrease race from Duluth to Grand Portage and back three times "and never made a cent," who never tired of answering our dog questions and who freely admitted to being obsessed with dogs. You know you're obsessed, he said, "when times get tough and you start lookin' around your house for stuff to sell so you can buy dog food!"

In our five days north of the Gunflint Trail, we adults all learned—by doing it ourselves, under Seim's hearty supervision—how to harness the sixteen Alaskan huskies he'd brought from his kennel near Grand Marais and how to drive at least a few of them.

He showed us how to feed them: You don't hand food to sled dogs because they're too eager to get it. Instead, we tossed pound-and-a-half chunks of frozen chicken right in front of their noses, so they wouldn't bite the hands that fed them.

He taught us to break up dog quarrels safely: Yell at them, so they know you're mad. Grab something and hit them on their wide, thick heads—never on their vulnerable backs, ribs or legs. But whatever you do, "Don't stick your hands in there!"

He filled us with mushing facts: A sled dog's racing life only lasts from about age two to age seven, though they can live to be fifteen. Racing teams are three times the size of the six-dog teams we were running—our limit, because of the dogs' great strength and our inexperience. To win a long race, a team has to average nine to ten miles per hour—but they can sprint up to twenty.

When they weren't working, the dogs were kept chained— they're not pets—far enough apart so they couldn't squabble. They managed it anyway, whenever they got the chance.

Seim explained the noisy nuances of dog communication: If they're all barking, it's probably a fight. If they're howling, "they're just talking to each other." But if they're doing both, they've probably spotted somebody carrying their sled harnesses. Pulling sleds is what they've been bred, raised and trained to do, and they love it.

Sled dogs do more than just get excited when they know they're going to run. They go wild, jerking at their chains and barking and howling in ear-splitting excitement. They keep that up until the instant they feel the sled brake loosen. Then they fall silent and start pulling, concentrating on what they do best.

"These dogs," said Seim, "are athletes." But we weren't, so Seim drummed into us "the first rule of dog mushing: Never let go of the sled!"

The dogs knew commands for right turns ("Gee!") and left

turns ("Haw!"), and they understood "'Straight ahead!" and "On by!" (for passing other teams or avoiding distractions) and "Hike!" (to pick up their speed).

But they recognized no command for "Stop!" Let go of a running team, Seim warned, and they'll keep right on going till they get into a tangle or hit something, either of which can mean a dogfight and injuries, even death, for the animals.

So we hung on tight. Or tried to. Sometimes it wasn't easy. I slid sideways off the brake when the sled tilted onto one runner on a steep portage going down onto Duncan Lake. We would have crashed if one of the trip leaders, standing at the side of the trail, hadn't given the sled a strategic shove. It righted itself, and we came down onto the frozen lake intact, but I was so scared I was shaking.

Another woman fell off the first time she tried to drive but managed to grab hold of the dangling brake and the snow hook—a wicked-looking steel claw used to keep a stopped team stopped. She stalwartly hung onto both while the dogs dragged her face-down across the ice until somebody finally caught up to the sled. That point, she said later, "was the highest for me—and the lowest!"

When it wasn't our turn to dogsled, there was cross-country skiing, a snowshoe trek, an overnight campout (yes, it is possible to sleep outside in winter, without a tent, without freezing) and, one night, a sauna on the edge of Bearskin Lake. The finale was jumping into the water—with much screaming—through a hole chopped in the ice.

None of these activities—not even the dog sledding—was pushed at us. Of the wilderness trips I've taken, this was the least macho, least competitive and least pressured, and the one that provided the most hands-on experience. "You let us do everything we think we can do," a 30-year-old man named Reed said to the leaders. "But you're always there in case we make a mistake."

Reed was talking about the day trip we took to Rose Falls, a twenty-foot-tall natural sculpture deep in the woods, with running water still chortling behind stalactites of blue ice. The leaders debated about going. The trail down to the falls was steep, they warned, and thick with snow. It could be difficult . . . .

Reed, who uses a walker because of injuries from a car accident in college, wanted to go anyway. "I could crawl on my hands and knees," he volunteered. That kind of pluckiness characterized the trip. Reed got to Rose Falls standing up, walking behind a plastic sled called a pulk and using its handlebar for support, with one of the leaders walking close behind him.

On our last evening at Camp Menogyn, we took stock of what we'd liked best. Robert, a 25-year-old New Yorker with epilepsy, summed up most people's answers in three short words: "Dogs," he said. "Sledding. Bijou."

Bijou was Seim's gentlest dog, a greyhound-husky mix who had patiently allowed us to pull, push and tug her padded X-back harness onto her head and under her front legs, over and over, until each of us got it right.

My faves included Gonzo, who had blue eyes and liked to put his paws on your chest and try to lick your face. White, named for his color, who enjoyed being picked up and cuddled—if you could get his more-than-fifty-pound weight onto your lap. Jasper, who was shy and wouldn't eat if people were too close. And Yassir, whom Seim named after Arafat because, he liked to say, that dog and his littermates were "nothing but a gang of terrorists."

The idea of such dogs and dog-sledding had enticed me onto this trip, and I came away more than satisfied. Actually, I came away hooked—something that happens to me every time I do something intensely interesting. I phoned home to say so.

The patient voice of home, who is accustomed to calls announcing a sudden and dramatic life change, took a deep breath before replying. Okay, he finally said, so how many dogs do you need to get started?

"Six," I said. "I think six."

He knew before I did that I wasn't *really* going to get around to running the John Beargrease—just as he'd known I wasn't really going to take up glider flying that time or build my own sailboat or open a bed-and-breakfast just because I liked Victorian furniture. But he also knew this wasn't the time to say so.

A Scorpion's Tale

1990

——

"THIS," I REMEMBER THINKING, "shouldn't be happening." Rummaging for my alarm clock on my last night in Costa Rica, I had slipped my right hand into a side pocket of my duffel bag and felt a sharp pain at the base of the ring finger. Within seconds, my finger, then my whole hand, began to pulse and throb.

I thought I'd broken a blood vessel or cut it on the pocket's zipper. Neither had happened, but something else certainly had. Yet there was no sign of damage. I was mystified. The family I was staying with were not. A biting ant, they suspected instantly, or an *alecran*—a scorpion.

Oh, come on, I thought, as flames of pain shot up my arm. Scorpion bites are for adventure comics and Indiana Jones movies, not real life. But I had forgotten where I was. In Central America, scorpions are part of real life, even though—in more than a dozen trips there—I'd never seen one.

My hostess, the good lady I call Mamá, insisted on examining the duffel bag. On top of it she found a tiny, mostly mashed insect, about the size of a termite. "*Alecrancito*," Mamá declared. Baby scorpion.

At least it wasn't a big one, I thought. If little ones could hurt like this, what could a big one do? Then Mamá examined the pocket itself. There were six more baby scorpions squirming unpleasantly in the bottom. This did not satisfy her. "Where there are baby scorpions," she said quietly, "there is always a mother."

And then, like a dream monster emerging from a child's closet of fears, the mother scorpion crawled slowly out from under the pocket flap. My memory has added the "Star Wars" sound effects.

The mother scorpion was pale beige and about two inches long, but to me she looked as big as a rat. She seemed to know she was powerful. She almost swaggered, tail stinger poised, as she moved majestically onto the top of the duffel bag.

There were five adults in the room, and all of us, even the men, gasped. I remember that everyone except Mamá also jumped up on the nearest piece of furniture, or maybe it was just me, hopping up onto the sofa. It was some moments before any of us recovered, and then I pulled off one of my shoes and smashed the mother scorpion flat. And kept on smashing, until there was nothing left of her but a white paste.

The mother was the one that stung me, not her offspring. But the perpetrator no longer mattered: Pain, awful pain, had enveloped my arm like a sleeve of red-hot nails. It flickered through the muscles in sickening waves, and any movement, however small, pounded the burning nails in deeper.

Weirdly, my arm looked normal—no discoloration, no swelling. This was dismaying: The least it could have done was look as horrible as it felt. But scorpion venom, I learned later, is a nerve poison. It hurts, but unless the sting gets infected, it doesn't show.

Within an hour, the burning pain had consumed my entire arm, all the way into the armpit, and I was scared and panicky. What would happen when it got to my head? Everyone now agreed that I should go to the local hospital. If I'd been in the States, we'd have called an ambulance. But the hospital was nearby, so Mamá and I did what we always do on short jaunts in Costa Rica: We walked.

Each step touched off dazzling explosions of pain around and through my arm, a regular aurora borealis from hell. I wondered, the whole way, whether the effort of walking was driving the poison deeper into my body. I began to wonder whether I would die.

The hospital was small, more like a neighborhood clinic. There was only one doctor on duty, and the open-air waiting room was crowded, even now, at midnight. "I think I got stung by a scorpion," I said in Spanish to the nurse. She told me to wait. Apparently, a scorpion bite in Costa Rica doesn't exactly rank with having a heart attack, but there was no comfort in the thought. I cradled my arm as we waited, not that it made any difference to the pain.

"I got stung by a scorpion," I said to the young doctor when we finally got in. He looked exhausted. He leaned against the wall, closed his eyes and replied, in English, "No problem—be happy."

I would have laughed, if I hadn't been so scared and if the pain hadn't kept on getting worse. The doctor suggested an antibiotic injection but could do nothing more. Mamá walked me back to her house, where I took five ibuprofen tablets and tried to sleep. The pills didn't make a dent.

Pain and fear kept me awake most of that night, and I kept

going over the whole hideous event in my mind. How could it have happened? I'd been so careful. Ever since I was little, when I'd been impressed by some tropical adventure movie, I'd known how to keep scorpions and other icky things out of suitcases and shoes:

You keep your luggage closed, except when you're using it, so nothing dangerous can hide inside. When you take off your shoes, you stuff them with socks for the same reason. I had done that religiously on all my trips, starting in childhood, even in scorpion-free Europe. I'd done it on this trip around Central America too. Or thought I had.

But in Belize, I'd stayed in a beach hut, its floor only a few inches above the warm sand, perfect scorpion habitat. I'd been extra careful there, because I had had to keep my duffel on the floor—there was no place else to put it. When I was leaving, I noticed that one small pocket was unzipped.

Good thing it was such a flat pocket, I thought, zipping it shut. But the mother scorpion had already squeezed inside and claimed it for her nest. She must have crawled all over the whole bag to find that little slot.

So she rode along, out of Belize, across Honduras and into Costa Rica. During the trip, her babies hatched. And if I hadn't gone rummaging for my alarm clock the last night, I wouldn't have opened that pocket until I got home. I imagined the scorpions escaping into dark crannies of my Minneapolis house, lying in wait, stinging my dog, killing him.

As the night wore on and the pain worsened, I began to fear that if I fell asleep, I wouldn't wake up. I thought back over my life and the people in it and wondered if I'd see them again, but eventually my mind faltered, and I dozed.

When I woke up, it was 4:30 A.M., it was still pitch-dark, and my arm was still screaming. None of it mattered. I thought it was the best morning I'd ever seen—for the simple, stupid reason that I hadn't died. I felt euphorically happy. Life seemed good and easy; the air had a clean taste, and food was heaven. I just didn't dare move my arm.

It took fourteen hours for the searing pain to ease, and I spent most of that time on airplanes, flying home. Slowly, the pain crept back down the arm, the way it had come, but it got more and more intense, as if it were being concentrated, squeezed into a smaller and smaller space. And then the pain went out, *poof,* like a candle flame.

It was a week before I could feel anything in my right hand again, a month before the arm stopped tingling when I moved it. Almost anything touched off the tingles—gripping the steering wheel too hard, putting on or taking off a glove, picking up a pen.

The sensation was a weird, invisible prickle, like hitting your funny bone or wearing a ring of burrs. But every time I felt it, I remembered: I had been bitten by a scorpion, and I hadn't died.

Never mind that scorpion stings don't normally kill adults. Never mind that the biggest dangers, once you're over the panic, are allergic reaction or infection and that I'd had neither. Never mind that there was no residual nerve damage. The pain had been bad enough to make me feel that I'd survived something big.

I didn't even regret that it had happened. When my life changed suddenly a few weeks later—a marital separation, a leave of absence, a temporary job in a different state—the scorpion bite made everything easier. Every time my hand tingled, I remembered that feeling of victory, waking up the morning I didn't die, and the memory made daily life look good again. When the last of the tingles finally faded away, I was almost sorry.

Riding the Wild River North

2001

————

S HE WASN'T MUCH TO LOOK AT, tied off at the dock in Yellowknife just past the floatplanes: a small, no-nonsense rectangle of blue and white sheet metal, boxy, blunt-bowed, more tow boat than clipper ship. But the sturdy little Norweta—her name derives from "Northwest"—wasn't built to be lovely. She was built to work. Her "wow" factor comes from where she goes.

Each summer, the Norweta offers the continent's most unusual cruise, taking a handful of passengers the length of the great Mackenzie River—more than a thousand miles, from the river's birthplace in Great Slave Lake north to the maze of channels in its delta, where the Mackenzie finally empties into the Arctic Ocean.

I thought I knew cruises. I'd taken a couple in the Caribbean, done the Mississippi on the Delta Queen, cruised the Great Lakes, crossed the Atlantic on the Queen Elizabeth II. All were great experiences, but none—none—came close to the Mackenzie.

Going downstream—north, that is—the little boat is helped by the powerful current, but the thousand-mile journey still takes nine days. In all that time, in all that distance, the Norweta passes only eight tiny villages.

Picture it this way: That's roughly the length of the Mississippi between the Twin Cities and Memphis, Tennessee, but without Minneapolis, without St. Paul, without St. Louis, without Memphis. Without everything—except wide blue water, untouched forest, midnight sun and those eight hamlets, the largest of which—Fort Simpson—has only 1,200 people, fewer than Frontenac, Minnesota. Can't quite picture Frontenac? That's what I mean.

(The Mackenzie and its tributaries, by the way, are the second-longest river system in North America; the Mississippi-Missouri combo is first.)

Riverboats used to ply Canada's rivers the way they did ours. Air travel put an end to them—except for the Norweta. Launched in 1970, she was built as a passenger boat. In the 1980s, she was used as a standby ship for oil rigs in the Beaufort Sea, that part of the Arctic Ocean above Canada's Yukon and Alaska. The current owners bought her as a retirement project and put her back in the cruise business in 1991.

The Indians in this region call the Mackenzie "Deh Cho," meaning "great river." It fits better than the official moniker, which honors British explorer Alexander Mackenzie, who canoed it in 1789. By either name, the river starts and ends in what Canadians call "North of 60"—the lands north of the 60th parallel.

Because the Mackenzie flows north, like the Red River on the Minnesota-North Dakota border, locals talk comfortably about going "down north" and "up south." A popular map reflects that point of view. It shows North America upside down, with Greenland at the bottom. When you're North of 60, a map like that makes a lot more sense.

With only seventeen other passengers, a mix of Canadians and Americans, most of them retired, I took the Norweta "down north." We pulled out of Yellowknife, the small, quaint-sounding but perfectly modern capital of the Northwest Territories, at noon on a sunny day in late June. Even making eleven nautical miles an hour, it took all that night and into the next morning just to cross the western end of Great Slave Lake—there was still ice in some of its bays—and enter the Mackenzie itself.

The cabins, like the boat, were plain and serviceable. Mine had a good bed with a warm comforter, a small desk, a closet, a compact sink and shower and a toilet that flushed with silty river water. It also had a built-in space heater, welcome at night, even though daytime highs could reach more than 75 degrees.

The Norweta's chef was used to cooking for men on oil rigs, so she made meals that were big, hearty and frequent: Breakfasts included homemade muffins and breads; lunches and dinners featured steak or roast beef or pork chops, always with homemade pies and cakes. Because the British tradition survives in Canada, there was also afternoon tea, always with freshly baked cookies, served in the dining room, the only gathering place that could hold all the passengers at the same time.

Day or night, moving or stopped, whenever I pulled back the curtains in my snug cabin, the view from the porthole was the same: an expanse of wide blue water, a strip of shore, a wall of green trees and the vast Canadian sky. It was nearly midsummer, so the sun was always up; it flirted with the horizon, but it never set. In the clear, endless light, I felt as if my eyes were open all nine days.

Our first landfall was the hamlet of Fort Providence, population 700. Fighting clouds of mosquitoes in early morning sunshine, I walked to the town's blue metal school building and encountered Angie Matto, a small, soft-voiced woman who was its aboriginal culture instructor. She was a Dene Indian from the village who visits each classroom every day, teaching the children things they would once have learned from their elders: a little of the tribe's traditional South Slavey language, the uses of local plants, how to make mittens and moccasins, how to feed a fire, how to honor the river. That meant giving it gifts, in hope of protection, important because of the river's fierce power. A woman, she said, might give it money or a bullet, letting it fall from her hand into the moving water.

Then she taught me, as she does her students, how to shake hands properly. It's different from how whites do it. The Dene way is very gentle and bonding. You take turns, one person holding his hand still, the other doing the shaking. "You don't grab," she cautioned.

We bypassed the village of Jean Marie River (time was a factor and so was its very steep bank), but we stopped at all the rest between Yellowknife and Inuvik: Fort Simpson, an 1803 Hudson Bay post that is the oldest town on the Mackenzie; Wrigley, 130 people atop picturesque bluffs; Fort Norman, population 450; Norman Wells, an oil-producing and shipping port with 750 people; Fort Good Hope, population 630, narrowly missed by a forest fire six years earlier and almost as old as Fort Simpson, and Arctic Red River, population 160, on a commanding point of land north of the Arctic Circle.

The villages looked much alike: a boat landing beneath high riverbanks, a gravel road sloping up from the water, a few dirt streets, standard pastel government houses, maybe some cabins, plus a church, a school, a store and sometimes a Royal Canadian Mounted Police station.

The majority of villagers are Dene. In the United States, they would be called Native Americans; Canadians call them First Nations people. Most of them, we were told, live in government housing, on government assistance. Some still hunt and fish for their families, but commercial hunting and fur trapping don't pay anymore. "It's not worth it to go out there," a young Dene man told me in Fort Providence.

Sadly, the villages shared other things too: "A lot of beatings, a lot of mischief, a lot of fights—all related to alcohol," said a young Mountie in Fort Good Hope. "There's a lot of bootlegging," he added. "It's flown in from Norman Wells," where well-paid oil workers have a lot of money and a lot of mobility. Drugs were coming in from there, too.

Even diet was a problem that was aggravated by remoteness. In villages on the Mackenzie, junk food is cheaper than fruits and vegetables, a nun who runs the Catholic school in Fort Norman told me as we sat in her small apartment, full of knick-knacks and potted plants: "An apple costs $1.50. So if they have a dollar, they can buy a candy bar, but not an apple."

Between villages and occasional stops to explore the empty, rocky banks, days on the Norweta followed a pattern: Get up, scan the river banks for wildlife, have breakfast, scan the river banks, have lunch, scan, have tea, scan, eat dinner, scan some more and then play cards or knit or read or talk till bedtime. If, that is, you spent all your time in the Norweta's dining room-cum-lounge.

It was more exciting up in the wheelhouse, where the captain, Russ Brown, and the crusty old pilot, Buster Helmer, both veteran rivermen, took turns standing six-hour shifts around the clock. Up there, you could see the Mackenzie the way they did—unrolling the maze-like navigational charts, spotting buoys that marked hazards, taking the binoculars to look for the range markers that indicated when to start a turn.

You could also listen to their limitless supply of river stories, bad jokes and reminiscences that summed up the realities of life in the Canadian North. It was like hearing voices from the old frontier.

On one early morning shift, Helmer—who'd been on the river for more than fifty years and officially retired a decade ago—told me about the childhood accident that cost him his left forefinger.

"I was born and raised on a trapline north of Fort McMurray," he said. "I was seven years old before I seen a town. I was eleven years old, workin' on that trapline, when I chopped my finger off. So I got a plane ride to McMurray." It was the nearest place with a doctor.

Helmer laughed. "When I got back, my brother was standin' there. I said, 'I been closer to heaven than you!' He said, 'All you got was a good start to hell!'"

Another time, as we were leaving Fort Norman, passing a bluff with three huge oval stains that the Dene say are the skins of giant beavers, Russ Brown recalled a bend in the river where he turned too late while piloting a towboat with seven barges.

"Took out seventy-five feet of bank and trees," he said, grinning. His captain chewed him out, "barkin' like a little bulldog. He was a little Newfoundlander—ruff, ruff, ruff!"

"On the next bend, captain says, 'I'll take it.'

"I said, 'OK.' And he tore right into the bank."

"Ah," said Brown to the captain, "so that's how it's done!"

And the captain blew up and stormed out of the wheelhouse, "ruff, ruff, ruff!"

Then Brown's voice softened. The little captain from Newfoundland had come to a bad end. "The guy got killed. Slipped on ice and got tangled in the equipment." He was crushed between two barges.

"Nothing anybody could do," Brown said. He paused. "It was quick, if that's any consolation."

Though it never got dark, the Norweta stopped for the night so we could sleep. Around suppertime, she nosed into the muddy, rocky riverbank; deckhands threw lines around the likeliest boulders or trees, and everybody—passengers and crew alike—ventured briefly out on shore, into the endless sunset and the endless hordes of mosquitoes. I thought I knew mosquitoes the way I knew cruises, but there was no contest here, either: Canada's were worse than Minnesota's.

The river was never less than a quarter of a mile across; usually it was a mile, sometimes it was nearly three. Surrounded by water and ever vaster wilderness, the boat seemed littler and littler as we pushed farther and farther north, until finally we were infinitesimal.

How big the land is, I kept thinking, and how empty. Between villages, the signs of human occupation were rare: an abandoned cabin on the bank, or a Canadian Coast Guard boat re-setting buoys, or a towboat pushing barges down to Norman Wells or Inuvik. A whole day could pass with only one event like that.

Canada is the second-biggest country in the world, after

Russia, but its population is only a fraction of ours: 31 million in a country bigger than the United States. The entire Northwest Territories has fewer than 42,000 people in more than 45,000 square miles.

Wildlife—at least, big wildlife—seemed about that sparse too. Plenty was out there, we knew, but this is all we saw:

A nest of bald eagles—two worried parents and two hungry chicks disturbed by our engines when we tied up the second night. Three "really big dogs" that we spotted romping on the bank a half day's travel from any human habitation. It dawned slowly on us all that they had to be wolves.

And three black bears. Most of us saw only the last two black bears. The only person to see Black Bear No. 1 was a passenger named Fred. He didn't mention it till the bear was gone because, Fred said, he "wanted to be sure." Passengers within earshot groaned at that.

The sameness of the days made small events fascinating. The best were conversations, like the one at Fort Good Hope, shouted between our boat and the shore. We were watching from the Norweta as four men loaded half of an unbuilt building—two-by-fours, window frames, screens, a cupboard and a table—into an open fishing boat. Then, with less than a foot of clearance above the water, they added gas tanks, two big black dogs and themselves. Their clearance was now down to inches.

Norweta: "What ya building?"

Guy on shore: "Cabin."

Norweta: "Where ya going?"

Guy: "Forty miles."

And then the men gunned their outboard and roared off downstream, as casually as city teenagers might head for a mall, unperturbed that their boat's wake was higher than its stern.

The Norweta's last port of call was Inuvik, where the Mackenzie split into a fan of narrow channels and flowed on, through its wide delta, toward the Arctic Ocean. But we disembarked here, to look around for a day before we flew out. A planned town, Inuvik dates only from the late 1950s. It has all of 3,500 people, but after the river villages, it seemed like a metropolis. It had a choice of stores. Souvenir shops. Postcards and a post office for mailing them. A college. Restaurants. Bars. Stuff to do.

For me, though, journey's end had come earlier—not when we tied off at the Inuvik riverbank, but the afternoon before, on our last stop for a shore walk through the middle of nowhere.

The river was glass-smooth, the sun was hot, and the mosquitoes hadn't found us yet. I walked a long way from the boat and sat down on a big log that could have floated down from British Columbia—the nearest place with big trees—and that would end up, when the next flood took it, as driftwood on some Arctic beach.

I intended to sit there and think, but it was one of those rare, pristine moments when life looks simple and your path is as clear as the air. I didn't think so much as feel—the warm sun, the great wilderness, the wide, strong river.

It was perfect contentment—except for the pang I felt when I remembered that this was a one-way journey. At Inuvik, another group of passengers was already waiting to take our places on the Norweta for the return voyage "up south" to Yellowknife.

Sitting there on my log in the sunshine, I was jealous of

those people. The Norweta was *my* boat now, and after nine full days—more water time than I've spent on my beloved Mississippi—the Mackenzie was *my* river. I didn't want to share either one.

Eating the World

2001

—◆—

FROM THE BALCONY of my room on the coast of Tunisia, I squinted into the glare of morning sun on water. Off-shore, I could see an open fishing boat and men dropping nets into the blue Mediterranean.

Two hours later, they were still there, but the boat had been pulled up on the sand, and the men were on the beach, straining to pull the nets out. One by one, each man grabbed a section of net and leaned back against its wet weight, digging his heels into the sand and stepping slowly backward for fifteen or twenty feet. Then each man ran forward, grabbed another section, leaned back and repeated the slow process. They worked so smoothly, it looked choreographed, like a stately dance.

I went down to the beach to see what they'd caught. But what had been an interesting ritual from a distance became, up close, a sad lesson in the ways of the modern world and a portent of what may come.

The fishermen had used two nets: an outer one with coarse mesh and an inner one, with fine mesh, so nothing would escape. The most remarkable victim was a young sea turtle, about two feet long, lying on its back in the sand. An air-breather, it had become tangled in the nets and drowned. Now it lay motionless, its eyes opaque, flies already buzzing around it. The fishermen had abandoned it; they were busy farther down the beach. So it would not be taken to market, would not be eaten. It had died for nothing. Another member of a vanishing species, wasted.

The black mesh of the nets was accumulating around the fishermen's feet like mourning veils. Judging by where they'd started, there had been at least a quarter-mile of netting in the sea. As the men pulled and the circle of nets shrank, I kept watching the water, expecting to see the shrinking surface boil with fish.

It never happened. The men kept dragging the nets in and in, until all the netting lay in the inch-deep shallows at the wave line. There were so few fish that it took only one man to pluck them from the mesh. He dropped them into a couple of plastic bins; together, they made barely a bushel of fish.

I was shocked. So many men, so much work, so many hours—and not enough fish for their families to eat, let alone enough to sell in town.

Then I noticed a tiny flicker of silver in the netting that the men had finished with. I walked over, looked down, reached down. What was flickering was an infant fish about four inches long—too small to be sold, too big to get through the netting. It looked like a miniature swordfish, with round unblinking eyes and a long, sharp snout. It was caught by the gills.

I started working the netting over its back; when I got it free, it lay in my hand like a living knife blade. I tossed it gently toward the water and watched it slice into the wavelets and disappear.

The next one I found was smaller, only a couple of inches

long, its bill like a sewing needle. I tossed it into the water, too.

In all, I saved six creatures that morning—five fish and one gray, wiggly prawn. Even as I was doing it, the effort seemed silly—as pointless, as hopeless as the fishermen's. But it was all I could think of doing.

We are eating the world, I thought as I did it. Our numbers are growing, and we will keep on eating. We will eat until the oceans are empty and the forests are desert. We will gnaw at the world until it is as dead as that sea turtle.

And then we will die, too. On that bleak morning, under the hot Tunisian sun, I thought that was exactly what we deserved.

A local man, who had come down to the beach about when I did, walked over to me while I was saving the fish. He wore a crisp cotton shirt, pressed slacks and a gray sweater, which made him stand out from the ragged fishermen, and he spoke some French, marking him as an educated man.

What kind of fish are these? I asked him, holding out my latest rescue.

"Sardines," he said.

Not swordfish?

"Sardines," he said again.

"They're catching the babies," I said. "If they keep taking the babies, there won't be any more big ones. Then there won't be any more fish."

"Yes," he said, sounding sad.

How odd, I thought. We agreed on the facts. We even agreed on the emotion. But we hadn't drawn the same conclusion.

For me, conditioned to think in American ways, the logical next step was: Stop catching little fish.

For him, it was: The fish are running out. Period. He saw it as something inevitable—as if overfishing and overpopulation had nothing to do with it. As if it couldn't be stopped.

Such moments always bring me to the same point of despair. We Americans consume more than any other culture, but we aren't ruining the world by ourselves anymore. Virtually every other country has joined in. And the results show. Any traveler can see them now, on any trip, whether it's the smoke of forest fires in Borneo, or the haze of pollution over Mexico City, or the sea of lights that burns as brightly around Bangkok as around New York.

We will lose the tigers, I think at such moments. We will lose the whales. And at this moment in Tunisia, all I had done about it was to save a shrimp and five minnows. That was nothing at all.

I worked the last baby fish through the netting and threw it back. "I'm sorry," I whispered to it, as it swam away.

Adventures in Porcelain

1995

———

WHENEVER I GIVE TALKS about international travel, I try to teach tolerance. "Other people's ways aren't wrong," I say, "they're just different, and differences are what we travel for." I even say that about foreign bathrooms. But here's the truth: When it comes to plumbing, I think some of those differences *are* wrong. In my experience, some have been downright malevolent.

I've encountered their most extreme forms in the Third World—so many and so often that I now suspect there's some cosmic force that requires a developing country to have weird plumbing. I know, I know—this is extreme Yankee hubris, of the worst, most culture-biased kind. I'd be ashamed of myself if I weren't talking to my closest friends.

Perhaps it's that a few steps in technological evolution got skipped. I mean, maybe your culture had to be in on the process when bathroom fixtures evolved from holes in the ground to chrome-trimmed ceramic shrines. If, that is, you hoped to end up with fixtures that worked. When the future springs fully clad in porcelain from the mind of Zeus and just gets dropped on you, it's already too late.

We in the West must have stood at such a juncture once—somewhere in the early Middle Ages, perhaps, when anybody could be a designer: You just put pencil to paper and *whammo!* You had Chartres Cathedral, or else a bidet. What an exciting time! But we've gotten things pretty well under control since then. Most of our plumbing flushes when it's supposed to and stops running when it's done, and in between we can all relax. Go too many steps out of the Good Old U. S. of A. and Canada, however, and you'd better pack a tool kit.

It isn't toilets that bother me so much. I've learned how to fix toilets. They're fairly straight-forward, honest gadgets—stolid, well-meaning, kind of like ceramic sheep. Showers are another matter. Showers are demonic. Showers lie and sneak. If they want to, showers can even kill you.

On that note, and purely in the interest of travel safety, let me introduce my top picks for the Miss International Difference Pageant. Consider yourselves warned.

The Electrocution Shower

This clever attempt to avoid buying a water heater is ubiquitous in Latin America. It involves a knife-switch—the kind that shows up in old Jimmy Cagney prison movies, right before the governor's pardon comes through. A couple of raw wires connect the knife switch directly to the shower head. People who own these showers believe them to be safe and highly efficient. Really. This is how they use one:

1. Turn on the water.
2. Flip the switch.
3. Get in the shower.

4. Believe that hearing water sizzle as it passes over an electric heating element just above your head is perfectly normal.

And this is how tourists use one:

1. Go into the shower your first morning in Country X.
2. Scream "Wires? Wires? Why are there those wires?????"
3. Go back out and ask somebody in your host culture if they're serious. (Pronunciation guide: "Aaaaarrrr yooooo peeeeple craaaaaazzzy?")
4. Decide you weren't all that dirty anyway.
5. Wait a week. If it's rainy season, wait two. ("Oh, gee, thanks, but I don't need an umbrella!")
6. Get so dirty you don't want to live anymore.
7. Turn on the water, flip the switch and wait for the lights to dim in the Big House.
8. Take a deep breath and get in.
9. Go on, get in there.
10. Be amazed that you didn't die. If you didn't.

The Bait-and-Switch Shower

On my first trip to Honduras, I had no illusions about the shower in a ratty hotel on the north coast (you could see through the slats in the outside walls—that ratty). The shower head was a tuna-fish can, punched full of holes and loosely wired onto the end of a single corroded pipe. A rig like that couldn't possibly have hot water, so I wasn't disappointed.

The bait-and-switch shower, on the other hand, passes for normal just so it can dash your hopes. I met my first one on that same trip, in a nice guesthouse in a nice neighborhood in Tegucigalpa. The place advertised hot water, a major reason for choosing it.

The bathroom had green tile walls and color-coordinated fixtures, and it was spotless. Good sign. Two water pipes fed into the sink. Better sign. Both sink and shower had working pairs of faucets. Terrific sign. Even allowing for the frequent confusion over C and H in Spanish-speaking countries—where the letters on imported faucets are sometimes interpreted as "Caliente" and "Hmmm"—the shower in this place *had* to be hot.

All faucets produced nothing but cold. I nearly wept from the betrayal. Why have two pipes if one wasn't going to be hot?

The management kept insisting they had hot water, but morning after cringing morning, I would try it, and the shower was always frigid. I suspected other travelers were using all the hot water first, so I kept getting up earlier and earlier, trying to beat them to it.

Finally, on yet another cold-water dawn, I traced what should have been the hot-water pipe down to the still-dark kitchen, where a middle-aged Honduran woman in braids was expertly building a fire in the cookstove.

"When will there be hot water?" I asked her, in my best I-am-not-your-typical-gringo Spanish.

"First, I have to build the fire in the cookstove," she said. "Then I build the fire for the hot water."

"But water takes a long time to warm up," I said, trying not to whine. "Couldn't you build the fire under the hot water *first*, and *then* build the fire in the cookstove?"

"No," she said. "*First*, I build the fire in the cookstove. *Then* I build the fire under the hot water."

She knew her job, and she was going to stick to it. If she had stopped there, I'd have retreated, cowed by her confidence. But then she threw in a little health advice, and I lost it. "Hot water isn't good for you," she added. "That's why Americans get so many colds."

I morphed into an Ugly American before her very eyes. "Don't tell *me* about hot water!" I snapped. "We *invented* hot water!" Which guaranteed that I wouldn't be getting any that morning, either.

The Burning Ring of Fire

In another place and time, the inventor of this shower could have been Thomas Edison. Or at least Johnny Cash. Instead, he was the manager of a bare-bones hotel in Copacabana, Bolivia. I stayed there one night in the mid-1970s, after a disagreement with my brother and our traveling friends. We'd been on the road for a couple of months, usually staying in fifty-cent-a-night dives. (No matter the local currency—*pesos, escudos, soles, colones, balboas*—they always turned out to cost fifty cents.)

In Copacabana, a pleasant town with beautiful Mediterranean light, we had fanned out to look for lodgings, and I'd found a gem: big rooms, scrubbed wood floors, French doors onto balconies *and hot water*. Guaranteed. True, you had to pay for it: The room rate worked out to a whole dollar, and the shower was twenty-five centavos more.

Too expensive, my brother and company said. They'd locked

in on yet another fifty-cent bargain. It looked like a military bunker—one light bulb, rows of dingy bunks and what I remember as dripping walls. There was no point in hoping for hot showers.

I stalked off to splurge alone at the expensive place. I signed the inevitably lengthy guest register—name, address, nationality, coming from, going to, passport number, philosophy of life—and asked hopefully if I could take a shower right now.

Why not, said the manager, who was also the porter, the night desk clerk and the resident plumber. He pointed to the shower room, a kind of concrete closet standing like a blockhouse in the middle of the courtyard.

"You get undressed," he said, handing me a towel from a stack under the counter. "I'll get the kerosene."

My Spanish is pretty good, but I don't do well with surprises. I went into the bunker, stripped as ordered, wrapped the very small and threadbare towel around me and kept trying to translate that last word: Kerosene? Did he really say *kerosene?*

The man came in carrying a ladder and a big red can with a spout. For a moment, I felt uneasy about being nearly naked in a windowless room with a stranger. Then it got worse.

He climbed up on the ladder and poured the kerosene into what looked like a circular lawn sprinkler suspended near the ceiling. Now I felt uneasy about having the stranger burn me to death.

The man turned on the water and tossed a match at the ceiling thing, which went *FOOMP!* and erupted like a miniature volcano. "Get in," he said, and left.

But I couldn't. The shower was raining fire, and I just kept standing there, spell-bound, flattened against the farthest wall, watching as blue flames turned the sprinkler into an unearthly chandelier.

Fist-sized gobbets of blazing sapphire kept detaching themselves from the ring and riding the water down to the floor, where they went on burning, like napalm. It may be memory that has added the sound effects—a kind of *zoom-plop-hiss* as they dropped.

Then the flames burned out, and I jumped in. The water was freezing. I leaned out the shower room door and shouted at the guy. "It went out! It didn't even get warm!"

He shrugged. "That's all you get for twenty-five centavos."

Ocean of Grass

1987

——◦——

ROM THE LOW HILLTOP where we stood, the empty
Mongolian grassland rolled away like a calm green sea and
lapped gently at the horizon all around. While I tried to fit it
into a camera lens—an impossible task—my Chinese guide
kept droning on about the heap of stones, called an *aobao*, that
brooded beside us.

Over centuries, Mongolians have built these stone piles on
top of every grassland rise, even ones that an American flat-
lander wouldn't count. Some hills are so low that you wouldn't
notice them at all without the *aobao* to tip you off. Though the
connection seems remote, the heaps are related to the *mani*
stones that travelers in the Buddhist Himalayas traditionally
pile up and string with prayer flags at every mountain pass.
Mongolia was a Buddhist country, too, with strong cultural
links to distant Tibet. It wasn't Mongolia's fault that it didn't
have mountains to work with.

"One month ago, local people hold ceremony here," my
guide was saying blandly, while I changed lenses and tried the
landscape again. No go, not even with a wide-angle.

"'They sacrifice sheep," he said, and finally I started to pay attention.

There were indeed two blood-crusted sheep skulls on the heap of stones. There was also a small black-and-white drawing of an Asian man in traditional robes. The picture had been torn from a magazine and weighed down with pebbles so it wouldn't fly away in the grassland's strong winds.

"Who's that," I asked casually, starting to focus my lens on the bloody skulls, "the Dalai Lama?"

"No," the guide replied, "Genghis Khan."

I nearly dropped the camera. "Genghis Khan!" I thought the guide must be joking. "The local people believe Genghis Khan is a *god?*"

"Genghis Khan is an *immortal,*" the guide corrected primly. "He is ancestor of all Mongolian people." That was why they had sacrificed the sheep to him.

Wow. Inner Mongolia may not have much to look at, but what there is can send chills up your spine. Or at least mine. Genghis Khan, of all people. *Genghis Khan.*

I'd gotten to this ad-hoc shrine for the Great Khan by taking a crowded overnight train from Beijing to Hohhot, the capital of the Inner Mongolia Autonomous Region. Hohhot, pronounced as if you were panting, had about 1.2 million people, nearly all of whom were not Mongolian. Much of the place looked like every other big city in China: blank-faced concrete apartment houses, hordes of black bicycles, a fringe of little trees along the boulevards, and everywhere people, people, people.

The great grasslands of Inner Mongolia lie two hours' drive from Hohhot, north beyond the Daqing Mountains. They don't look like the rest of China. They are empty.

Compared to cities like Shanghai and Beijing, where tourism is heavy and capitalism is enthusiastically practiced in
everything but name, Inner Mongolia has an austere quality
that the unadorned landscape strengthens.

In late spring, before the grass was fully up, the countryside
looked utterly barren, except for an occasional mud-walled
village or isolated farmstead. Alone or in clusters, the mud
houses faced south, turning windowless backs on the north
winds. With their slanting, awning-like roofs, made of earth
tamped over straw, they looked like Neolithic experiments in
solar heating.

Mongolia is a frontier, and that made it a little rough for
traveling. It seemed more politically dogmatic than the usual
tourist's China, more Maoist, more like the revolutionary
China that Americans used to fear. Which is another way of
saying that it was a touch behind the times.

Even the clothing was a throwback, with military style still
predominating, though it was no longer required. My guide
was typical: A man of about 45, with black hair going gray at
the temples, he wore a high-collared, navy blue uniform jacket
over khaki trousers, and he answered my questions like an
army officer. He ran my life the same way, meaning that I saw
what had been ordained for me to see.

From him and others, there was still a lot of talk about cad-
res and communes, even though Mongolia's herders and farmers, like those all across this huge country, were now working
on what China calls the "responsibility system." Even the place
names hadn't fully changed back to their original ones.

"What is the name of that village?" I asked as we left one
hamlet.

"Brigade Three," my guide said, snapping out the words.

This lingering rigidity doesn't mean Mongolians look back fondly on the old commune system. As one farm wife said, government policy before 1984 "just means 'one big pot.' You work hard, I don't, but you get just the same."

Now, she said, hard work and smart farming pay off. She and her husband can decide how many sheep and cows to raise, slaughter or sell each year, and they can keep their profits.

The people who live on the grasslands used to be nomads. Though most still raise livestock, they are almost completely settled now, pinned to the land by permanent housing and government policy, and they are no longer the majority in Mongolia. That distinction belongs to the Han, the dominant ethnic group in China. Of twenty million people in Inner Mongolia, only about 2.6 million were ethnic Mongolians.

For tourists, the only way to tell the Han from the ethnic Mongolians is to ask. Clothes won't tell you: Traditional Mongolian dress—handsome, long-sleeved, side-buttoned tunics and brightly decorated leather boots for men and women alike—is now worn only by folk dancers and people who work with tourists.

The face of the grasslands is changing, too. More and more fences are going up, as they did across the American plains a century ago. And near the villages, orderly stands of young trees are beginning to break the sinuous wild horizon.

But those new landmarks are still easy to dodge. They disappear around the next hill or over the next rise, leaving the region's old sense of emptiness and space.

Flocks of sheep still move over the vacant land, watched only by a solitary herdsman and sometimes a dog or two. The sheep feed as they walk, steadily tearing up tufts of green. Their grazing makes a soft ripping sound, alien to city ears. But the sheep don't touch the clumps of white and purple flowers that dot the spring landscape like bouquets.

"Headache plant," my guide announced. "They know if they eat it, they will get headache."

A headache was exactly what I didn't have. You can see for miles in the grasslands, and that is their principal delight for a China-weary traveler. No bikes. No cars. No people. No noise. At night, bedded down on the padded floor of a traditional Mongolian yurt, there was no sound whatever—just moonlight, shining through the panels of the yurt's low door, moonlight and soothing silence.

The undulating landscape looked even eerier then, like something from another planet or at least another time. In the Mongolian nights, I thought again of Genghis Khan: The grasslands hadn't changed appreciably since his horsemen swept across them seven centuries ago.

Yurts hadn't changed much either. Part wicker basket and part tent, these circular dwellings are made of thick sheets of white felt tied around a lattice of small poles. Finished, they look like giant bundles of laundry waiting for pickup.

Like the portable lodges of the Plains Indians, yurts can be set up or taken down in a matter of hours, and they stay snug and warm even in howling winds. But virtually nobody sleeps in yurts anymore, except tourists, and then only in a handful of villages that maintain yurt camps. I stayed in one called Xilamulun Sumu, a former commune about 55 miles from Hohhot.

Most of the food served at the camp was Chinese— mounds of rice, myriad plates piled with vegetables and a few with meat, all chopped in little pieces for ease in eating with chopsticks. Even so, strong Mongol flavors—and Mongol customs—crept in.

Breakfast consisted of hot, chewy fried bread and bowls of milky tea served with rock-hard cheese curds and millet grains like BBs. The idea was to soak these items in the tea until they softened; mine never did, no matter how long I left them in the tea cup.

Lunch one day was a gray, bony chunk of boiled mutton with a couple of paring knives stabbed into it. It was accompanied only by small bowls of a dark brown liquid that I thought was broth. Two locals were seated at the same table, and the four of us took turns sharing the knives. When it wasn't my turn for a knife, I tore off the meat with my fingers and dipped it into what turned out to be mouth-puckering—but grease-cutting—vinegar.

The camp's dining halls used to belong to an 18th-century Tibetan Buddhist monastery. The main temple, a few steps away, survived the destruction of the Cultural Revolution but just barely. In the temple's chanting hall, where monks used to gather to sing prayers, the wall paintings and silk hangings were garish and new, and the golden Buddhas in the altar chamber were obviously recent.

The most authentic thing left in the temple was its caretaker, an elderly monk with sad eyes and a face like smoked leather. He was the only monk, where once there would have been several hundred.

"Isn't he lonely?" I asked my guide.

"Oh, no!" he said. "This monk have wife, children, grandchildren." The rules on celibacy for monks had changed in

Mongolia and the rest of China with Sun Yat Sen's revolution of 1911.

Sightseeing on the grasslands was also different than in the rest of China. Despite the vast emptiness of the plains, it was more intimate. One cold, rainy afternoon, my guide took me to a farmstead near the yurt camp. The main room was nearly bare, except for a few folding chairs, a couple of cupboards and a small television under a hand-embroidered white cotton dust cover.

We sat on the heated brick platform that serves Mongolian people as both bed and sofa, while the lady of the house served us tea with the inevitable cheese curds and millet. Eventually, my guide talked her into removing the TV cozy, and we all moved closer to the set. The only thing playing was Chinese cartoons, but everyone, me included, watched without complaint. It made Mongolia feel almost homelike.

My last morning in Xilamulun Sumu, I got away from my guide long enough to walk back to the temple compound, so I could say goodbye to the old monk. Without someone to translate, I couldn't even say that, but it didn't matter. The monk beckoned me into his cramped rooms and poured me a bowl of tea. An old woman who must have been his wife appeared, holding a plump two-year-old who must have been their grandchild. And then we just sat there together, in good-natured silence, until my guide hurried in to fetch me back to Hohhot and the busy outer world.

Where the Veil Thins

1994

——

G LASTONBURY IN SUMMER, one of its residents told me, is "like living in a deck of tarot cards." Walking down the High Street in this West of England town of 8,000 people, I quickly saw what she meant. There were plenty of traditional English types strolling there, people you might see in any village: sweater-clad matrons clutching market baskets, rosy-cheeked young mothers pushing baby carriages, gentlemen in tweed jackets with the leash of the family terrier firmly in hand.

But here they mingled with the current version of hippies—a youth in a jester's cap, a cluster of kids in solid black, girls floating by in rainbow robes like saris. Waves of New Age music spilled from staid, old-fashioned storefronts, along with wafting banners, soap bubbles and more incense than I've smelled since the 1960s. The names on the shops summed up the atmosphere: The Gothic Image. The Crystal Star. Back of Beyond. Pendragon. The Goddess and the Green Man.

None of this is exactly usual for an English village, which makes Glastonbury one of the most intriguing—and troubling—places in Britain. Not that it hasn't been all along.

This place has been a religious magnet for about two thousand years—far more if you include worship in prehistoric times. There is so much here to believe in, or at least to wonder about, that seekers after meaning can find whatever they want. And they do.

Glastonbury stands in what is called the Isle of Avalon, once a region of islands rising from a shallow sea, which some believe was the last stronghold of Europe's ancient matriarchal faith, the pre-Christian religion of the Goddess. Until the marshes were drained to create more farmland seven hundred years ago, the two highest islands would have been what are now Wearyall Hill and the larger, oval-shaped Glastonbury Tor, 520 feet high, ringed with terraces and topped with a 15th-century tower.

"The Isle of Avalon is the heart chakra of the planet," said Kathy Jones, a teacher and psychic healer. "It's a place of pilgrimage. Spiritual seekers have always come here." For New Age practitioners like her, Glastonbury is the site of great convergences, a place where the world's "ley lines"—conduits of universal power—intersect. In such a place, "the veils between the visible and the invisible worlds are thin," she said, "so you can see things you cannot see . . . the fairy realms, the otherworldly realms."

That isn't the only belief system in play here, however. The Rev. Patrick J. Riley, a vicar whose parishes include Glastonbury, said it best: "There *is* an alternative religion in town, and it's the Christian one."

But even Christianity is complicated here, and the credit—or blame—goes to Joseph of Arimathea, the rich man who offered his own tomb for Christ's burial. You hear a lot about Joseph in Glastonbury: How he was a trader in tin and lead, plentiful in this part of England. How his walking staff, jabbed into the earth of Wearyall Hill, grew into a holy thorn tree whose descendants still bloom at Christmas. How he built a church, the first in Britain, and dedicated it to the Virgin Mary, who was his niece.

And how once he brought a grand-nephew with him on a trading trip, a boy who was the son of a carpenter . . . . That tradition is the kernel of one of Britain's most powerful hymns: *"And did those feet in ancient time / Walk upon England's mountains green?"* Those feet would have been Christ's.

Joseph of Arimathea is also said to have brought the Holy Grail to Glastonbury, where he hid it in a well that still exists. Known as Chalice Well, it is actually a spring, whose cold, iron-rich waters have stained the surrounding rocks blood-red.

Tradition says the Grail was the cup or chalice from which Christ drank at the Last Supper and which may have been used to catch his blood during the Crucifixion. But the Grail was never part of official church doctrine, Rev. Riley said. "It's a legend, and you don't ask whether a legend is true or false. You ask, 'Is it helpful or unhelpful?'"

The Grail, he said, is "the image or picture used for the search for inner truth." People talk about a personal grail because "it's a basic truth about themselves, their relationship with God and their relationship with each other."

Extend that image, and everyone who comes to Glastonbury is on a Grail Quest, whether they are aided by crystals, by drugs, by fate or by the Bible. The idea pervades the town.

When I casually asked the conservative-looking, middle-aged proprietor of my bed-and-breakfast how he happened to move here, he replied, "completely by chance." Then he immediately corrected himself: "Everybody else says that's impossible. I mean, I was *meant* to be here. *You* were meant to be here."

As my visit went on, I began to agree.

In Glastonbury's smorgasbord of beliefs, it is hard to tell where religion leaves off and legend begins. Sometimes they blend, as in 1191, when monks at Glastonbury Abbey announced they had discovered King Arthur's grave. Directed by visions and old manuscripts, the monks dug up two bodies—a huge man lying beside a small blonde woman. Who could the couple be but Arthur and Queen Guinevere?

The abbey's museum downplays this, hinting that the whole thing may have been a medieval publicity stunt. The abbey had had a disastrous fire and was destitute. Pilgrimages—which meant financial support—picked up after word of the find got out. "The story of Arthur is at the heart of the traditions of medieval European romances," said one exhibit. "By the late 15th century, the strands of Arthur, Guinevere, the Round Table, Joseph of Arimathea, the Quest for the Holy Grail, Excalibur, Mordred, the Siege Perilous, Avalon and Camelot had become so intertwined that it is now impossible to unravel Glastonbury's true part in the story."

But that doesn't keep people from trying. "I don't think it matters whether it's real," said Frances H. Gordon, a former BBC film director who was now running The Gothic Image, one of the New Age stores in the center of town. "The people who've come here on these pilgrimages—it's meant something to them. It's given their lives a meaning."

More recently, a different sort of pilgrim began arriving, members of a mysterious-sounding group called the Travelers. I'd been in town quite a while before I remembered that in Britain the term refers to Gypsies; the concept was more intriguing when I thought it had a capital T. Glastonbury's travelers aren't real Gypsies—they're mostly jobless young people who typically live out of their cars or vans. Rev. Riley thought many came "to find a sort of Nirvana here" and fell instead into "a morass of drugs and drink."

"When people come on a spiritual quest, they always assume that the spiritual life is benign," he said. "It ain't."

Kathy Jones said much the same thing. "Avalon in legend was the Western Isle of the Dead, so this is traditionally a place of death and regeneration and rebirth," she said. "People come thinking it's going to be kind of light-filled . . . . They soon find their lives disintegrating because it's a place where illusions are broken."

Today, Glastonbury Abbey itself is broken, reduced to romantic ruins, its stone arches jutting like gray bones out of gentle green lawn. Even so, the abbey still draws about 150,000 visitors a year, and both the Roman Catholic Church and the Church of England sponsor pilgrimages to it each June.

"The Gospel has much more of a cutting edge in Glastonbury than anywhere else," said Rev. Riley. "Everything is much sharpened here . . . . You can't drive through Glastonbury and be neutral to it." The vicar was right: By then I wasn't neutral. I had no spiritual reason to be in Glastonbury—I had come just because I thought it would be fun to see some King Arthur sites. But I got far more than I bargained for. You can take the rest of this tale any way you want.

I did all the standard tourist things, which included climbing Glastonbury Tor not long before sunset one afternoon. Legends and stories swarm thickly around the Tor. It has been linked with Neolithic astronomy and with the Celtic idea of the underworld. Some regard its terraces as a maze that symbolizes the Primal Mother, while an astrological tradition holds that nearby fields are shaped like signs of the Zodiac, if you view them from the air. I stayed on top of the Tor a long time, reveling in the golden light that shone on the green patchwork of the fields below, even though I couldn't make out any Zodiac signs.

Coming down, I thought briefly of walking back to town through those pastures—there was a path—but that route was isolated. The year before, I had been attacked on a path near my house in Minneapolis, and hiking alone was something I could no longer bring myself to do. I walked back on the main road instead, in the accidental company of four young Europeans who chattered about ley lines and convergences until we came to a public fountain on the edge of town. They stopped to drink, and I did too.

This fountain draws its reddish water from Chalice Well—holy to some because of the Grail connection, to others because it is associated, like other springs in Europe, with the religion of the Goddess.

The next day, I went to see the spring itself, now the centerpiece of a walled garden full of flowers. Except for its blood-colored rocks, it was ordinary and small, only a couple of feet across, under an arcade of leaves. I sat down in the shade beside it, shut my eyes and rested. Even though other people—strangers—were all around me, I felt safe there. At peace, as I had not been in a year.

Then suddenly I was praying, harder than I had ever prayed before, for the deepest sort of spiritual healing, asking for the fears that remained from the attack to flow away like the waters of the spring. When I opened my eyes, I felt cleansed, inside and out, as if I had been bathed in that red water. And I felt stronger.

Only then did I notice something else, something unusual. Nearly all the other people in the garden were women, and most of these women had red hair. It seemed to be more than coincidence. I turned to the nearest one, a girl whose long russet curls flowed down her back like a copper veil. "There are so many red-heads," I said. "What does this mean?"

She answered as if she'd been expecting my question. "It means," she replied, "we have more power than we think we do."

I didn't ask her where my sense of healing came from. I am still pondering that. In the absence of an explanation, I keep falling back on something I found in "A Course in Miracles." It has become one of my favorite meditations: "Every loving thought is true." I found it easy to think such thoughts in Glastonbury.

OFF-SEASON

Death Valley in July

1986

———

MUCH HAS BEEN WRITTEN—some of it by me—about the rewards of off-season travel, and it's true: It *is* worth doing. But I suspect that most people read articles about un-crowded Europe in the dead of winter and secretly agree with the tourists who stayed home: Too cold. Or they read about the great deals you can get in the Caribbean in summer and think: Too hot.

Probably I would think the same things, if I hadn't done so much traveling in the wrong seasons over the years. It started when I was a teenager, on a family camping trip to the West Coast one July. My parents decided to detour through Death Valley, just to see if it was as hot as its reputation.

It was.

Death Valley in July—in a station wagon without air con-ditioning—rewrote the definition of *hot* in our household. But it also taught my siblings and me some things we never would have known otherwise.

We learned that you could indeed cook an egg on the front fender. The yolk didn't do much, but the white turned opaque and firm before my father made us scrape it off the car.

We learned that movies had given us the wrong impression about the canteens that cowboys, prospectors and cavalrymen always swigged from. The water in them would not have been refreshing. It would have been just the way it was in the Boy Scout canteen one of my brothers brought along—hot. Hot as the scalding air.

We learned that there was still a threat of death in Death Valley. The national monument's rangers had put up warning signs at the entrances to all side roads, telling summer travelers to stay out because the roads weren't well-patrolled. If your car broke down, and you had to walk out without a water supply, you'd be risking your life.

We also learned that we wouldn't have missed Death Valley in July for anything. Yes, it was hot. But it was also incredibly *cool*.

Now when I take a trip at the wrong time of year, my main reason isn't that it will be less expensive than peak season or that there won't be so many tourists. It's that I'll be catching my destination not just off-season but off-guard, when the place is back to normal, and I can imagine myself as part of the community rather than part of a mob of spectators. It's like being around a troupe of actors after the play is over, when they pull off their wigs and remove their greasepaint and go back to being real.

If I hadn't been in the wrong place at the wrong time, I'd have missed Venice in winter, made magical by a sudden fog, when sounds seemed as muffled as the light, and the narrow streets promised mysteries.

I'd have missed Yucatan in August, when the beaches were empty and the hotels nearly so, and my sister Elizabeth and I got caught by a sudden thunderstorm atop a Mayan ruin at Chichén Itzá. We stayed up there, fascinated, while black clouds billowed overhead, wind tormented the green jungle, and rain pelted the ancient stones. It was like watching a painting come to dramatic life.

I wouldn't have seen the French Riviera in January, when the weather felt like a Midwestern October—hot sun and cold shadows—and a friend and I had the mountaintop hamlet of Eze, one of the region's "perched villages," all to ourselves.

Or a snowy midnight in Vienna, when I walked near the Stephansdom for a look at Mozart's house and encountered a young couple waltzing around the old cathedral in the falling snow, oblivious to everything except their own private music.

Or Paris on a shockingly cold New Year's Eve, when the streets were paved with glare ice, and the air rang with fender-benders. Elegant couples in evening dress kept slipping on the sidewalks, giggling and squealing "oooh-la-la!"—they really *do* say that—and the lights on the Eiffel Tower shone into the night like icy sequins.

Or Christmastime in a German village, when the all butchers' shops hung dressed-out rabbits in their front windows, the way our grocery stores display turkeys, and people put real candles on their Christmas trees, introducing an element of danger into the holidays. Twice I saw candles start a decorated tree on fire, and everything you ever read about how fast they burn is true. But my German friends just clustered around it and calmly blew out the flames.

I wouldn't have missed any of that. But as with so much in life, you can overdo off-season travel. During a year I spent roaming around Latin America, I went through three winters. I left for Costa Rica in the middle of *our* winter, reached Chile and Argentina in time for *their* winter, and came home in time for the start of our *next* winter. The trip was fascinating, but if I had it to do over, I think I'd aim for a triple summer.

Two Roads Diverged

2007

⸻

I WAS IN ECUADOR, on my way to a folklore performance, sharing a ride with two other tourists—a middle-aged Canadian woman and a young computer guy from California. They started comparing notes on their Latin American travels. I didn't join in. I'd seen the continent edge to edge over the previous twenty-five years, but I didn't want to interrupt their conversation by saying so. I just stared out the window, only half-listening.

Then I heard something that snapped me alert—something that made me feel as if I'd been kicked in the chest, as if my heart had stopped, as if I couldn't breathe.

"You know the place I liked best?" the young guy said. "Easter Island!"

The Canadian gushed in agreement. There was *so* much to do there! New hotels! The new museum! All the tours there were to take! And they've put so many of the statues back up . . . .

My God, I thought, suddenly strangled by memories. My God, my God. They're talking about Easter Island as if it's a *place. Just another place!*

At the folklore show that night, I applauded when the rest of the audience did, but I wasn't there. I'd been thrown a quarter century into my own past, back to a forty-five-square-mile triangle of black lava and wind-blown grass in the middle of the Pacific Ocean, 2,200 miles from Chile, 2,400 miles from Tahiti.

La Isla de Pascua. Rapa Nui. *Te pito o Te Henua.* The navel of the world. "The place farthest from anywhere." By all its names, Easter Island felt like home to me, the only place in the world that ever truly did.

I had been under its spell since before I could read, ever since my father first showed me its pictures in books—haunting pictures of giant stone heads perched on grassy slopes, lips pursed, eyes blank, staring out to sea.

I was a shy child then, and I grew into a shy adolescent, ill at ease with people, lonely but most comfortable alone. I took refuge in daydreams—always about somewhere else, somewhere distant and strange, where a stranger like me might find a better fit. When I was old enough, I started traveling, trying to make my dream world real.

By the time I got to the South Pacific, I was in my early thirties, and I'd been looking for home all my life—for the place I belonged, the place where I should have been born. I felt I'd found it on Easter Island, the moment I stepped off the plane. It was as if the island had been waiting for me, all that time, the way I'd been waiting for the island.

Yolanda Ika Tuki met me at the airport. Actually, she just met my plane, she and a pickup truck full of other island women, all hoping to rent out rooms to tourists. There were only a couple of flights a week from mainland Chile and not many visitors. Most of them were already booked into the island's only formal lodging, a six-room motel, but the local women met the plane every time anyway, crowding up to the stairs before passengers had a chance to get out, piling luggage into the pickup and pleading for guests.

Yolanda met the plane, met me, met my eyes. It felt like fate.

Her small house stood on a shady, sandy lane on the outskirts of Hanga Roa, the island's only village. She had one room to rent, a sunny, recently added annex that felt instantly familiar. The walls were varnished plywood, like a summer cabin up north, and the furniture looked like the stuff in the government clinic where my father worked—chrome tubing, green leatherette cushions.

The reason made me smile. Everything in that room— walls, furniture and louvered windows—was indeed U.S. government issue, liberated by the locals after our Air Force abandoned a satellite-tracking base on the island in the 1960s. Even the varnish smelled like home.

Yolanda was short and thick-bodied, like most of the older island women, with dark skin and thick black hair. She might have been 40 or 50 or even 60. I never knew. She cooked for me, interpreted the island for me, introduced me to her neighbors, included me in her household. It felt like a family but wasn't quite, so I fitted right in.

There was a quiet man I assumed was her husband, whom I saw mainly at dinner, and a pretty little girl who was a neighbor's out-of-wedlock child—Yolanda said the mother's new husband didn't want the girl around. There was also the child of another neighbor, a slender boy of about eleven whose history had a different twist.

He was half-American, one of about thirty youngsters that the U.S. airmen had managed to father while they were here. It was a significant number, in a population of less than 2,000 people, 600 of them kids. The islanders loved children—people joked that babies were Easter Island's biggest product—but this boy wasn't happy. He yearned to find his father and go live with him in the States.

"I know my father loves me," he said, "because he wrote to my mother once." One day the boy showed me the precious letter. The American man had promised nothing, hadn't included his address or even his last name. He was just saying goodbye.

This is what outsiders have always done in Polynesia, starting with the first European explorers and their crews— love 'em and leave 'em, right down through the centuries. It made me feel ashamed, but the islanders didn't seem to mind. All good stories, in fact, seemed to begin with the same words: "When the Americans were here . . . ." They had brought the modern world with them—electricity, piped water, Coke in cans, movies, the airport. "We *loved* the Americans," one islander told me.

Islanders didn't feel that way about people from Chile, which has governed Easter Island since 1888. They said Chileans couldn't be trusted, were lazy and given to stealing. Chileans said the same things about them.

Among themselves, the islanders spoke their own language; it was soft, rounded and full of vowels, like all its cousins across Polynesia. With me, they spoke Spanish, the island's second language and mine as well. But while I heard about local problems—feeling discriminated against by mainlanders was mentioned often—no one dragged me into them. I think it was because I was under Yolanda's wing—not a member of the community, but not an ordinary tourist, either. She treated me more like a daughter.

Sometimes, when she called me for breakfast, she would come in and perch on the foot of my bed and chat. She also gave me advice. It wasn't always wise, but it was always the same: *Disfrute su vida, Catalina,* she said. Enjoy your life, Catherine. And I did.

I began to exist in the present tense, as if I had no past regrets and no future fears. It was something I'd never done before. That, and the incredible distances surrounding us, lent me an exhilarating freedom. I likened it to hiding in a childhood tree fort with the rope pulled up. "No one knows where I am," I kept thinking. "No one can find me."

My days quickly fell into their own gentle rhythm: Go out walking after breakfast. Explore a cave, a volcano, a vista. Take pictures. Talk to people. Go home for lunch. Nap or write or poke around Hanga Roa. And in the late afternoon, walk over to Tahai—the row of giant statues, called *moai,* that stood closest to town—and watch the sunset paint the sky in the direction of Tahiti. Sometimes on Easter Island, it seemed that all I could see was sky.

After supper, the island's only TV station went on the air, and I joined Yolanda's household around the set. The programs, flown in once a week, would have been odd anywhere, but here in the uttermost corner of Polynesia, the mix was especially peculiar: decades-old "Beanie and Cecil" cartoons, a British-made series of English lessons ("Why are there no onions in the onion soup?"), a quiz program on Chile's fishing industry, and American reruns, subtitled in Spanish—"The Six Million Dollar Man," "The Rockford Files."

"Is there a lot of that in the United States?" an adult asked reasonably after one of Rockford's chronic car chases. The children thought the Six Million Dollar man was real. I couldn't get over the station's signature logo: three dancing *moai*, wiggling their world-famous bellies on the screen.

One evening I stayed in my room to write. Between gusts of wind that rattled the trees, I caught gusts of soft music. It was coming from the church down the lane, and I realized that the people were singing Polynesian hymns. If I'd known nothing about this culture, that music alone would have told me they'd been seafarers. There was a canoeing cadence in it, like the throb of waves or the steady pulse of paddle strokes.

There was distance in it too, and a touch of sadness. It made me think of the complicated, crisscross navigations that populated the Pacific in ancient times, and the vast emptiness that those early voyagers sailed into without knowing what lay ahead, and how many must have been lost before others finally happened upon this tiny fleck of land.

"Wind and music and nothing to do," I wrote in my journal that night, "Sunday on Easter Island." But it didn't feel like Sunday. It felt like Saturday. Every day on the island felt like Saturday.

I knew what my favorite place would be before I saw it— Rano Raraku, the extinct volcano where the giant statues had been quarried and carved. They were already old friends. Face to face, they looked exactly as they had in the books of my childhood—an army of elongated heads frozen in mid-journey down the grassy slopes.

This was where, in the late 1600s, the ancient carvers put down their stone chisels and never picked them up again. The reasons aren't fully known, but shrinking resources likely led to warfare, devastating the old culture.

The heads at Rano Raraku were the ones that never reached their destinations, travelers stranded in mid-trip. Islanders said these *moai* were blind. They had not yet received their stone eyes or been given stone topknots, and they would never stand on an altar like Tahai's.

The cylindrical topknots—like top hats the size of corn cribs—were quarried at another volcano, Puna Pau, where the lava rock was rusty red instead of grayish black. Abandoned ones lay on the ground there like giant red boulders. They all had been hollowed out inside, the better to fit onto a statue's head. One afternoon, I curled up inside a topknot and spent an hour watching white clouds drift across brilliant blue sky, over a landscape of yellow grass; it reminded me of a Kansas prairie.

The weather reminded me of Hawaii—frequent showers, followed by clearing skies and rainbows. But the resemblance stopped there. The island was mainly a big pasture edged by cliffs. It wasn't tropical, and it wasn't lush. Outside of gardens and protected valleys, there were almost no trees, and the beaches were black rocks.

Yolanda told me there was another American on the island, a woman about my own age. I ran into her one sunset at Tahai, and we struck up a friendship. She had visited the island before, drawn by its archaeology, but she was back this time because of a boyfriend, an islander. She wanted to see where that relationship was going to lead. I soon knew what she was wrestling with.

One night, Yolanda took me to Hanga Roa's little disco—

about half the village was there—and an island boyfriend found me too. That meant I was swept into another extended family—parents, sisters, cousins and armfuls of little nieces and nephews. There were more gatherings in homes, lots of talking, loud card games that I usually couldn't follow. Their favorite was a complicated four-person game called "bree-hay"; it turned out to be bridge, pronounced in Spanish.

The most beautiful spot on the island was one I'd never read about—Orongo, the place of the birdmen. My islander borrowed horses—much easier to borrow than cars, because there were more of them—and we spent a day riding up there and back.

Orongo was a fringe of low stone huts on the lip of a high, sheer cliff, with the blue sea crashing at its foot. Seabirds nested on the cliff front, and in the past, island men used to risk their lives to climb down and gather eggs each year. The rituals they performed at Orongo didn't die out until the 1860s, and the cliff was still dangerous. There were no protective guard rails, just the stone huts, a rim of grass and that sheer, dizzying drop to the limitless sea. Standing up there was like standing on the edge of the world.

From the beginning, Yolanda had been urging me to stay longer. I'd only planned on a week, but as plane day got closer and she kept talking, I had weakened. Yolanda was right, I decided. There was really no reason to leave so soon. The only thing waiting for me was a small internship on a newspaper in Buenos Aires, and the start date was more than a month away. Besides, there was no penalty for changing my reservation. What harm could it do to wait?

I missed one plane. And then another. And another . . . .

And while I waited, my newly simple life grew complicated. I was enmeshed in a love affair, all right, but it wasn't exactly with the man I'd met. It was with Easter Island itself. My island.

I could see a future opening up for me here, and every time I cuddled one of the little nephews on my lap, it seemed more real, more possible. How many people, I wondered, get to live their dearest wish? How many people really find paradise? How many dare to stay once they find it?

That was the biggest question, and the longer I was there, the harder it was to answer, and the less like paradise my paradise appeared. I loved the "wind and music" part, but I was no longer sure about "nothing to do."

I watched the men and began to understand why every day felt like Saturday. It was because so few of them had real jobs. I watched their wives and noticed that the idle men didn't help them with all those babies. I saw how few options there were for everyone, even the children, and wondered how many options there would be for me.

Yolanda kept on telling me to enjoy my life. But my Minnesota conditioning had begun to kick in. *Be careful what you wish for*, it whispered in my ear. *Be careful . . . .*

My American friend confided that she and her island boyfriend were having problems—sometimes he drank too much, and then they argued. It scared her. It scared me too, and I started to undermine my happiness with questions:

What would I do when the magic wore off? Who—what— would I turn into if I stayed? Could I really grow old here? Would days of childcare and evenings of bree-hay be enough? This wasn't just some other town—this was another world. It had taken me a lifetime to reach it. What if it took that long to get away?

I couldn't tell whether I was being realistic or just a coward, didn't know what I wanted to do, let alone what I should do. Maybe I preferred daydreams to reality, after all. Didn't I, on almost every trip, imagine what it would be like to live there? And didn't I always go back to normal, back to family, house, job, no matter how tempting the place was? Yes. Yes, I always went back.

And now I did again.

I made the final decision fast, on almost no notice so I couldn't be talked out of it by my boyfriend, by Yolanda or even by myself. I must have said goodbye to the people I was leaving behind, but I don't remember doing even that. All I know is that when the next plane left, I was on it, and when the clouds closed behind me over Easter Island, whatever future I could have had there vanished into mist.

Everything I have written since then—every story in this book and a thousand others—has come from that decision. Leaving Easter Island broke my heart, but it also turned me into a travel writer.

It's hardly a normal way to live—a kind of paid homelessness, a career dependent on permanent exile: Go away, have experiences, find stuff out *and then come back* to tell it to the folks at home. It means being always on the outside looking in, longing to stay and never staying. I was perfect for it.

I still looked for "home" when I was on the road, and sometimes—on other islands, in tiny towns—I found it for a while. But never again with the same fore-ordained, consuming clarity I felt on Easter Island. I wasn't surprised: All acts have consequences, and you can't defy destiny without paying some sort of price.

I have never gone back. I can't. When asked, I say it's

because I don't want to see how the island has changed (all those hotels, all those tours . . . .)

But the real reason is that I don't want to feel like an outsider there. I don't think I could bear being just another tourist in a place where once, however briefly, I belonged. And I don't need or want another look at the path not taken; I've been seeing it ever since I caught that plane.

Over the years, readers have asked me about what I do. One question comes up again and again, usually from women in full stride, doing the great American juggling act—husband, children, home, career: "Aren't you afraid," they say, "traveling around the world alone like that?"

No, I tell them. Leaving home's a cinch. It's the staying, once you've found it, that takes courage.

Bananas and Wool

1989

—-—

O NCE, IN A VILLAGE in the steamy banana groves of north-coast Honduras, a little girl handed me a roll of Chiquita Banana stickers, an unsolicited gift given as we waited under a porch for the rain to quit.

The roll was six inches in diameter, and it held thousands of stickers. Her father's job, she said, was to paste a sticker on each banana shipped out of the plantation—one by one by one. She and her mother and brothers and sisters helped him.

Until that moment, I'd never given a thought to the stickers on bananas in grocery stores back home. But ever since, American produce departments have made me think of that tired family. Around their village, fields of continually ripening bananas stretched out for miles. The task must have felt like counting sand on a beach.

I keep that roll of Chiquita stickers among my most valued souvenirs. None of them came from souvenir shops, though a few came from public markets, and none are fancy, though some are complicated and took a lot of skill to make. Mostly, they're ordinary objects that local people used in their daily lives. I love them because they carry stories.

One I would willingly give back, if I could: It's the sharpened leg bone of a llama, used by Peruvian weavers to tamp down the yarns as they work. I bought it before I knew better, from a weaver I met on a road near Cuzco. I spent a long time talking with her, and she showed me everything from how she spun the wool by hand to how she strung her loom. When I left, I wanted something to remember her by—a typical tourist mistake, because it was the human encounter, not a souvenir, that mattered.

She had no finished weavings to sell, so I offered to buy the llama-bone tool she was using. She nodded slowly, took my money—I think she asked for a dollar—and handed over the artifact. It was worn smooth, like a small sculpture, and it fit solidly in my hand; I still find it comforting to hold, though it always makes me sad.

As she parted with it, the weaver's face sagged a little. Long after I'd taken it away, I realized why: She could get another llama bone, but she couldn't replace that one. It had been a companion. Years of work with her own hands had worn it smooth. She had shared her life with it, and she wouldn't have sold it if she hadn't been poor.

A souvenir I wouldn't give back is a little Turkish prayer rug. It too trails bittersweet memories, but most of them aren't my own. They belong to the elderly Jewish man who helped me choose it, in a rug shop in Istanbul.

The shop owner had led me to a pile of beautiful carpets, but their price tags were daunting. Then the old gentleman appeared at my elbow and quietly explained, in accented English, what I should be looking for—the number of knots per inch, what the pile was made of, whether it was worked on cotton or wool.

Finally he found a small carpet I could afford. It was finely woven, like traditional prayer rugs of wool and silk, but so low-priced that I was puzzled. "The work is the same," he explained softly, "but it is wool and polyester. If it were silk, it would cost several thousand dollars." I thanked him for his honesty and bought the rug for a song. And then he gave me the real souvenir: He told me his life story.

He had been a concert violinist in Germany in the years leading up to World War II. The woman he was in love with—I think she was in the same symphony—was not Jewish. When the Nazis came to power and anti-Semitism worsened, the young couple was afraid to be seen together; to protect her, they had to walk on opposite sides of the street.

The man managed to get out of Germany in time and so escaped the concentration camps. Eventually, he settled in Istanbul, where he continued his music, staying on there after he retired. Now, in old age, he was a permanent refugee, and he was lonely. That was why he liked to stop in at the rug shop, to chat with the owner and translate for tourists he took a liking to.

And the woman in Germany? He never saw her again, and he never married. What he wanted most now, he said, was to meet a lady with whom he could spend his last years. Any nationality would do, any personality: "All I ask is that she be able to accompany a Mozart sonata adequately on the piano."

Back home, I mentioned his wish in a travel article about Istanbul, hoping an eligible woman would see it and find him. I'd like to think one did, and that he had music and happiness to the end of his life, but I never heard. The little rug he chose for me still hangs in my home. I know it is not wool and silk, but it gives that impression—adequately—and I think of the old violinist every time I touch it.

In Flanders Fields

1988

———

WE FOUND THE MONUMENT at twilight, unexpect-
edly, at the cemetery we had decided would be our last.
We couldn't endure any more World War I cemeteries that
day, my friend and I. We hadn't been prepared for how many
there would be. Maybe we couldn't have been. Maybe nobody
could.

The British called this part of northwestern Belgium the
Ypres Salient, because Ypres was the main town. It's pronounced something like "eep" in French, but the English-
speaking soldiers who fought here called it "Wipers."

Their dead are buried where they fought, in little groups—
sometimes a dozen men, sometimes a hundred, sometimes a
thousand—in scattered cemeteries that look like miniature
parks or suburban yards, as prettily groomed and green as private lawns. Sometimes, where a town has grown over an old
trench line, the cemeteries are part of real suburbs. It was startling to drive past those—house, house, cemetery, house—as
if there were no difference between homes for the living and
homes for the dead.

Ypres lay on the Allied-German front and was in the line

of fire for four years, beginning in 1914. By war's end, it was little more than rubble. Most of the rebuilt town is drab, like other war-ravaged communities in northern Europe. But the Grote Markt, the central marketplace at the heart of town, is meticulously handsome again, right down to the arcades of its 13th-century Cloth Hall.

The marketplace was where we'd started out, late that morning, following Route '14-'18 out of town. It's a memorial road, marked by blue-and-white signs, that loops out from Ypres and winds through the former battlefield, one of that horrific war's most horrific places. Think trench warfare. Think "going over the top." Think slaughter.

We counted thirty-seven small cemeteries within a two-mile radius of Ypres alone, and those were just for the British. We didn't include the French or German cemeteries or Tyne Cot, the largest of the British ones. Tyne Cot, our guidebook said, contains 26,000 named graves and even more unknowns.

At each stop, we found booklets that explained the fighting there and listed the names of the burials, when known. The booklets, prepared by Great Britain's Commonwealth War Graves Commission, were kept inside stone or metal boxes near the cemetery gates. The boxes were not locked; the commission wanted these names and stories read.

The first two or three of the cemeteries on Route '14-'18 were interesting, and we read their booklets carefully. But "interesting" wore off fast.

The next four or five cemeteries made us angry. The cemeteries after that made us numb. We stopped reading the booklets, finally, because they blurred together. And the cemeteries just kept coming. The narrow country road twisted and turned, and cemeteries popped up like stone dandelions in the spring-green landscape. Their frequency was mesmerizing, and so were their names:

Duhallow Cemetery. Bard Cottage Cemetery. Talana Farm Cemetery. Larch Wood Cemetery. Chester Farm Cemetery. Hedgerow Trench Cemetery. Perth Cemetery. Belgian Battery Corner Cemetery. Railway Chateau Cemetery. Oxford Road Cemetery....

And on and on, until we couldn't absorb any more and had to stop. By the time we reached that point of emotional shell-shock, it was getting dark, and we were getting snappish. On the surface, we were tired from a day's driving in unfamiliar country, and hungry because we'd skipped lunch to gain sightseeing time. But those were just excuses, a mask for our real feelings. I think we were exhausted from holding the real ones in.

OK, we told each other, we'll see one more and quit. We came around the next turn, and there, at Essex Farm Cemetery, was a roadside monument to the soldier we had been talking about all day.

"John McCrae," the large stone read. "In Flanders Fields."

It was dated May 3, 1915, the day McCrae wrote his now-famous poem to honor a fallen comrade. We had been repeating part of that poem to ourselves for hours. You likely know it too. You would have learned it the same way we did, in grade school, and repeated it when we did, every Memorial Day.

In Flanders Fields, the poppies blow
Between the crosses, row on row ....

There are 1,180 burials at Essex Farm Cemetery, but the poet isn't among them. He's linked to Essex Farm because he was a physician who ran a field hospital nearby in the spring of 1915. McCrae died three years later, in France, of pneumonia and an infection of the brain.

Like the other cemeteries, Essex Farm had a guest book for visitors to sign. Most of that day's signatures belonged to British schoolchildren, on end-of-year field trips. Their comments were trite and forced—the kind of thing seventh and eighth graders write because they think they should, because they're afraid the teacher is watching.

"Speachless," wrote a girl from Nottingham.

"RIPs," scribbled another.

"Too many graves," a boy scrawled. "It should of never happened." No, we agreed, wincing at the grammar, it shouldn't.

Reading their entries, I wondered what McCrae would have thought of them, these kids on a bus trip so far removed from him in time. They were among the people for whom he had written the challenge at the end of his famous poem:

> To you from failing hands we throw
> The torch; be yours to hold it high.

Then we turned the page and found the last entry in the book. We read it together, and it made us both break down in tears. Signed by a Belgian couple, it said what the British students had not.

Simply this: "Thank you, English Army."

The Cabin

1991

———

S PRING IS COMING. I know that not because of the returning Canada geese honking overhead, or the mud smell
on sunny afternoons, or the fact that the creeping charlie in the
front lawn is turning green. I know it because the Vermont
Country Store catalog has just arrived, and I've once again
circled the Toilet Tank Drip Catcher (one for $12.95, two for
$22.95).

I did the same thing last year, too, about this time. It means
I'm thinking about the cabin again. The Cabin. The Lake. The
Place Up North. Every Minnesotan's dream. It also means I'm
remembering the reality.

Why taking care of a summer cabin should be more work
than a regular house, I'm not sure. But it is. The reason we need
the Toilet Tank Drip Catcher is because warm, moist summer
air condenses on our cabin's toilet tank, kept cold by deep well
water, then drips off and rots the flooring underneath.

My father came up with a partial solution a decade ago: He
routed the hot-water pipe into the toilet tank, which cut down
on the problem—and guaranteed that no guest would flush
while seated. At least not more than once.

But the tank still drips, albeit more slowly, and the floor is still rotting. Vermont Country Store to the rescue. If I ever get around to placing the order.

Therein lies the trouble with cabins: In a real house, you see its problems every day, and you have the whole year to fuss with them. In a summer cabin, you're aware of the problems only in season, and the season's short, and there's the beach calling, and the boat . . . .

Oh, yes, the boat. If I remember right, we put that away in a hurry last year. There's a layer of green scum on the hull that will have to be scraped off before we put it into the water again. Unless—oh, frabjous joy—green scum dries up and flakes off when you keep its host in a garage over the winter.

Sure. That's like believing the carpenter ants will move out of the guest-room wall without professional help or that the new black stuff on the kitchen ceiling won't be mold.

For years, we kept a New Yorker cartoon posted on the cabin refrigerator. It showed a hopeful family arriving at the front door of their summer home, while a menagerie of birds, squirrels, skunks and other wild cuddlies flees out the back. That, my mother used to say, was how the first weekend Up North always felt to her.

One year, one of the bats that had wintered inside couldn't find an escape hatch. It fluttered around while the newly arrived humans panicked, and then, harried by brooms and tennis rackets, it dive-bombed the sleeper sofa in the alcove. So far as we know, it never came out.

A big part of the vermin problem is that our cabin has no basement. The air vent in the pantry floor leads straight into the crawl space below the house, which makes it a mouse freeway. They move in whenever the place is left empty for more than a week, and they take complete control after close-up every October.

So come mid-May, I know what I will find the first time I turn the key in the front-door lock: Tiny black droppings, like dismal confetti, on every surface in the kitchen. Paper towels and bars of soap chewed to dust. The traditional handful of acorns that winter mice always stash in the desk drawer in the entryway. And why hasn't anyone sealed off that air vent in all these years?

Repair procrastination is our family malady. Sometimes a new adult marries in or a young relative comes of age and is inspired to save us, but only temporarily. Sooner or later, the family malady infects them too.

Title to the cabin has dropped down through another generation and come to me, but I follow ancestral tradition. Consider that missing bat carcass. My mother never looked for it, and I don't plan to either. But sometimes I imagine it's still inside the sleeper sofa, and the metal springs and levers under the mattress are now festooned with bats—a miniature Carlsbad right in the middle of our knotty-pine haven. And any night now . . . .

Outside, things can be just as perilous. We used to have three maple trees, real novelties among the skinny birches and sky-darkening pines. One summer we arrived to find all the bark stripped off one of the maples. Fearing for the others, my father wrote to the Department of Natural Resources, seeking advice. The DNR cheerfully suggested that we put out pans of sugar water, because the culprit must have a dietary need. Dad had been hoping for the name of a good poison.

The real enemy of a summer cabin, though, is exactly what you want one for: shade. Cool shade. Cool, damp, endless shade.

The perpetual shade of all those trees is deadly to cabins, at least to ours.

Shade is what grows that stuff on the kitchen ceiling (please, let it just once be cooking grease). It is what sent countless wooden porches and a few window frames moldering into our patch of Minnesota earth. It's what makes us go around the cabin every summer, kicking at the lower reaches of the siding. That's like kicking tires anywhere else, only your heart sinks more when you kick wood that goes "squoosh."

My brother John remembers his youthful summers Up North as an ongoing battle against the encroaching forest: "The trees—or me." But if you cut the trees down, you get a summer cabin on what appears to be a suburban lot. So you aim for balance, and there isn't one. That's even more true if the cabin is as old as ours: We've had it for three generations, with a fourth in training. It is quite possible that no summer home was intended to last this long.

The adults who figured in its early stories are gone now, but we heard so many of them growing up that they have entered the family's collective consciousness. Sometimes it seems as if I was there when they happened, looking on in 1938, for example, while the cabin was being built. I can even picture the ancient, alcoholic mason—seldom sober enough to hold a conversation—who still managed to split granite cobblestones with a single blow and turn them into a fireplace that remains a minor work of art. He held each big stone in one hand and hit it with a mallet. The hand that cradled the rocks had grown twice as big as the other.

My father, then in college, spent that summer up there with some of his friends, allegedly "helping the workmen." Meaning he and his buddies rolled out of bed about five in the afternoon, just in time to see the workmen leave, and then went dancing till dawn at the old Spotlight, a sleazy white-frame nightclub in nearby Nisswa, the village where the rest of us still go for groceries and Dairy Queens. The Spotlight, to my sorrow, burned down when I was a child, ruining my plans for a wasted youth.

The story I like best is about my parents' honeymoon. On a tight budget, they were married in a Minneapolis minister's study and then headed for the cabin, where, in the middle of their wedding night, neighbors they'd never met emerged from the dark woods, shouting and banging on pots and pans.

It was a shivaree, an authentic country tradition. But my father didn't have enough money to buy them off—an authentic shivaree requirement—so the neighbors just hung around the cabin, making noise until the fun went out of it. For everybody.

Then there are my own memories. Some are of things that rotted away, like the lovely little pram—a small rowboat my father and grandfather built one winter—and the old bearskin rug that had claws and teeth and a frozen pink snarl. I look for their replacements still.

Other memories are of things that never were—the sleeping loft Dad talked of building, the totem pole we were all going to carve together. The most precious memories are of things that can never be again—times when my brothers and sisters and I were little together, with our parents, with our grandparents.

Down through the generations, though, despite McMansions springing up around the lake and a diminishing number of outdoor privies, surprisingly little has changed in our cabin's life. Certainly not the annual rituals:

Three generations of spring clean-ups—airing out mattresses, brushing mayfly husks off the siding, arranging to have the dock put in, the plumbing patched, the water turned on.

Three generations of summers spent weeding poison ivy out of the pathways, knocking down wasps' nests from under the eaves, chasing the bats, hunting the mice, rebuilding porches, sniffing for mold.

Three generations of fall close-up—covering the furniture with sheets, turning the dishes upside down on the kitchen shelves, making sure there's no food left anywhere for mice to get into (not even a cracker or a tea bag), taking up the dock, closing the chimney flue, locking the windows, pouring anti-freeze down the drains.

And three generations of winters spent remembering fires in the fireplace, loons calling to each other like lost spirits across the water, evenings of popcorn and card games, cookouts and s'mores, the forts we rigged from beach towels, shouts from wet, sandy little kids trying to catch minnows in the shallows . . . .

Nostalgia is a hard jailer. It's why I can't let go, even though I know that soon the cabin will become too much for me to handle, too hard to keep up, too valuable to hang onto. "They're not making any more lakeshore," as people up here often say, explaining the ever-rising property values and why they're going to sell someday.

The previous two owners of our cabin got off easy, I sometimes think: My grandfather and my father each died before they had to make the decision that faces this generation—that faces me. But maybe not *this* summer. Maybe I'll just give it this one more summer, one more good one, and then I'll decide what to do with the old place.

It's like this every spring. I start out grumbling about toilet tanks, mold and mice. Then I ruminate on death and taxes. Then I start planning for another summer. I haven't even seen the first robin yet, and we'll probably get another blizzard. But I've already had my equinox: The cabin is back on my mind.

VIETNAM

Chewing Betel in Hanoi

1997

I WOULDN'T HAVE CONSIDERED doing it if the old lady beside me hadn't looked so much like my grandmother. Same bulky body. Same high cheekbones. Same beaming smile. The resemblance was so strong that I felt at home, as if I were once again sitting beside the woman who had let me spend my childhood feeling like a princess.

Now, nearly halfway around the globe from my grandmother's grave, the presence of this aged Vietnamese woman made me feel like a princess again. Her name was Dao Thi Thanh, and she was 73, but for the rest of this encounter, I thought of her as my grandmother, come briefly back to me.

Except that this grandmother was chewing betel nut. She had just invited me to share this traditional Vietnamese pleasure with her and her friends. I was hesitating. Betel-chewing is an accepted tradition in much of Asia, but if you're a Westerner, it's undeniable proof that you're in a foreign culture. Really foreign.

The old lady took my hesitation for ignorance and began to demonstrate what betel-chewing is all about. Still smiling, she opened her mouth and pushed the cud she was chewing forward so I could see it—the way little kids gleefully show you their bubble gum.

But instead of neon-pink Bazooka, this was a tongue-load of well-chewed green leaf and wood, swimming in a bath of blood-red spit. It looked as if her gums were hemorrhaging and gave me the distinct impression that my grandmother had reincarnated as a vampire.

I knew that betel turns saliva scarlet—that explained the wet red and dried brown blotches on Asian sidewalks. But knowing this didn't make the sight less unnerving.

I also knew I would have to join her. My traveling self is usually a good sport. But my secret self, which mentally behaves as if it's about eight years old, began to throw a tantrum: "No fair! How come I always have to do stuff like this?" Because I say so, that's why. "Grammie wouldn't have made me!" True.

I hadn't come to the Banh Ma Pagoda, on Hang Buom St. in Hanoi's Old Quarter, to chew betel. I'd come because the little structure is famous, and my new friend Barbara thought I should see it. Barbara had been a psychiatrist with U.S. forces in South Vietnam in the early 1970s and had vowed to come back after the war. When she did, in the early 1990s, she made Hanoi her home.

The Old Quarter, whose streets are named for the ancient guilds that plied their trades there, is a maze of tiny lanes, crowded with pedestrians and pedal cabs piloted by men with strong leg muscles and khaki-green pith helmets. It is Barbara's favorite part of her favorite city.

The pagoda honors the spirit of Hanoi, its patron saint, in a way—a magical white horse that appeared about a thousand years ago and showed an early Vietnamese ruler where to build the fortress around which Hanoi would grow. The horse rose from the ground at this spot, ran around the area to the west of the Old Quarter, north of Hoan Kiem Lake in central Hanoi, then came back here and disappeared into the ground. "I will build my citadel on the footprints of the horse," the ruler pledged.

Famous it may be, but this isn't the kind of pagoda Westerners think of when they hear the word. It's not a tower but a small one-story building with stucco walls and a tile roof. Step through its gate, and you're in a courtyard with rooms on each side. Ahead is the entrance to the shrine, and inside that is an altar with religious figures, including a horse; fragrant sticks of incense; lots of red and gilt, a bowl of fresh fruit and garlands of tiny Christmas-tree lights.

Barbara and I joined Dao Thi Thanh and two of her elderly friends at an oil-cloth-covered table in the courtyard, where they had gathered the way their Midwestern counterparts might gather in a church basement. Each old lady had a round tin box, like the ones Christmas cookies come in, sitting open on the table in front of her. The boxes held the paraphernalia of betel-chewing—substances as mystifying to an untutored American as the potions and powders in an alchemist's shop.

From time to time, the ladies dipped into these kits to build a fresh chaw. Build is the right word. You start with a leaf—a bright green, oval leaf about three inches long that comes from a special pepper plant. On top of the leaf, you put a chunk of what looks like pine wood—that's the betel nut, actually the seed of a type of palm tree. Then a bit of peeled twig—a spice, perhaps? Then some stuff I couldn't identify. And finally a purplish-gray dollop of lime powder mixed with water. This last ingredient looks like Hawaiian poi. Or old library paste. Or the stuff dentists use to polish your teeth. Take your pick.

You fold the leaf around all this, making a little packet. Then you pop the packet into your mouth, chew it into mush and tuck the mush into your cheek, like a cud of chewing tobacco. Chemicals from the cud leach into your system, and when your mood needs a boost, you just give it another little chew.

Besides turning saliva red, betel also stimulates the saliva glands, so you regularly need to spit out the gaudy juice. When you've absorbed all the kick it can give, you spit out the whole cud and start making a new one.

The key ingredient, according to the Encyclopedia Americana, is "the alkaloid *arecoline*, a mild stimulant that produces a feeling of well-being." It can also be used, the encyclopedia added, as "a de-wormer in veterinary medicine." That's my best fact this year.

However you explain it, betel-chewing is supposed to make you happy. Judging by the blissful red smiles all around the table, it works. Barbara leaned across the table to me and began a running commentary, explaining betel use in fast, cheerful whispers. "It's like offering someone a drink," she said. In Vietnam, "the men have drinks, the older women have betel—it's a social lubricant." So social that I couldn't weasel out of trying it.

Dao Thi Thanh popped her cud out of her mouth several times, to make super-sure I got the idea. But I couldn't shake the image of bleeding wounds, and it nearly made me gag. "You're handling this well," Barbara encouraged. "Some people think this is pretty gross."

My mental eight-year-old was indignant: "Think? *Think?* This *is* pretty gross!"

Most cultures have something like this, whether it's chewing coca leaves in the high Andes or having a glass of wine in

France. But those practices don't make your mouth look like a prize-fighter's after he's taken a punch to the face.

I took a deep breath, smiled at my grandmother's surrogate, picked up a shiny green leaf and started to create my own mouth-sized compost pile. She nodded approvingly.

Then I tucked the finished packet into my mouth and bit down. Leaf, nut, lime and spices crunched together. Mouth, lips, tongue and throat instantly went numb. I don't know what I'd expected, but this scared me, and Barbara responded to my panicked expression.

"Take it out," she hissed, "and act really happy!"

I spit the pulp into my hand and started to pantomime ecstatic joy. Great! I beamed. Terrific!! Really! It's really, really *great!*

I wasn't fooling Barbara or myself, but the dear old ladies bought it. Crimson grins all around. Another cultural bridge crossed. And a spiritual visit with my grandmother, to boot—even if this incarnation did wear a vampire smile.

Thanksgiving Meets the Guy

2002

TRADITIONS CAN GET GARBLED when they leap an ocean. I never saw it as clearly as I did one evening in London, when English friends and I managed to tangle three holidays of ours with one of theirs.

I thought of it again on the first Thanksgiving after the terrorist attacks of September 11, and by then, that noisy evening in England had taken on an unexpected poignancy.

A couple of Novembers ago, I was visiting my London friends John and Margaret. It was Guy Fawkes Day, which commemorates the foiling of a guerrilla plot against the king, four centuries earlier.

My friends gave me a choice for the evening: We could go down to Lewes, a town in Sussex known for its Guy Fawkes celebration. Or we could spend the holiday shooting off Fourth-of-July-style fireworks with their grandchildren.

There was only one possible answer. "Let's go see your grandchildren," I said, and we drove over to their house in the London suburbs, where I was introduced to John and Margaret's son, a musician; his wife, who was a caterer, and their three beautifully-spoken, well-behaved small children.

In my memory, the little ones practically curtsied when they said hello.

After that, it became a rather American evening. But with twists. Everybody agreed on pizza for dinner, knowing Americans love it. But they ordered "Mexican pizza." It was so spicy I could barely eat it, though it went over fine with everybody else, whose tongues grew up accustomed to blazing-hot Indian curries.

Then the children begged for the fireworks. Their mother confided that it scared her to death to shoot them off, but she dutifully set up rockets in the back yard, told the kids to take cover and started striking matches.

For the next twenty minutes, she dashed back and forth between porch and launch pad, lighting fuses, then taking cover herself. In back yards all around us, other mums and dads were doing the same thing. It sounded as if a neighborhood blitz had broken out. Bombs burst in air, balls of colored light exploded over garden fences, and it was exactly the kind of Fourth of July menace that Minnesota had banned when I was growing up.

At last, when the noise stopped and only the smell of gunpowder lingered in the air, we adults settled down to talk. My hosts explained the Gunpowder Plot of 1605, in which Guido (a.k.a. Guy) Fawkes, an explosives expert who had served with the Spanish army, was caught trying to blow up the Parliament while the king was inside. The plot failed, and November 5 was named a day of thanksgiving, still celebrated with fireworks and bonfires and a catchy little verse:

Remember, remember
The Fifth of November

Gunpowder treason and plot
We see no reason
Why gunpowder treason
Should ever be forgot!

When it was my turn, I described the costumes, the trick-or-treating and the candy of American Halloween, whose roots include Guy Fawkes Day as well as the ancient Celtic festival called Samhain. Then we segued onto another American holiday.

"I've always wanted to know," John said, peering at me over his spectacles, "on Thanksgiving, what *is* it you're thankful for?"

Until that moment, America's Thanksgiving was not a holiday I'd analyzed. I didn't even question it in childhood—I just swallowed the Pilgrim story whole, without a second thought. And I'd certainly never been called on to explain it, let alone to an adult audience on the other side of the Atlantic.

In my family, Thanksgiving has always focused on the food. If John's question had involved my mother's apple pie or the right way to make dressing—the time-honored Watson way: without sausage—I'd have been on solid ground.

But that wasn't what John was looking for, so I took a deep breath and plunged into the saga of Plymouth Rock, instantly aware that it sounded like a fairy tale. And equally aware, as I never was before, that it was the classic, no-doubts, no-nuances, politically incorrect, grade-school version. I almost wished I'd said "once upon a time" at the beginning.

My English audience already knew—as I hadn't until well into adulthood—that many of the Pilgrims had been living in Holland for a dozen years before the Mayflower took them to the New World, while a good many others were more interested in free land than in freedom to worship.

But I soldiered on anyway, painting a golden picture about how hard the newcomers' first year was, and how so many of them died, and how Squanto and other Indians helped them grow corn by planting it in mounds of earth with a fish inside, and how grateful the Pilgrims were.

This did not satisfy John. "Yes," he said. "But what are you *thankful* for?" I said something lame about its being a family holiday, and the conversation mercifully moved on.

Guy Fawkes Night was on my mind again in November 2001. At Thanksgiving dinner, so soon after the loss of life in New York, in Washington and in the airplane crash in Pennsylvania, I told my siblings, nieces, nephews and friends about that English evening. By then, I could have answered John's question with confident passion. As it had for so many other Americans, the tragedy of September 11 had refocused my heart.

At that Thanksgiving, my family began what has become a tradition: We went around the table, and each person, from child to grown-up, told what they most valued. The answers were surprisingly similar. Then we drank a toast in honor of the lives lost in a guerrilla plot that had tragically succeeded.

What was it we were thankful for that day? "Everything," I would tell my friend John now. "Each other. All of us. Being together. Being alive."

TURKEY

The Land of Cones

2000

———

THE AFTERNOON SKY GLEAMED like blue crystal, the golden sunlight was perfect, and the rocky pinnacles before me were among the most remarkable I'd seen in Cappadocia, one of the world's strangest landscapes.

Hmmm. Maybe the pinnacles were a little *too* remarkable. Putting it nicely, they looked like tall morel mushrooms. Putting it not so nicely . . . .

Halfway through a roll of film, I lowered the camera and took a critical look at my subjects. They weren't just dramatic— they were frankly phallic. I continued shooting pictures in that exquisite light, but it seemed wise to stop framing individual pinnacles in graceful openings in the rock.

When I got back to my hotel that evening, I telephoned Minnesota and talked to my best friend, trying to describe Cappadocia to him. As usual, he understood. "I get it," he said, when I detailed the afternoon's photo shoot. "Porn Shop of the Gods!" Well, that was one way to put it.

Cappadocia (pronounced cap-uh-DOE-kee-uh) is famous for these geological peculiarities. The region is even nicknamed "the land of cones." That's another way to put it.

The cones, also known as "fairy chimneys," yet another way to put it, exist because this part of south-central Turkey is covered with a thick layer of tuff, a soft, easily eroded volcanic rock. Over eons, water worked its way through the soft stone, sometimes leaving a boulder as a protective cap, and created spires, cones, turrets, mushrooms and so on. I emphasize the "so on."

The stone is easily carved by people, too. Starting with the Hittites several thousand years ago, locals began burrowing into the rock—sculpting rooms, homes, chapels, stables, even multilayered underground cities out of the cream-colored geology. It's as if colonies of gnomes had settled in an anatomical version of the Badlands and carved hide-outs in the hoodoos.

Cappadocia lies in a triangle bounded by the small cities of Kayseri, Aksaray and Nigde, about three and a half hours of fast driving southeast of Ankara, the national capital. My friend Jim and I, exploring the western lobe of Turkey, based ourselves in the still smaller and more picturesque town of Goreme (roughly, GOR-ruh-may).

Goreme itself is dotted with rock cones, but we arrived at night, and they were invisible in the darkness. We found rooms in a cozy guesthouse near the center of town. The lobby looked like an old-fashioned Turkish living room, with red and blue handmade carpets draped on the floors and sofas. We were the only guests, and the night clerk invited us to sprawl on the rugs and watch Turkish soccer with him on TV. Jim took him up on it; I begged off.

Upstairs in my snug room, under an arched ceiling hacked out of local rock, I fell asleep to the bleating of a very loud, very nearby cow. The cow had a distinct Minnesota accent. It was a one-note, no-diphthong cow, so when it said "moo," it sounded like Governor Jesse Ventura saying "no" or "go."

"Mo," said the cow, over and over. "Mo. Mo." I found it comforting.

The cow was silent the next morning, and—except for a couple of donkey carts—so was the wide street outside my window. All of Goreme was quiet, for that matter, all the time we were there. This was puzzling, because it's in the heart of one of Turkey's most visited regions. Normally, about a million people a year come to see Cappadocia's fantastical landscape of cones and pinnacles, but the numbers were off during our visit.

The soccer-watching night clerk, still on duty at breakfast, tried to explain how foreign tourists had been scared off. "After they catch Ocalan, the Kurdish terrorist, somebody set off bomb in Istanbul. Not a big bomb. Put something in a bottle . . . ." He struggled for the term.

"Molotov cocktail?" Jim and I chirruped in unison, sounding like professional guerrillas.

"Molotov cocktail!" our host agreed, and we resumed snacking on breakfast: plates of tangy olives, creamy yogurt and fresh bread, washed down with glasses of hot, sugary apple tea.

Istanbul was a long way from little Goreme, which felt safe and almost sad, because it was so empty. We could see the effect on the local economy everywhere—in the sleepy streets, the neglected cafes, the highly available guides at local sights. Restaurants appeared to be waiting just for us. Even the normally aggressive Turkish carpet dealers sounded forlorn when they invited us in, as if they had no hope we'd come.

One night, at dinner in a cone-shadowed restaurant, we had three waiters hovering at our table: We were the only diners. As we finished eating, the tall young man who owned the place came over and joined us, settling down for a chat; there was nothing else for him to do.

He picked up Jim's empty coffee cup, swirled its residue of thick, espresso-like grounds and started to read Jim's fortune. There would be some sadness, the young man predicted—"three times cry"—but what he saw also foretold money and a long life.

I hadn't ordered coffee. "Hold out your hand," he said to me. I thought he was going to tell my fortune too, something I try to avoid. But he only traced some of the lines on my palm. He said they formed the name of God.

"All people have 'Allah' written in their hands," he said. "My father told me that. See it?"

Turkish has been written in Roman letters since the 1920s, thanks to a decree by the country's great leader, Kemal Ataturk. The result looks like English with a few extra dots and curlicues. Even so, Jim and I couldn't see the name of God in my palm, or his either. But we liked the idea. We said we saw it, and our new friend was pleased.

The missing tourists were missing a lot. It was spring; there were wildflowers and roses blooming in the cone-dotted valleys around Goreme; the weather was warm and sunny, and for sheer exploring potential, Cappadocia was unbeatable.

The top sight, our guidebooks said, was the Goreme Open-Air Museum, a glen of stone spires riddled with caves that had been Orthodox Christian churches in the eleventh and twelfth centuries. We got there very early, but sun-wise, you cannot see anything in Cappadocia early enough. It was already squint-your-eyes bright in the museum valley, and the place looked like a bone yard. An oven-hot, shadowless bone yard.

It was also Sunday, and it was crowded. Uniformed troops of Boy Scouts swarmed the cones; families with little kids roamed in and out of the cave openings; grandmothers balked at the steeper staircases; jeans-clad teenaged girls giggled up ladders and through once-holy rooms. Most of the chapels were plain or so poorly preserved that their frescoes were crumbling off the walls.

I like to think I'm a professional sightseer, but this wore me out. I craved shade, solitude and a Coke. But we hadn't seen the Dark Church yet, the one the guidebooks praised most heavily, the one that had been freshly restored. We waited for a lull, then made for its entrance. And stayed.

There were angels on the archways, painted saints in every corner, and even the shadows throbbed with color. The surprising beauty of it hushed my boredom, took away my thirst. The walls were covered with Bible stories, painted in a flat, childish style. The baby under the Star of Bethlehem resembled a miniature mummy, and the starlight fell on him in stick-straight lines like arrows from the sky, but the combination looked like innocence.

When we'd seen enough manmade caves above ground, we tackled the ones below—Cappadocia's underground cities. Three of them are easily toured, our guidebooks said, and we set out to see them all. Normally, Jim and I do our own research and guide ourselves; it suits our cranky, independent personalities. But at Kaymakli, our first stop and the best-known of the underground cities, we—um—caved. And it was a lucky thing. It would have been impossible on our own.

A short, gray-templed guide in a brown suit offered to take us through for five dollars, and we agreed. I crouched down until my knees wouldn't bend anymore and duck-walked behind him into the dark maze. Within minutes, I knew I'd have paid him ten times that much to get me out.

In cross-section, the place would look like a human-sized ant farm: room after room, tunnel after tunnel, level after intertwined level, with nothing to keep you oriented and nowhere near enough light bulbs. Our guide said the underground city once held five thousand people, and I believed him. It managed to be simultaneously immense and tightly confining.

For the first time in my life, I had claustrophobia—had it to the verge of nausea. "I am okay," I told myself, over and over, trying not to retch. "This will be okay. I'm with a guide . . . ."

But it wasn't okay. It took only seconds to get lost, and I kept doing it. Several times, Jim and the guide disappeared around a corner or into a branching tunnel, and I couldn't tell which way they'd gone. I would be choked with panic until I heard their voices. The worst moment came when I followed the sound and then realized it wasn't them at all—the voices were coming from tourists on the next level down. Now I understood how people feel when they're lost in the woods: If there had been room to run around wildly and get even more lost, I would have.

I found my companions almost accidentally. They hadn't been looking for me, hadn't even noticed I was missing, which meant they would never have found me. I protested that they'd let me get lost. Yes, the guide said cheerfully, "it's a labyrinth."

When we finally got out again, into that hot, blazing, now-welcome sunlight, he asked if we'd like to see the other two underground cities. Thanks, I said, but one was plenty.

People were still living in Cappadocia's cone houses and man-made caves until the 1950s. The slight middle-aged man who ran a carpet shop next to our guesthouse was one of them.

Hasan Uludag was born in a cave home, which made him a true troglodyte, or cave dweller, as every book on Turkey calls the locals at least once.

"They kept you cool in summers and warm in winters," Hasan said, with a touch of nostalgia for the old rock refuges. They were dry inside, and you never had to repair the roof. But it was hard to put in modern plumbing and electricity. When the government began providing healthier housing for troglodytes, most were quick to trade picturesque caves for free-standing modern homes.

Hasan told me this while I carpet-shopped. When I finally bought one of the beautiful handmade rugs, he was so pleased—or had so little business—that he took a whole morning off to show Jim and me around the neighborhood. "I used to be a guide," Hasan explained, as he escorted us to the Rose Valley and the Honey Valley, more cone-dotted, cave-pocked landscapes nearby.

He led us to stands of tall fairy chimneys that weren't in the guidebooks and helped us crawl into caves where he remembered there were carvings, mostly huge crosses, on the ceilings. Along the way, we walked up narrow dirt roads overhung with walnut and almond trees, amid silvery shrubs and purple iris.

Occasionally, we met local farm women walking toward town. They wore traditional—meaning modest—peasant dress: long skirts or baggy trousers, a long-sleeved sweater buttoned to the neck, no face veil but a head-scarf as big as a shroud. They were a striking contrast to the teenage girls in tight jeans and T-shirts back at the museum village.

I knew that female modesty is important in Islamic countries, but the rules vary, not just in Turkey, but all over the Middle East. Perhaps it was the landscape, so dominated by male forms, that made me bring it up now. Whatever the reason, when another heavily dressed peasant woman crossed our path, I asked Hasan why it was necessary for Muslim females to cover up like that.

"The Koran says yes," Hasan explained gently, "because women are very important. They are like jewelry that you should keep in good boxes." He sounded so kind and sincere that I bit my mental—and thoroughly Western—tongue. It already had permanent dents from avoiding this topic elsewhere in the Middle East. One more dent wouldn't hurt.

"Umm," I said, sounding a little like my monotonic cow, and we kept walking. I hoped Hasan thought his answer had cleared this question up for me. It was, after all, a lovely day, and there were more of those phallic cones he wanted us to see.

SPAIN

Tornado Alley

2000

———

MADRID DOESN'T SLEEP MUCH, and for that I was
thankful. It was the first night of a trip, and I was too
jet-lagged to sleep. I parted the curtains at midnight, and the
street below my downtown hotel window looked like an urban
block party. Half the city seemed to be out there, walking, eating, laughing, embracing and generally having a good time. I
got dressed again and joined them.

I shot some crowd pictures, ate an ice-cream cone and
spent fifteen minutes watching a white-faced mime stand perfectly still, while his pet kitten sat perfectly still on his head.
Even that didn't make me sleepy.

Fortunately, the movie theater across the street was having a late show: "Twister," which I'd missed seeing at home.
I bought a ticket and went in. I expected a sound track in
English with subtitles, but the film was dubbed—not in the
North American schoolbook Spanish I know, but in Madrid
slang. This rendered Helen Hunt—and most of the plot—
incomprehensible.

But there was no misunderstanding the scenery—the low-

– 250 –

ering sky, the evil light, the ominous rise of the wind. It looked like the Middle West on far too many summer afternoons. It looked, in short, like home. Midway through the movie, when cows and semi-trailer trucks were bouncing down out of the clouds, I glanced around at my spellbound seatmates. From their expressions of utter disbelief, they might as well have been watching "Jurassic Park."

Tornados can occur anywhere the world, even in Western Europe, if the weather conditions are right. But compared with the great flat midriff of America, they're so rare in Spain that this movie had to seem unreal—another American myth to add to the stereotypes we've earned in the rest of the world's collective mind: How we all talk like Texans, we're forever getting into car-chases on the way to work, and we all go around packing six-guns.

The tornado on the screen gave me a twinge of Midwestern pride. I wanted to tell the Madrileños that this was different, this was real. Except for that ending: Where I come from, everybody knows that you don't survive a direct hit from a funnel cloud by lashing your belt to a pipe and holding on. At least not usually.

We also know what a tornado looks like, even if we've never seen one in person. At least, we ought to. I thought I did until a recent summer, and while the way I found out wasn't like a movie, the experience certainly humbled me.

It happened on a Fourth of July weekend in northern Minnesota. My sister Jane was driving her kids and me from our family's lake cabin to Brainerd, the nearest big town, because Brainerd always has terrific fireworks. I was idly looking out the window when Jane noticed something odd.

"Why would a bunch of people run out of Bonanza and lie down in the ditch?" she wondered, as we passed a popular roadside steakhouse.

"Maybe there was a bomb threat," I said. We kept driving.

Then Jane noticed something else peculiar. "People in oncoming cars keep looking at something behind us and pulling off the road," she said.

I turned around and checked, but there was nothing to worry about, nothing even unusual—just bright white clouds prettily back-lit by the evening sun. I looked again, just to make certain. No, nothing threatening, though I did notice that one of the clouds was stubby and V-shaped and that it appeared to be squatting on the highway directly behind us.

"If it were black, I'd think it was a tornado," I said, "but this one's white. Tornadoes aren't supposed to be white." They also aren't supposed to be short and stubby—they're supposed to be long and snakey. We kept driving.

At the amusement park called Paul Bunyan Land, we made a left turn toward Brainerd, and something happened to the clouds. They'd stopped being pretty and white. Now they were coal-black, as if a giant hand had snapped off the lights.

Jane rolled down her window then, and we heard sirens. "Maybe we should turn on the radio," she said. I fiddled with the settings, and we caught the panicky voice of a young announcer urging all Brainerd listeners to take immediate cover in the basement of city hall.

Jane spun the van around and floored it toward sunlight. Now we were going away from Brainerd and away from our cabin. Minutes later, a vicious storm passed behind us and smashed into the city.

You're supposed to wait longer than we did, but when

the sky cleared, we turned around and went back to the cabin over the roads we'd just driven. The damage was appalling, and I was ashamed of my stupidity and stunned at how lucky we'd been. Hundreds of roadside pines—tall stands of trees that I remembered from my childhood—now lay on the ground in whorls, like giant cowlicks, flattened by the spinning air, their trunks twisted and splintered.

I expected we'd find the cabin splintered, too, but our lakeshore neighborhood had been spared. There wasn't even a broken branch. I picked up the phone and got a dial tone—it was lucky that the lines weren't down—and called home to say we were safe.

The next day, our neighbors told us what a close call everyone had had. The storm system was huge, and it had spawned many tornadoes. Besides the one that hit Brainerd, another had killed a child in a campground a few miles away, and another had touched down "right out there!"—not far off shore in our own lake. The neighbors said the tornado pulled lake water up into itself, and the rising water made the funnel look green, like glass. That was another color I thought tornadoes weren't supposed to be.

Day of the Dead

2003

DEATH WAS EVERYWHERE, even in the food, and I didn't like it. But everybody else seemed to, which made Mexico at the end of October even more colorfully foreign than usual. The country was getting ready to celebrate *el Dia de los Muertos*—the Day of the Dead—and my friend Mary Ann and I had gone to see what it was like.

The Day of the Dead, we quickly learned, is not the same as Halloween—most decidedly not—even though it takes place at the same time. This is the big difference: In America, the ghoulies and ghosties and witches and bats are supposed to scare kids or at least give them a scary thrill.

In Mexico, the candy skulls and miniature graves and sugar coffins and dancing skeletons aren't supposed to be scary at all. They're cute. And they're familiar. They help Mexican kids grow up at ease with the concept of death.

At ease, I am not. I don't like reminders of the Grim Reaper. Most Americans don't. We're taught not to. From birth, our frenetic culture submerges us in the present moment; our high-quality health care lets us pretend that life-threatening illness is merely a problem to be solved, and our national emphasis on youth keeps aging and death in the background, if not at bay.

The Day of the Dead teaches Mexicans just the opposite. It teaches them the truth about death. It teaches them that we are always within its reach.

The holiday is celebrated all over Mexico, though in different ways. In some places, it's more like Memorial Day: People place flowers on loved ones' graves and maybe go to church. But Mexican families also build special altars in their homes. Called *ofrendas*, they honor dead relatives. And in some regions, like the state of Michoacan, west of the capital, people take the Day of the Dead much further.

From midnight on the night of November 1 till dawn on November 2, the dead are believed to come back. Back to their families. Back to life. In villages around the town of Pátzcuaro, for example, relatives not only decorate loved ones' graves, they spend the night in the cemetery, enjoying the company of beloved spirits. That picturesque middle-of-the-night vigil is what attracts thousands of tourists to Pátzcuaro every year and what had attracted us.

We got to the pleasant colonial town on the evening of October 29. We thought that would be early enough, but the place was already booming, so full of visitors that we got rooms downtown only by chance. (I was at a hotel's front desk when a cancellation came in; the concierge had just finished telling me I should have booked a year in advance.)

The main square was jammed with giant white tents—a *tianguis*, or handicrafts fair, is part of Pátzcuaro's celebration— and candy skull sellers had set up shop under the arcades of the old Spanish buildings along one side.

From morning to night for the next three days, whenever

we stepped outside our hotel, we were part of a moving, growing crowd, most of them shopping the sugar stalls. School kids in uniform, moms holding toddlers, grandparents, foreign tourists, country people—the men in cowboy hats, the women wrapped in traditional blue shawls called *rebozos*—all were engrossed in choosing just the right items for the ofrendas and for each other.

Candy skulls were everywhere I looked—stacks and tiers and heaps of skulls, thimble-size to life-size, plain sugar or chocolate. There were piles of miniature sugar coffins, sugar models of fruit, sugar enchiladas, sugar tacos, sugar angels, sugar rocking horses, even sugar tequila bottles. A plainer necessity, *pan de muerto*, bread of the dead, was there, too; the lumps on top of the round loaves represent human bones.

Eventually, I got used to these macabre mementos—was even able to judge candy skulls on quality of decoration or skill of design—but I was never comfortable with them. Not until the very end.

It did not sound as if the dead were expected back from Christian heaven. It sounded as if they were returning from an ancient underworld. Indeed, Mexicans told us, the Day of the Dead is an old tradition, a pre-Hispanic custom, with Christian beliefs welded on top of it. The orange flowers on the ofrendas were proof of its roots.

Ofrendas vary in style from family to family, like Christmas trees, but they all feature masses of big, brilliant marigolds. Mexicans don't call them by their Spanish name. They use a word the Aztecs would recognize: *cempasuchitl*. It means "many-petaled," and the color of the blossoms honors the sacred life-giving sun.

So many marigolds are needed that they were brought into

Pátzcuaro by the semi-trailer-load. People bought them from street sellers or directly from the trucks, walking away with their arms so full of flowers that they could hardly see over them. Their faces glowed orange from light reflected off the marigolds they carried.

Ofrendas also need to include the four ancient elements—earth, air, fire, water—because the dead are coming from the ground, wind helps their spirits travel, candle flames lead them home, and they need water when they arrive because they will be very thirsty.

Some people, we heard, lay out new clothes for the dead, because their burial outfits will be dirty and dank; some even give up their beds for that night, because the dead might want to rest.

The dead need to be nourished too, so ofrendas display things that they loved in life—foods, mainly, but also sugar models of toys for the children, favorite brands of cigarettes or tequila or beer for the adults. And everybody in the family, living and dead, gets sugar skulls with their names on them.

This food doesn't go to waste. "You know, the next day, when we eat the fruit, it has no flavor," a woman selling sugar skulls confided. She meant that the dead, who cannot really eat, soak up aroma and flavor instead and leave the food behind. "People say that isn't possible," she said, "but it's true."

I kept puzzling over those candy skulls. "It's like this," an older man explained. "I put your name on a skull and give it to you. You put my name on a skull and give it to me. It's fun." I nodded, but it didn't sound like fun to me. It sounded creepy.

If the candy skulls were fun, skeletons were hysterical, even more so when they put on clothes. That explained the ubiquitous skeleton figurines in the market and all the shops—

skeleton ladies in big plumed hats, skeleton Last Suppers, skeleton doctors treating skeleton patients, skeleton dance bands, skeleton everything.

There are even skeleton nursery rhymes, like this one, whose syllables do a nice job of sounding like clacking bones:

La Muerte calaca,
Ni gorda ni flaca,
La Muerte cacera
Pegada con cera.

My own translation didn't make sense: *Lady Death's skeleton, neither fat nor thin, Lady Death caretakes, patched up with wax.*

Obviously, I was missing some fine point. Mary Ann, who speaks better Spanish, couldn't crack it, either, so I copied the rhyme down and tried to get bilingual Mexicans to translate it for me. Invariably, they burst out laughing when they read it, shook their heads and said they couldn't.

A dealer of skeleton figurines in Pátzcuaro came the closest. "It doesn't matter if you're skinny or fat, at home or getting medical treatment," he said in English, "death will come for you anyway." And everyone who understood him burst out laughing again. Except us.

On Saturday, November 1, the mood in town changed. The stalls under the arcades were just as busy, but the school kids and local families had given way to a thickening flood of tourists. Nearly all were Mexican, and most were young. As they poured in, downtown Pátzcuaro took on the mood of a mini-Cancún during spring break. The college crowd hadn't come for handicrafts and graveyard vigils. What they wanted was live music, jungle drums, drinking and each other.

All that day, anticipation mounted. Music got louder, drums more frenetic. When it began to rain, hard, in the afternoon, all the restaurant tables under the arcades filled up solid and stayed that way the rest of the evening. Afternoon drinkers turned into night-time drunks.

The most famous place to go for the night of the dead is Janitzio, an island in Lake Pátzcuaro. That was where we'd planned on going, but so had everyone else. By 9 o'clock Saturday night, there was a traffic jam in the direction of the town pier, where launches were leaving for the island.

Rain, open boats, drunks, crowds—Janitzio sounded like a bad idea. We decided to go to Tzintzuntzan instead, a small town about seven miles away, billed as the area's second-most traditional cemetery observance.

We got a taxi the way we'd found a room, by serendipity. A woman slid out of the back seat of an old vehicle right in front of us, and we slid in behind her, becoming instant pals of the crusty little driver, Juan Pineda. His every third word was a curse, but he swore—by many saints and several body parts—he'd get us to Tzintzuntzan despite the traffic. And did. In twenty minutes.

"We had luck," he said.

He parked on the roadside a quarter of a mile out of town, in a line of tour buses and SUVs, and walked in with us. Mexican tourists carrying drinks in plastic cups were swaying and singing along the road, locals were charging outsiders to park cars in their gardens, and the whole thing felt like a tailgating party without the football.

Except for candles on the graves, a few flashlight beams and the sporadic strobes of an American TV crew, the cemetery was pitch black, and the rain had turned it into a swamp. I couldn't see my feet. People slipped, mud sucked at my shoes, and Juan Pineda, trying to watch over us, swore even more. It was—to my American sensibilities—appalling.

We slip-waded to two decorated graves, with the families standing grim-faced beside them, while tourists turned their vigil into an amusement park, until I finally froze in place, afraid that I'd lose a shoe if I moved or, far worse, my camera.

Juan Pineda reached for my arm. "Let's go," he said. "I will take you somewhere smaller."

He drove us back toward Pátzcuaro, against the traffic, and took a highway turnoff for a town called Ihuatzio. We drove under a tall arch of marigolds, and the mood was instantly better. The way into town was lighted every fifty feet with little fires, like a marigold path, and we were almost the only car on the road.

The cemetery was small, rocky, unlit and packed with graves. It wasn't muddy, but I stumbled anyway, tripping over unseen rocks, stepping into shadowed sinkholes, hoping I wasn't walking on graves or treading on feelings, afraid that I was doing both.

Around the graves, families were setting up big wooden frames covered with marigolds and decorated with apples, bananas and oranges. Some of these temporary walls were already finished, and women, men and kids, wearing winter jackets or wrapped in blankets against the damp, were sitting inside them, at graves that now looked like parade floats, strewn with marigold petals and lighted by three-foot-tall candles. I asked permission to take pictures, and each time it was granted. People were proud of what they had done for their departed.

One woman stood out. About my age, in a long skirt with a dark-blue shawl around her shoulders, she sat serenely next to a decorated grave, looking like a Diego Rivera painting. Her face was radiant in the candlelight.

"We are afraid of death in my culture," I said to her. "But everyone here looks so happy."

"Yes, we are happy," she said, beaming up at me. "We are happy because, for one day of the year, they are *with* us."

Her voice was strong. She meant it literally, and the power of her belief filled me with awe. I stood there in that dark, lumpy cemetery, hesitating to move lest I step on another grave, and envied that woman her faith. I started to tell her so but choked on words and tears.

At that moment, I wished that I, too, could build a marigold room and furnish it with food and candles and sit inside—even for just a few hours—and know that my own dead were truly, *truly* with me again.

After the Day of the Dead was over and we were back in Mexico City, packing for the trip home, the friendly maid at our hotel gave me a farewell gift. It was a little human skull made out of chocolate, with a turquoise candy flower on its forehead and turquoise sequin eyes.

A week earlier, I would have found the skull repulsive—a grisly little reminder of something I dread. Now I understood. The skull was a gift from one friend to another, a reminder not only of death, but also of life and the things that truly matter in it. I thought of candlelight glowing on the faces in the graveyard at Ihuatzio and accepted the skull with thanks.

A Galena Christmas

2004

———

WHEN YOUR HEART LIVES in one place and your body in another, it's hard to know where to spend the holidays. Do I stay in Minneapolis, where my siblings live? Or do I go to Galena, Illinois, my favorite town, my own personal Dept. 56 snow village?

For nearly two decades I have asked myself those questions, and for nearly two decades I have answered them the same way: I will do both, even though the twelve-hour round-trip to Galena adds to the craziness of this crazy time of year.

This means that I celebrate Christmas twice. It doubles both the blessing and the pressure. But I can't help it.

I fell in love with Galena thirty years ago, on a newspaper assignment, and finally, after ten years of dreaming about it, I gave in and bought a beat-up little house there. My mother was dying then, and my sense of home was dying with her. The little Galena house came into my life as she was leaving it.

I have never once, in all the time since, stepped through its front door without feeling instantly safe, loved and *home*. The house is like a giant, full-body hug. That's most true at

Christmas, the season for which historic Galena's red-brick and green-shutter color scheme seems to have been intended.

Over the years, my view of this village of 3,600 has changed. Not for the worse, just for the real. I fell in love with a two-dimensional picture postcard. Now I know it's a living, changing place, full of quirks and personality. My house is the same way.

I never manage to get more than a few days in Galena before Christmas or a few days afterward, but I decorate as if I'm staying forever. The house demands it, and the house, I have learned, can be stubborn.

One year, early in my ownership, I'd decided not to do a tree because I was going back to Minneapolis too soon. Then, on the night of Dec. 23, it suddenly seemed essential to change my mind.

Galena's tree lots were empty, so I drove to the nearest big town, Dubuque, Iowa, fifteen miles away. I got the last tree in the only still-open lot I could find. Literally *in* it: The scraggly thing had fallen over and frozen into the ice. The needles on its down side pulled off when I pried it loose. Never mind. It was a Christmas tree, and the house had to have one somehow.

There have been other Christmases since then, when I spent most of a day decorating a tree, only to leave it the next. I have even put up trees the day *after* Christmas, just to be able to sit beside one in that dear little house at midnight on New Year's Eve.

Meantime, the house has taken on a life of its own. Or maybe picked up where it left off in some earlier time. It has its own traditions now, and its own Christmas style—white lights on the front porch pillars, white lights on the tree and glass ornaments in shades of rose and pearl. Only rose and pearl. Back in Minneapolis, I don't even like pink, but apparently that's what the Galena house wants. And so, when I'm there, do I.

The Christmas after my mother died, Galena was where I took refuge. I planned to stay right through the holidays, because I needed a haven for my heart more than a turkey dinner with my brothers and sisters. Or so I thought, until Christmas Eve. Then I chickened out and dashed north in darkness to be with them.

That has been my pattern ever since. I still haven't spent a whole Christmastime in Galena. But Galena is where I keep Christmas, and that is something different and, to me, far sweeter.

THE GALAPAGOS

Sailing with Darwin

2002

——-—-——

A S MY SHIPMATES TRAILED our guide through the
cactus-dotted landscape of South Plaza, our last island,
one woman and I lagged behind, savoring the sweet, small
world around us: The piercing blue of the sea, the hosts of
nesting birds, sea lions grumbling on the rocks, and whole
fields full of yellow flowers and giant yellow-tinted lizards—
iguanas, amiably munching on blossoms.

Animals in the Galapagos are not just unafraid of people,
they're oblivious to them. On this island, we'd already stood
next to seabirds while they mated and walked close enough to
sea lion colonies to hear their babies nursing. It was like being
invisible.

Now the path made a small bend, and we found an iguana
at our feet—a full-grown golden one, dressed in its mating colors, which made it match the flowers and the sunshine. Iguanas would look like dinosaurs if they were bigger, but they are
big enough. This one was about three feet long, counting its
spiny tail. We crouched down in front of it, barely a hand's
length away. The iguana didn't flinch.

These islands are a world treasure, as well as one of

Ecuador's national parks, a place where—rightly—visitors are forbidden to interact with the animals. But it was the last day of our trip; it was the last island, and it was a reverent impulse. I don't think my companion even planned it.

She pinched off one of the yellow flowers and—very gently—held it up to the iguana's nose. I held my breath.

The iguana looked at the flower, rolled its slit eyes upward and looked at us, rolled them back and looked at the flower again. And then—just as gently—it took the gift.

It thrust its head forward, opened its wide pink mouth and bit down on the petals. And stayed there, chewing calmly, its bumpy prehistoric face only an inch from human fingertips.

There was nothing we could say to each other, or to the rest of the group later, or to you now, that could convey the impact of that moment. Two alien species, sharing the same flower: Even after a week of close encounters, this one was miraculous.

We lingered as long as we dared. Then we remembered another Galapagos rule—stay with your guide—and hurried up the path in the direction the others had gone. The iguana stayed where it was, blinking in the warm sun, chewing its delicate meal. The curve of its jaws gave it a kind of smile.

I have had my share of wildlife close-ups in many parts of the world, but in the Galapagos, they were longer, closer, more intense and lots more frequent, with many more kinds of creatures. What made it all the more wondrous is that the archipelago is such an unlikely place for so much richness: thirteen mounds of volcanic rock big enough to call islands and more than one hundred too small to deserve the title. They lie smack on the equator, 600 miles from the coast of Ecuador, at the eastern edge of the Pacific Ocean.

Modern travelers come because of the unique wildlife, but the islands have been scientific shrines for a hundred and fifty years, thanks to a young English naturalist, Charles Darwin, and a ship named the Beagle, which carried him there in 1835.

The differences between these islands are obvious to any eyes: Some have cactus forests, some are barren, some have sheer cliffs, others gentle beaches. But Darwin noticed differences among the birds. Finches on different islands, for example, had differently shaped beaks. He concluded that the birds had changed over time to better survive in differing conditions. He called the process "natural selection." His book, "On the Origin of Species," came out in 1859, and from that came the theory of evolution. It rocked the scientific establishment then; it's been rocking many others ever since.

The Galapagos had been on my wish-list for half my life. It's a complicated journey. First, you have to get to Ecuador. Then you fly an aging plane from Ecuador's national airline to an old landing strip on the tiny Galapagos island of Baltra. Then you board a passenger boat, which becomes your home and your transport, taking you from island to island, cove to cove, vista to vista.

Mine was a one-hundred-year-old sailboat named the Sulidae. But when I ran into tourists from other boats, I just said I was on "the pirate ship." Everybody knew which one I meant.

The Sulidae is a 63-foot-long gaff-rigged ketch, with a wooden hull, a high stern, two stout masts, red sails and a nicely sinister black paint job. The only thing missing was the Jolly Roger—the infamous pirate flag with a white skull and crossbones emblazoned on black. The crew said their old one had worn out, and the new one hadn't come yet.

I had chosen the Sulidae over the protests of my travel agent, and she turned out to be correct. It *wasn't* very comfortable. The cabins were small, the toilets smelled, and there were cockroaches in the corners, in the cracks in the walls and eventually in my toiletries kit. I loved it anyway.

The five-man Ecuadorean crew was friendly and casual, padding around in shorts and bare feet. The food was good and abundant. The eleven other passengers—four Britons, four Canadians, three Americans—were compatible companions. We'd all chosen the boat for its small size and romantic looks.

Plus, there was an undeniable thrill in pulling into an anchorage and watching tourist heads turn on other boats. Sometimes we even attracted sightseers, who zipped around us in motorized dinghies, taking pictures. In return, we pirates on the Sulidae planned imaginary raiding parties: how we would clasp our Swiss Army cutlasses in our teeth, clamber over the sides of unsuspecting sissy yachts and order everybody in matching T-shirts to walk the plank. It amused us between landfalls.

Our energetic guide was the bonus. He took us to nine islands in seven days, giving us bragging rights: People who'd been on the largest, plushest cruise boat we saw admitted later that they'd only visited three.

"We are going to see even more than Charles Darwin," our guide promised the first morning, as he laid out the day's timetable—when and where we'd land; how long we'd stay; what animals to look for; whether it would be a "dry landing," meaning hiking boots were okay, or a "wet landing," meaning sandals and swimsuits, and, in between, how to protect the islands from us.

Each island is a separate eco-system, so after every landfall, we had to wash the sand off our shoes, so we wouldn't carry contaminants to the next. Such carefulness is relatively recent: Islands that were still uninhabited in 1959 were declared a national park; the first rangers were appointed in 1968.

Before then, human beings came very close to ruining the Galapagos, and the islands are still vulnerable. Goats, brought in by 20th-century settlers, went wild, breeding so fast that they now number in the thousands on some islands, where they have devastated natural food supplies. More recently, throngs of poor Ecuadoreans crowded in from the mainland, looking for work, overfishing sea cucumbers and poaching sea lions for their pelts.

"Colonization has been stopped," our guide said, but the human population now stands at about 16,000, and on less-visited islands, poaching is still going on: One day, we came across the carcass of a sea lion that someone had killed and skinned.

The hardest-hit creatures were the giant land tortoises, now the emblem of Galapagos National Park. Starting with explorers and pirates in the 1500s, seafarers captured so many for meat that they were almost wiped out.

Most of the survivors live at the Charles Darwin Research Station on Santa Cruz Island, where researchers are breeding them. The most famous is Lonesome George, the last known example of his particular species. "Perhaps there is a Georgina in a zoo somewhere," our guide said, holding out a thin thread of hope. Tortoises can live a century, and George is only about 30, so there's still time to find her.

Much as I liked my sailboat, the Sulidae never actually sailed. It couldn't. There was too much distance to cover and not enough wind. So we motored between islands, often running all night, in ocean waves that made the boat buck and pitch like an angry Brahma bull. Yet each morning, when I woke up stiff and cross from lack of sleep, I'd step out on deck and instantly forgive the Sulidae her every fault. That's how beautiful the islands were.

What we saw, however, was not always beautiful. Nature is brutal—it doesn't take a Darwin to tell you that—and a good national park lets it have its way. But we were soft-hearted tourists, and the glimpses of life and death struggles, however natural, were wrenching.

The saddest came at the beginning, at sunset on North Seymour Island, our first stop. The beach was busy with female sea lions and their pups. But some of the babies were alone, and they were starving to death. Their mothers had swum out to feed and, for whatever reason, hadn't come back. "Maybe killed by a whale," our guide said.

Desperate, the hungry babies wandered the beach, crying piteously. They went up to other mothers and tried to nurse, but the females always snarled and drove them off. As they weakened, their bodies shrank, and their sleek brown coats grew loose and wrinkled; by the end, they were only rough-furred sacks of tiny bones. We saw them in all these stages of dying, and it broke my heart.

While I watched, a starving little one—chased away by every female it approached—finally gave up and lay still, waiting to die. I couldn't get its pathetic image out of my mind. Wasn't there anything we could do? Someplace we could take it? A vet who could put it out of its misery? No, our guide said. That is not the way.

"It's too hard," I wrote in my journal that night and wondered if I had been right to come.

Life lured me back into the trip. The next morning, dying infants were replaced by living ones, in scene after astonishing scene, each straight out of a National Geographic special.

On the island of Española, we stepped from the Sulidae's dinghy onto a concrete pier, and there, just a couple of rocks away, was a healthy baby sea lion frolicking in the surf, under the watchful eye of its mother. It was playing like a human toddler at the edge of the waves, letting the pulse of the water roll it over and over, in pure joy.

Then it suddenly spotted the long tail of a sleeping iguana dangling off a nearby ledge. I could see the baby think this through. Then it flip-flopped over to the iguana, stretched its head up as high as it could, chomped down hard on that tail and held on. The iguana woke up and tugged back. Finally it pulled its tail out of the baby's mouth, crawled out of reach and went back to sleep. The disappointed youngster swam back to mom for comfort, and she gave it, reaching down and nuzzling its nose with hers.

Whole mornings, whole afternoons, were filled with exquisite moments like that. On-land lessons alternated with ones taught by the sea. One afternoon, the group was snorkeling around an outcropping on Floreana Island, when the loveliest fish in the world flashed through the clear water beneath me—a two-foot-long parrot fish with hot-pink scales, each edged in brilliant turquoise. I'm not much of a snorkeler, but I followed that fish for most of an hour, as smitten as if I were in love.

On one of Floreana's beaches, when evening light had

turned the sea to silver, we found wide bands of familiar-looking chevron tracks in the soft sand. I was instantly indignant: How could the national park allow ATVs and tractors here? Then I understood.

These weren't man-made trails. These were the tracks of huge female sea turtles, coming ashore at night to lay their eggs out of sight of predatory birds. Out in the water, little black dots were already bobbing in the waning light—the heads of turtles waiting for darkness to hide them, waiting for us to leave.

On the last night of the trip, we lingered at anchor after supper, close enough to South Plaza Island to eavesdrop on the conversations of sea lions by the water's edge. They sounded like a herd of cattle sharing a bad cold—a constant chorus of grunts, coughs, groans, barks, snuffles and snorts.

By then, I was used to such noises—used to the whole phenomenal Galapagos experience: sea lions rolling happily in the surf, blue-footed boobies looking cross-eyed on the rocks, dive-bombing pelicans, green coastlines with no trace of humankind, parrot fish in impossible colors, water so clear you could see stingrays lying on the bottom twenty feet down, flower-eating iguanas, the whole natural miracle of it.

But being used to miracles doesn't make them less miraculous. And it didn't mean I was ready to let them go. Lying on the warm planks of the wooden deck that night, I watched the Southern Cross through the swaying rigging and knew—knew in my heart—that life at this moment, aboard this boat, in these wild islands, was the only life I cared to have.

Art School in the Desert

1993

—·—

"REALISTS! Meet in five minutes by the granola!"
It was our daily call to prayer—the regular morning
meeting with my fellow art students in the semi-wilds of northern New Mexico.

We would gather around the cereal bar just after breakfast
and get our marching orders, then head out to paint, burdened
with easels, drawing boards, folding chairs, sun umbrellas,
rolls of paper towels, cans of turpentine, sketchbooks, sun
hats, sunglasses, sun block and, oh, yes, brushes, oil paints and
chalk pastels.

Artists, I would notice afresh each morning, certainly do
lug around a lot of junk. And to think I had wanted to be one.

I'd been briefly seized by that passion the previous spring,
when I heard of a floating art school in the southwestern
landscape that Georgia O'Keeffe immortalized. O'Keeffe had
spent half a century painting the raw, magnificent geography
around Abiquiu, New Mexico, west of Taos, and here was a
chance to follow in her brushstrokes.

But showing up in O'Keeffe country with a kit of oil paints
does not, alas, make you Georgia O'Keeffe. Or Cezanne. Or

Monet. Or anybody else you might want to be, maybe not even yourself.

I tried explaining it to my family after I got home. They didn't get it. My sister looked at the few pictures I'd managed to finish and gently pronounced them "gooooooooooood," sounding the way she did when her kids brought art work home from grade school. My brother just laughed. "Painting the desert?" he said. "All I can see is twenty-five people with spray cans aimed at a mesa."

It wasn't quite like that. But it has been hard to define. I came to think of it as somewhere between summer camp and boot camp, with brushes and palettes in our knapsacks instead of jackknives and signal mirrors.

And there were moments when I thought of it as the hardest thing I'd ever done.

My painting experience was limited to childhood paint-by-number sets, but suddenly, reading the brochure, I wanted the real thing. I wanted to know how to make the colors of shadow, wanted to look so closely at something that its light would shatter into fragments, wanted to learn to bend my mind and flatten reality, to turn 3-D distances into 2-D shapes on a piece of canvasboard.

I also wanted a complete break with my normal mental life, which involves a steady torrent of words. I wanted to paint all day in mental silence—only seeing, not narrating what I saw. I wanted, it seemed, a vacation from myself.

I got it, too, but what I learned in those fourteen days wasn't how to paint. It was how to fail at something—and survive.

I went in late September, into a country of fifty-mile vistas, towering mesas and dusky mountains with yellow aspens sparkling on their flanks like flames. The course involved a week at Ghost Ranch, near Abiquiu; then a weekend in Taos, and another week at Philmont Scout Ranch, near Cimarron.

We students—ranging in age from late twenties to late sixties—gathered in Santa Fe, tarried long enough for me to buy half a ton of art supplies, then drove north to Ghost Ranch, whose red rocks and yellow mesas still protect one of O'Keeffe's homes.

I was instantly glad I'd come—and instantly certain I was in over my head. Of the two dozen people in the class, three-fourths were experienced artists. They came from all over the country—watercolorists from California and Illinois, a muralist from New York, graphic designers from both coasts. Several had taken the class before and were back because of the dynamic teacher, Gary Faigin, a New York-trained artist who specializes in figure drawing and meticulous landscapes in pastel.

"For me, the big things are light, color and distance," Faigin told us the first night. "I want to record a feeling—a sensation—of place." That sounded just like photography, which I love. But it wasn't like that at all.

The first day of painting, I found myself stalling—looking for the perfect spot, fussing with tubes of paint, choosing the right brush—anything to avoid facing the blank canvas. I was actually afraid. I felt as if I were about to jump off the mesa I'd chosen to paint, and I didn't know if I'd land on my feet.

Usually I look for details when I shoot pictures, so I did the same now. It wasn't what Faigin wanted. Forget the details, he kept saying: Look for big shapes first. I didn't get it. "It's like I'm asking you to paint a pearl necklace," he said finally, after I'd lost my way again. "I want you to paint the whole thing. And you're trying to paint it pearl by pearl."

So how big *are* these big shapes, anyway? Sky? Rock? That big? Yes, That big. I must have looked as bleak as I felt. "This is why you go to art school," he reassured me gently.

Our days began with demonstrations—watching as Faigin explained perspective, clouds, tree shapes and value theory, which ranks colors by their intensity, like grays shading from white to black. Other people got very good at color values; I didn't. "What value is this sky?" Faigin would ask. "Two point five," they would chorus. That tree? "About a four." The shadows on the grass? "Definitely five." And I would think, "Huh?"

After the demos, we'd set up on a ridge top or down in a canyon and work all day, fighting winds that toppled easels, blew powdery pastel dust off the paper and drove insects into still-wet—always wet—oil paint. Once I laid a small oil sketch down among the sagebrush to dry, and ants clambered all over it, attracted as if by syrup. They were particularly partial to red.

We students learned from each other—although in my case it went pretty much one way. I told people I liked their drawings. They responded with things like, "If that gate has five pickets, it's got to have more than three shadows." Oh, right. Good point.

We also learned to trust our surroundings, agreeing that we felt safer amid empty acres of semi-desert than we ever had in cities. I even grew used to the unlocked doors. Ghost Ranch is a Presbyterian-run conference center now, and trust is an important element of its philosophy; its rooms don't even *have* locks. The biggest leap of faith was leaving canvases and equipment set up all one night at the upper end of a box canyon. That involved trusting local rodents, snakes, scorpions, humankind and the weather. But everything was fine when we came back in the morning—just as we'd left it, except for a few gnats in the drying paint.

I had hoped for peace, but from the first moment, painting in the desert was anything but peaceful. I worked increasingly hard—and felt increasingly incapable. Worse, I began to question the underpinnings of my life. My entire life.

Between brush strokes, under blazing sun, I admitted that this was the first time in years—decades—that I'd risked failure. Then I admitted that I didn't take many risks of any kind, not even when I traveled—it just looked as if I did.

After one really bad day, another discouraged beginner confessed that she'd been shooting photographs on the sly, "because that's something I know I can do!" I'd been doing the same thing, for the same reason.

The reward of this journey was its setting: hills dotted with piñon pines, the rich fragrance of sage, air so clear you could drink it like water, sunsets that covered half the sky and, everywhere around us, the landmarks of Georgia O'Keeffe. Just about everybody, including me, took a crack at painting the Pedernal, a blunt-topped mountain that O'Keeffe regarded as a personal possession: God had told her she could keep it, she once said, if she painted it well enough. She got to keep it; I had to give it back.

From the first moment, the class lived, breathed and talked nothing but art. What we did in the rest of our lives—careers, families, houses—came up only incidentally. Instead, conversations revolved around which brand of pastel had the truest red, which paper had the best "tooth," which portable wooden easels had the sturdiest hardware (French, by a landslide).

I marveled one afternoon as two painters debated which

colors of oil paint dragged the most when you stroked them on canvas. White, they agreed, was slowest.

I marveled more at the art jokes. One night, a bunch of us watched a videotape of "Dances with Wolves," and at the first wide-open scene of the Dakota prairie, somebody shouted, "yellow ochre, value three-point-five, in the foreground!" Much hilarity, my notebook records, but you had to be there.

It was a lot like being trapped in a convention of nuclear physicists. "Hey," I kept wanting to protest as conversations approached the artistic equivalent of the quark, "I'm supposed to be on vacation!"

But their intensity was contagious. On only the second morning, I woke up thinking I should have mixed more crimson with my cobalt blue the day before. On the third morning, I stared groggily at the bedsheets and thought for a split-second that I was looking at stretched canvas. And somewhere on day four, the process of painting evolved into a new philosophy of life.

I had worked that day on a yellow mesa that stood like a crisp paper cutout against deep blue sky. I got the sky color right, the mesa shape right. Then I started adding shadows, and the picture began to fail. Soon the mesa looked like melting vanilla ice cream with chocolate sauce running down its sides. When I put more purple in the shadows, it looked like ice cream drenched in blood.

I was horrified. This wasn't what I meant. This wasn't what I saw in my mind. I kept trying and only made things worse. I worked for five hours on that mesa and quit for the evening convinced I'd made a big, expensive mistake with this class and should go home—should never, in fact, have come.

"This doesn't yield," I told my journal. "If you can't be good, why bother?"

Then came a flash of insight, and suddenly the class wasn't about art anymore. It was about commitment. I had been trying to paint without it. I hadn't really *looked* at the shadows on that mesa. Hadn't connected with them. Hadn't *seen* them. So I wasn't painting reality, I was making it up.

Painting, I saw, is like ballet: Every mistake shows. If you're going to do it right, you have to give yourself to it one hundred percent. No half measures, no fudging. You have to really mean it. You have to commit.

From then on, things got better. I began to look—and look hard—at what was in front of me, and I tried to let that reality show me what to do. By the end of the course, I'd managed to paint a couple of pictures that I wasn't ashamed of. "Umhmm," Faigin said, looking at one in the final critique, "you can put your name on that." I felt reprieved.

Home now, I have stopped bragging about this achievement to friends and family, and I no longer blurt out, "I can do that tree!" every time I notice a cadmium-orange sugar maple against an ultramarine sky. None of that is important, anyway. But the lessons I took away were. This is what I really learned from painting school in the desert:

Be open. Be honest. Take risks. See new things. Stand back and look for the big picture. Don't sweat the details. Never defend a bad job, just start over. Dare to make mistakes. Don't waste the daylight. Commit to the shadows.

Cold War Within

2003

YELLOW, AMBER, ORANGE, TURQUOISE: It doesn't matter what color the latest alert is. I can't manage to react. I used up my lifetime ration of terror during the Cold War. I was a little girl then, and TV wasn't very sophisticated. But I saw the televised tests of nuclear bombs, and they scared me sick. Truly sick.

Fear was everywhere. Even "My Weekly Reader" carried stories about the Strategic Air Command and the reason we needed it. The reason was the Russians. Worse news was in the real newspaper, and it got worse for me when the Minneapolis Star decided to serialize the nuclear thriller "On the Beach." Every day after school, I came home and read another chapter, wide-eyed with horror, as the fictional clouds of fallout slowly laid waste to the world. The novel told how people were given poison pills so they could kill themselves when their suffering got too bad. They were supposed to give the pills to their children first.

One afternoon, the Star ran a target-shaped map that covered the whole front page. It showed how far the damage would extend if a Soviet A-bomb hit Minneapolis. Dayton's

Department Store was Ground Zero. Within the concentric circle where we lived, nobody would have survived.

My father announced an escape plan. We would all somehow get north, he said. We'd gather at the family cabin and "make our stand." I'd seen enough westerns to know what that meant, though I was confused about how we'd do the shooting. Nobody we knew owned guns.

Our teachers at Bancroft Elementary School made us practice taking shelter from atomic bombs. Sometimes it was under our desks. Sometimes we went into the basement hallway and crouched against the yellow tile walls and covered our heads with our hands. The teachers said that when the bombing stopped, "ducks" would come to take us home. My father explained that they weren't real ducks and drew me a picture of a World War II landing craft.

A classmate brought a bit of uranium ore for Show and Tell, and I touched it before I knew what it was. I thought I was going to die. I washed my hands over and over, to get the poison off. And kept on washing them. I washed them until they were raw. Then I started counting things.

Words, sentences, paragraphs, actions, I counted everything. Three was the best number. I washed my hands three times, touched things three times, read things three times. And if three was good, nine would be better, because nine was three times three. And three times three times three would be better still . . . .

The rituals paralyzed me. I had to do the counts perfectly or start over from scratch. I could not do schoolwork, could not read because I could not keep track of the counts. At first, I was only protecting myself, but the need for the counts spread, until I was protecting my family too, and finally everybody.

Everybody everywhere. Saving the world is a hellish burden for a ten-year-old.

What I am describing has a tidy label now—obsessive-compulsive disorder. Doctors say it can happen for many reasons, biochemical included. So maybe I'd have developed OCD without the Cold War. Maybe I could have blamed my phobias on, oh, "The Howdy Doody Show" or a bad episode of "Rin-tin-tin." But I don't believe that. I blame the fear in the air.

The turning point came one night in our kitchen. My mother was at the sink, cleaning a chicken for dinner. I was at the table, struggling to get through the Cedric Adams column in the evening paper, starting over every time I made a mistake. Almost at the bottom, I lost count. I wanted to know how it turned out, but starting over now would mean twenty-seven complete readings. I took a chance and sneaked to the end anyway, without counting. I remember the guilt I felt, then the overwhelming relief: Nothing had changed. I hadn't died, my mother hadn't died, nobody had died.

After that, my symptoms began to wane, but it took a long, long time for them to go away. Even now, fifty years later, there are moments when it would still be easier to lock the front door three times or buy the third blouse on the rack when there's nothing wrong with the first two. Nobody would notice if I did—those would merely be personal superstitions, not much worse than tossing salt over your shoulder to stave off bad luck or not walking under a ladder.

But I learned, long ago, to walk under ladders on purpose, to spill salt and let it lie. That is how you kill phobias. You do the thing you fear. You read to the end. Do that enough, and the fear goes away.

That is why I can't be scared when a color-coded alert

comes out. But the alerts make me feel a little sick, anyway: I know how scared some children will be and how the fear will stay with them, far longer than their families will ever know. My parents talked to me as softly and calmly as parents are being advised to do now. It didn't work. It won't work. You can tell kids they'll be safe, over and over, till you lose your voice, and there will still be some who won't believe you. Who will stay terrified down to their souls. Who will be scarred for life by that terror.

In the spring of 1979, I rode the Trans-Siberian Railroad across what was then the Soviet Union and got a first-hand look at the country I'd spent my childhood being afraid of. The truth hit me hardest in Irkutsk. The city is in Siberia, on Russia's equivalent of the Great Plains, and it was bigger than Minneapolis. Half the population was living in log cabins without indoor plumbing. My government guide insisted they liked it.

I watched old people, wearing heavy clothes against the cold, carrying buckets and trudging slowly along dirt streets to get to the neighborhood water pipe, and suddenly I was flooded with anger.

"For this?" I thought. "For *this*, I gave up my childhood?"

All that is why I'm not buying duct tape or plastic sheeting, or laying in a supply of canned goods and drinking water, or surfing the Internet for the best price on gas masks.

I am also not staying away from airports, airplanes or any other kind of public conveyance. Or from foreign countries. Or from the city of New York. Or from any place else. I refuse to be afraid this time around. I refuse. What I count now are freedoms, and my freedom to move around this world was too hard-won.

On the Bheri River, in southern Nepal

Catherine Watson was the founding editor of the Minneapolis *Star Tribune's* travel section and its chief travel writer and photographer from 1978 to 2004. Nationally, her honors include the Lowell Thomas Travel Journalist of the Year and the Society of American Travel Writers Photographer of the Year. Watson teaches literary travel writing and memoir in college-level workshops and is a mentor with the University of Minnesota's Split Rock On-line Mentoring for Writers program. When not on the road, she shares pizza and long walks with two small dogs and divides her time between a 1926 cottage in south Minneapolis and an 1869 farmhouse in the historic village of Galena, Illinois.